CW00393090

WORKING PAPER

ALFRED P. SLOAN SCHOOL OF MANAGEMENT

CORPORATE PLANNING: AN EXECUTIVE VIEWPOINT

by

Peter Lorange

WP 985-78   May 1978

MASSACHUSETTS
INSTITUTE OF TECHNOLOGY
50 MEMORIAL DRIVE
CAMBRIDGE, MASSACHUSETTS 02139

CORPORATE PLANNING: AN EXECUTIVE VIEWPOINT

by

Peter Lorange

WP 985-78   May 1978

Tentatively to be published by Prentice-Hall. This draft is preliminary,
it is not yet edited. Not to be quoted. Comments solicited

ABLE OF CONTENTS

CHAPTER ONE

Purpose of Corporate Planning: Strategic Decision-Making

1. Introduction

The purpose of corporate planning (also labeled long-range planning,
strategic planning) is to be a management tool in the strategic decision-
making process of a company. Its focus is clear: to aid in strategic
decision-making. If an activity that goes under the label of corporate
planning does not aid in the strategic decision-making of the firm it is
not planning (and it is also wasteful), even though the activity may seem
to involve many of the "right" elements of planning, such as elaborate five-year
plan documents. The problem frequently is that the five-year plan does often not
fluence the strategic decisions; the key executives rely on other decision-making
aids. Effective corporate planning, on the other hand, does not have to
be elaborate, complicated or voluminous, but logical and focused on the
strategic decisions that will have to be taken. The thrust of this book
will be to operationalize the concept of corporate planning as a strategic
decision-making tool.

How can we operationalize corporate planning beyond the general
decision-making thrust just stated? We think that there are at least four
aspects of this task that need clarification:

- corporate planning's role in the allocation of the company's scarce
  resources such as funds, management talent, or raw materials;

- corporate planning's role in assisting the firm to adapt to
  environmental opportunities and threats, identify the relevant
  options, provide for an effective strategic fit with the environment,

- corporate planning's role in the process of choosing strategic
options that duly reflect the firm's own internal strengths and
weaknesses; integration;

- finally, corporate planning's role in the process of building an
organization that is learning about itself; a strengthened sense
of professionalism

Let us discuss each of these aspects of corporate planning as a
strategic decision-making process in some more detail.

1 - 2. Allocation of resources

Resources, most obviously funds, will have to be allocated in order to
carry out a strategic decision. Let us discuss briefly a few examples of
such strategic resource allocation.[1] For instance, the Chief Executive
Officer (C.E.O.) and his senior management of a divisionalized company may
be faced with the possibilities of whether to make a major commitment to
expansion within a particular existing division or within another. Alternatively, maybe management should be making a somewhat more evenly split
resource commitment to both divisions? Another alternative might be to
invest in an acquisition instead of continual pursuance of one's present
businesses. Decisions of this type, taken explicitly or not, will represent an option of senior management to redistribute the balance between
the emphasis on the firm's different businesses. As such, the discretionary
resource allocation tool might have a profound impact on a company's strategic direction. Another example of strategic resource allocation might be
faced by a division manager who might make a choice with regard to how much
of the discretionary funds generated from his "leading" product line should

be placed back in the same product line in order to protect its future position versus how much funds he should want to divert into the development of new product lines. Again, the resource allocation pattern choice, this time with regard to the allocation of scarce resources between the various product directions, might have a profound impact on the strategic direction of a division. Even when it comes to a particular product line there might be radically different alternatives for how to allocate resources to build up a competitive strength, ranging from a heavy "investment" in R & D to taking over a competitor who clearly has the skill, from establishing a strong competitive position in one market to investing in a more diversified distribution system, and so on. The allocation of strategic funds will again shape the strategy, this time for this particular product line.

Strategic resource need not be funds only, but any resource that can be disposed of by the firm's management to create value to the firm. A list of such strategic resources might look as follows:

(a) Funds. These will have to be available and free for discretionary use. Thus, funds accumulated in a country from which they cannot be transferred but will have to be reinvested internally are not a strategic resource. Similarly, although a joint venture might be highly succesful the funds flows generated might typically not be disposed of at any of the owners' free discretion. Instead the more modest dividend payments become a strategic resource to the parent companies.

(b) Management skills. Managers are also scarce resources to the extent that they can be transferred from one area to another, and that they represent a scarce output factor for a particular company. For a company which on the other hand is in a position of having an ample number of qualified management to pursue its present strategic direction management skill is not a strategic resource. To underscore this, excess management cannot be "sold" to other corporations, only transferred from one usage pattern to another within the same organization. It is in this latter form that it becomes a strategic resource.

(c) Tax shelters. Tax shelters can now and then be transferred and used elsewhere too and as such are a scarce resource. We assume, however, that the tax shelter can be taken advantage of by other parts of the company, or that the tax shelter can be "sold". (Through leasing arrangements, for instance, the benefits from a tax shelter may be transferred from one company to another). If of no use internally and/or not transferable, the tax shelter is not a strategic resource.

(d) Energy is also potentially a strategic resource, measured, say, in BTU units, provided that freed up energy can be transferred from one part of a firm's operation to another, or, sold to outside users.

We do, however, normally focus on discretionary funds as the primary resource that we have to allocate strategically. The allocation of resources, either through investments or discretionary expenditures, is the demonstration of strategic direction - intended or not intended, explicit or implicit. Thus, the corporate planning process must be focused on the allocation of strategic resources, the resource allocation pattern is the key ingredient of the output of strategic planning.

1 - 3. Adaptation, identification of strategic options

Strategic success in most instances will require that the firm systematically look for opportunities and/or threats in its environment

to come up with the best alternatives that the firm can pursue. This
outward-looking search is crucial to improve the firm's chances to pursue
more advantageous directions and to employ its resources in such a way
that they yield the best return.[2]

Adaptation may be seen as the antithesis of extrapolation. Too often
plans are being developed based on a strong element of extrapolating from
the past what will be expected to be the activity levels of the future.
The epithomy of this can be found when activity level forecasts in the
plan increases in a harmonious manner, say linearly or with a steady,
fixed percentage every year. Even in cases where the plan is not built up
around such visible numbers extrapolations, there might, however, be a
strong element of "mental extrapolation" behind the development of the
plan. For instance, we may have become familiar with how a business has
been developing in the past. Consequently, we wish that such a pattern
will continue; we are comfortable with a scenario that we feel we can understand and relate to. Such extrapolation-based planning was probably
not all that worthless during the relatively stable decades of the fifties
and sixties. However, in a post-OPEC, post-recession environmental climate a continued extrapolative belief in an undisturbed growth seems far
less relevant. Thus, a focus on adaptation to emerging environmental
opportunities and/or threats has become more and more a critical element
of planning. Planning should facilitate an assessment of one's strategic
exposure to opportunities and threats in the future, and unlatch a creative
process to take advantage of this. Planning should never become an extrapolative, creativity-dampening process. Needless to say, for those
companies that succeed relatively better than their competitors in instilling an adaptive planning mode there is likely to be much more opportunities to excell performance-wise in an unstable environment.

Paradoxically, for the sophisticated, well-managed company environmental turbulence represents a welcomed opportunity to move ahead.

Adaptation might take place in several ways It might be an assessment of opportunities to move into a new business, including acquiring another company; or it might be an opportunity to improve one's position within one of one's present businesses, say, by bringing out a new or modified product line, or by breaking into a new market, or, it might be an adaptive assessment that is bound primarily to a particular function, such as a new technology opportunity that seems to be emerging for research and development. In parenthesis it should also be pointed out that adaptation might also take the form of a defensive move, such as divesting of a business.

Adaptation might not be equally important for all companies. Some companies may enjoy more than ample opportunities without carrying out an elaborate formal adaptation process. One example of this might be a company which is within a highly specialized segment of the electronics business, where demand is developing so rapidly that all the company's attention and resources are channeled into following up on the business opportunity that the firm finds itself in. Another example of relatively low adaptation pressure might be for a company within the oil-based energy field At least up until relatively recently the selling of the finished oil products was less of a problem, the company's efforts would primarily concentrate on how to increase oil thruput by getting more oil out of the ground and/or streamline production. Still other companies may have done such a successful identification of opportunities in the past that they have a backlog of opportunities and can thereby deemphasize formal adaptation efforts somewhat. An example might be an R&D-intensive company which has had a number'of new product successes and does not have the capabilities to follow all of them through. A final situation might be a company which does not have discretionary resources of any significance to commit during the foreseeable years, either because of weak economic position which will call for consolidation of present situation rather than expanding or because of a major recent commitment which will consume all of the firm's discretionary resources.

It also follows that the need to adapt might change over time too. For instance, the continued potential for growth and expansion within a business which has been highly successful up until the present might slacken off, or, alternatively technological innovations and/or entry of new companies might weaken the firm's position. Thus, while the company's mode of succeeding in its business previously was relatively straightforward, an increased need for adaptation is now being created in order to maintain an updated competitive strategic approach. Another example, which is very common, is that the general degree of maturity of a firm's product lines may be shifting somewhat from a rapid growth mode towards becoming more mature as time goes by. This potentially requires relatively less recurring investments to be "plowed back" into the business for the maintenance or increase of its market share, as well as the establishing of a production and/or R&D-position in order to continue in the business. The firm's cash-flow position will therefore typically change in terms of increased flexibility to allocate discretionary funds. However, an increased adaptation need has thereby been created, namely for identifying viable

options for where to allocate these resources in order to achieve best
possible continued growth.

1 - 4. Integration, narrow down options

A third important purpose of planning is to provide for an orderly
evaluation and choice of alternatives in such a way that a direction can be
established which reflects the firm's own internal strengths and weaknesses
Thus, the integration purpose of corporate planning is to facilitate the
"narrowing down" of the options in such a way that a basis can be provided
for achieving an efficient course of operation.[3] Integration, then, is concerned with how to develop ways of achieving a strategic direction, always
attempting as much as possible to build on the strengths that the firm
possesses and avoiding the weaknesses. As such we might say that there is
an extrapolative element in integration, namely now to achieve one's strategic goals in the most economical way, i.e. by building on one's present
thrust to the extent possible and avoiding undertaking changes in one's
mode of operation that are not required.

Integration can take several forms. a dominating aspect of the integration planning process is the strategic programming process, which will
emphasize the development of strategic programs for achieving particular
objectives. Typically there are many ways to achieve a particular objective
and to identify and choose among these alternatives is often a time-consuming
and difficult process. Another and related integration planning activity is
zero-base budgeting, which attempts to break down the choices among expenditures according to their strategic relevance when seen as part of a strategic program. Finally, the preparation of an operating budget or action

program in itself represents the culmination of the integration planning process in that the budget represents the "tip of the iceberg" of the agreed-upon strategies for the firm.

There are important relationships between the adaptation and integration purposes of the corporate planning activities While adaptation implies a focus on where for the firm to go, integration focusses on how to get there in the most efficient manner. Thus, above all the two purposes

complement each other. To carry out a corporate planning activity that addresses the adaptation issues of identifying the key options but fails to narrow down these options through an efficient integration procedure does not provide a useful strategic decision-making support; issues are left "hanging in the air". Similarly, a good integration approach which is not complemented by effective adaptation is equally unsatisfactory; by not systematically assessing the opportunities of the business environment one will easily end up with a "garbage in - garbage out" performance of one's corporate planning system. Although both adaptation and integration thus are critical aspects of planning, there are three aspects of the relationship between adaptation and integration which might call for differing degrees of emphasis between the two modes.

First, when the absolute emphasis is high on adaptation aspects of planning, then the absolute level of integration emphasis will have to be high too; this is merely an issue of "capacity balancing". For instance, a large, diversified corporation which is operating multinationally within several highly volatile businesses will have a higher absolute need for paying attention to adaptation than a company operating within a set of businesses that are relatively mature and, say, within the domestic market only. Further, when it comes to the integrative aspects of planning too, namely narrowing down the strategic choices in such a way that the firm's own strengths and/or weaknesses can be brought to bear, the first company will have to put higher emphasis than the second company on this too, with a considerably more multifaceted set of strength/weakness considerations to take into account.

However, we still have to address the issue of the relative emphasis between the adaptation and integration dimensions. A company may be in a situation in which it needs to emphasize adaptation more vigorously, say, because it is accumulating resources at a faster rate than it can utilize them. Adaptation planning should be emphasized relatively more than integration planning in such a case. Another company, however, may be in a tight financial situation due to a series of competitive setbacks. Relatively more emphasis on integration would be appropriate in such a case.

Finally, although a company typically will be in a position at a given point in time which would call for both a particular absolute level of adaptation and integration emphasis as well as for a particular relative adaptation/integration planning balance, these absolute levels as well as the relative balance will probably change over time, given that the needs of the firm will probably change, reflected in improved or worsened economic conditions, due to shifting environmental opportunities and/or threats and/or changes in the firm's internal strengths and/or weaknesses as well. For instance, a European-based corporation within the automotives businesses faced relatively less need for planning both for adaptation as well as for integration, a few years ago than it probably does today -- enjoying a relatively stable home market and high growth in its major export markets. With the emergence of a fiercer competition, both abroad and at home, as well as due to added fundamental changes in the "climate" for doing business,

above all the uncertainties due to the less and less clear energy policy
situation, the absolute "level" of planning needs will probably have increased. At the same time there has probably also been a relative shift
in emphasis from vigorously going after new adaptive opportunities, in
terms of markets and model changes, to paying very close attention to
internal integrative planning issues, above all in order to keep one's
break-even point under control in response to slackening demand, rising
labor costs and increasing government legal intervention which causes less
flexibility in trimming size of work-force and/or plant shut-downs. Thus,
the absolute emphasis on planning as well as the relative balance between
the two planning purposes should probably change over time. In fact, this
calls for an approach for managing the evolution of the planning system
so that an appropriate absolute emphasis as well as a relative balance can
be maintained.

1 - 5   Learning

A fourth purpose of corporate planning is to provide for more effective
managerial learning, so that the executive team of a company can systematically increase its strategic decision-making capabilities over time. A
properly designed and executed strategic planning approach might do this
in two ways.

First, the process of developing a plan and discussing it will provide
an executive with the opportunity to think through his strategic setting
in a relatively systematic and complete manner. This opportunity to state
his strategy and plans in an explicit way and to communicate these to others
might provide a valuable learning experience, particularly during the first
times around with planning

Potentially an even more important aspect of learning is planning's role as a self-improving system. By stating a strategy and a set of strategic programs for achieving the strategy a basis has been provided for monitoring subsequent progress towards these goals. Thus, posterior analysis can be made of why a particular strategic program, say, did not fulfill the expectations. Experiences can thus be accumulated in a systematic manner so that past errors can be avoided in the future. Further, experience can be gained about how to react to adverse developments. Important steps can thereby be made towards making the corporate planning system a self-correcting system.

Above all, then, the planning system should instill a mode of management style within the corporation which fosters professionalism. This takes the form of an accumulation of strategic understanding and strengthened aptitude towards managing strategically among a relatively large group of management. Also, it facilitates the transferability of strategic skills from one manager to another. Thus, planning may be seen as a vehicle for facilitating the "normalization" of the strategic management tasks within a firm. This might become an increasingly important factor for several reasons. First, given the dying out of the "old, entrepreneurial salts" that managed the business on their own, senior management transition from founder-entrepreneur to professional manager might be facilitated. Further, given the needs to "bring up to speed" managerial talent that has been brought in from outside the company, a relatively rational and explicit management style might be highly beneficial. Also, given the need to cause less disruption when transferring managers internally a common frame of reference to shared understanding of the firm's strategic directions might be essential.

- 6. Outline of book

All four specific purposes for corporate planning that we have discussed are merely aspects of the overall purpose of the corporate planning activity, namely to improve the strategic decision-making within the company. The purpose of this book is to operationalize the design and implementation of corporate planning systems that can provide effective support in this. The focus is thus primarily on the planning systems and processes. As such, the book addresses the issue of how to complement good substantive strategic decision moves. A corporate planning system alone cannot provide for corporate success; the quality of the strategic decisions is what matters. Many a company has prospered without a formal corporate planning system, because of intuitively strategically sound decision-making by the "old salt" senior management of the company. Similarly, a good planning system cannot substitute for the lack of strategic savvy of the management. It seems reasonable, however, to see a planning system as a useful complement which might improve the "batting average" of the management. Also, the planning system might be an important factor in making the strategic management of a company less dependent of the highly individual personal style elements of the leadership of a particular chief executive, thus improving the firm's ability to cope with management traditions. As discussed, it will probably be easier to bring new management talent "up to speed" in terms

of effectively functioning within a corporate managerial setting that is "normalized" in terms of its planning system's guidelines for strategic decision-making compared with what might be the case when brought into a highly individualistic, even at times eccentric corporate setting. Given the present state-of-the-art, it seems as if corporate planning is a tool which is likely to give management a competitive advantage, since corporate planning is no longer in its infancy, it seems questionable whether senior management can afford to dismiss it. There is just too much evidence about its usefulness to permit this.

The approach to be taken in this book is based on the belief that the needs for planning will differ from company to company as a consequence of differences in the strategic situational settings of the firms. Thus, a planning system should be tailormade so that it will possess the unique set of capabilities that the particular needs of a given company will call for. Hence, it is highly unlikely that there might exist a standardized approach to planning that will be universally acceptable. Despite this, we shall attempt to develop a generally applicable unified set of concepts about a contingency-based approach to the design and implementation of corporate planning systems. This approach is based on an initial conceptual framework for planning, which sets out a few general propositions about how to approach the fulfillment of the task of designing a planning system. From this initial base of general components for planning a series of steps will be suggested for progressively tailoring the planning system to the given strategic needs at hand.[4]

The outline of this book, then, is as follows. We shall start out in Chapter Two by introducing a conceptual scheme for corporate planning. We have been involved in the development of this over a number of years and we have implemented the scheme in large, complex corporations several times. O experience is that it is particularly useful to have an overall conceptual framework explicitly established when attempting to develop a corporate planning effort, given the complexity of such a system; the many elements of the system which will have to be fitted together in a consistent manner; the many executives who will have to be exposed to parts of the system and therefore must understand its rationale, as well as the political implications of strategic decisions calling for a need to develop and communicate an overall set of "rules" for executives' behavior in the planning process.

Having established our conceptual approach we shall argue that a logical and often necessary step will be to carry out a "strategic position audit" with regard to where the firm stands in terms of its <u>strategic planning needs</u>, the topic to be discussed in Chapter Three. This is important for three reasons. First, a clear and explicit perception of the opportunities and threats in one's environment as well as one's own strengths and weaknesses, i.e., one's strategic position, might be one of the most essential prerequisites for making good strategic decisions. Secondly, the strategic audit might point out inconsistencies between one's strategies and illogical aspects of one's organizational structure. Thirdly, the strategic position will provide one of the most important determinants for the tailor-making of the corporate planning system to the given situational setting, i.e. it will establish a focussed set of needs for planning.

Our first step in terms of modifying our general conceptual planning scheme to the particular situation will be to discuss a series of pitfalls that we have experienced when designing a particular corporate planning system, the topic of Chapter Four. Each of these problems relates specifically to a particular aspect of the planning process, and we shall point out what seem to be reasonable guidelines for handling each of them. Thus, we shall develop what amounts to a first check list to determine the usefulness of the design of the corporate planning system.

There is another important aspect of the issue of designing a useful system to the particular situation, i.e., to attempt to build into the planning system specific capabilities that reflect the particular needs of a given firm. This relates heavily to the balance between adaptation and integration planning, a consideration that comes up after all the pitfalls have been handled, as an attempt at further sharpening and improving the planning system's design. In Chapter Five we shall discuss this.

Since planning needs will change as a function of time, we shall also discuss the issue of how to manage the process of modification or evolution of the corporate planning process. What might be a useful design approach at a given point in time might be less appropriate during a different time period. The issue, thus, is to manage the system so that it maintains its usefulness, which might be seen as a third phase in the successive steps to add company-specific tailormade focus to the planning approach, a topic to be discussed in Chapter Six.

Give that a strategic planning process, just as any decision-making process, is behavioral in nature we shall continue with a discussion of what might be appropriate roles for various executive groups within the firm: line vs. staff, senior management vs. division management, general business divisional management vs. functional specialists, planning staff vs. other staff, and so on. These role examples shall stress the crucial need of seeing planning within an organization as a "main-stream" decision-making process and not as an "ivory tower" exercise detached from the line. This will be the topic of Chapter Seven. Finally, in Chapter Eight we shall undertake a brief summarizing of the planning approach proposed in the book.

_ 7. Summary

In this opening chapter of the book we have stated the overriding
purpose of corporate planning as we see it and as we shall advocate it in
this book, namely to assist a company's line management to better carry out
its strategic decision-making task   It might be argued that this task has
taken on added dimensions of importance due to wnat seems to be the
emergence of an increasingly violent and unstable environmental setting,
thereby creating a strong need for better incorporating alertness to
environmental opportunities and/or threats into strategic decision-making.
The approach of this book will be to focus on an operational approach to
strategic planning which centers around the firm's allocation of resources,
in such a way that it attempts to facilitate a modification of the firm's
strategic direction so as to adapt to emerging opportunities and/or threats
in the environment   Also, however, we shall emphasize the need to take a
realistic account of the firm's internal strengths and/or weaknesses when
choosing between strategic options; thus, we shall advocate an approach
which stresses this dual interrelationship between adaptation and
integration aspects of the firm's planning.

The focus of the book will be to bring up issues for discussion that
might be useful from the corporate executive's point of view, of relevance
either in terms of his desire to make more effective use of planning as a
strategic decision-making tool or in terms of his desire to improve of the
planning process itself. There will of course not be a set of definite
"do's" and "don't's" in the field of corporate planning, partly because
the area is so new that more definite and universal approaches have not
yet emerged, but above all because of the need to tailormake the approach

taken to planning to the particular corporate setting at hand. Thus,
although we shall see examples of emerging, relatively general planning
principles in this book, we shall never expect planning to lose its flavor
of being a discipline with a high degree of contingency-based tailormaking,
with few stable and lasting solutions. Despite of the "embryonic" state-
of-the-art of corporate planning we shall attempt to discuss approaches
that are founded in the forefront of actual corporate practices, not in
abstract theorizing. Several years of intensive field research within
several dozen corporations thus provides the basis for the synthetizing
that is attempted in this book. Examples will also be used extensively
throughout tne book to enhance its potential usefulness as a tool for
practitioning managers.

Footnotes - Chapter One

1. The resource-allocation purpose of strategic planning has been stressed
   by several authors, see, in particular Berg, Norman A., The Allocation
   of Strategic Funds in a Large Diversified Company, Unpublished Doctoral
   Dissertation, Harvard Business School, Boston, 1963, Bower, Joseph L.,
   "Planning Within the Firm", American Economic Review, May 1970, Bower,
   Joseph L., Managing the Resource Allocation Process: A Study of
   Corporate Planning and Investment, Division of Research, Harvard
   Business School, Boston, 1970, and Carter, E. E., "The Behavioral
   Theory of the Firm and Top-Level Corporate Decisions", Administrative
   Science Quarterly, Vol. 16, 1971.

2. The dual concepts of adaptation and integration have been discussed by
   several authors, although frequently with use of different wordings.
   See Cordiner, Ralph J., New Frontiers for Professional Managers,
   McGraw-Hill, New York, 1956, Sloan, Alfred P., Jr., My Years With
   General Motors, Doubleday, Garden City, 1964, Lawrence, P. R. and
   J. W. Lorsch, Organization and Environment: Managing Differentiation
   and Integration, Division of Research, Harvard Business School, Boston,
   1967, Lawrence, P. R. and J. W. Lorsch, "Differentiation and Integration
   in Complex Organizations", Administrative Science Quarterly, June 1967,
   Thompson, James D., Organizations in Action, McGraw-Hill, New York,
   1967, Rhenman, Eric, Organization Theory for Long-Range Planning, Wiley
   Interscience, New York, 1973, Whybark, Clay D., "Comparing an Adaptive
   Decision Model and Human Decisions", Academy of Management Journal,

December 1973, Lorsch, Jay W. and Allen, Stephen A., III, Managing Diversity and Interdependence: An Organizational Study of Multi-divisional Firms, Division of Research, Harvard Business School, Boston, 1973, Malm, Allan T., Strategic Planning Systems: A Framework for Analysis and Design, Student Litteratur, Lund (Sweden), 1975, and Normann, Richard, Management for Growth, Wiley-Interscience, New York, 1977.

3. See footnote 2 for discussions of integrative aspects of the planning tasks. Also, see Wilson, S. R. and John O. Tomb, Improving Profits through Integrated Planning and Control, Prentice-Hall, Englewood Cliffs, 1968, Van der Ven, A. H., A. I. Delbecq and R. Koenig, "Determinants of Coordination Models Within Organizations", American Sociological Review, April 1976.

4. The approach to be taken to strategic planning in this book is an extension of a conceptual scheme developed by R. F. Vancil and P. Lorange, see Vancil, Richard F. and Peter Lorange, "Strategic Planning in Diversified Companies", Harvard Business Review, Jan.-Feb., 1975. The notion of interrelationship between a firm's capabilities and strategic setting have been discussed in Ansoff, H. Igor, R. P. Declerck and R. L. Hayes, editors, From Strategic Planning to Strategic Management, Wiley Interscience, New York, 1976, Lorange, Peter, "Diagnosis and Design of Strategic Planning Systems in Diversified Corporations", Sloan School Working Paper, Cambridge, 1976, and Lorange, Peter, "An Analytical Scheme for the Assessment of a Diversified Company's Corporate Planning System: Needs; Capabilities; Effectiveness, Sloan School Working Paper, Cambridge, 1977.

CHAPTER TWO

A Conceptual Approach to Corporate Planning

2 - 1. Introduction

As discussed in Chapter One, the purpose of the present chapter is to present a conceptual model for corporate planning, as our first step towards an operationalized planning approach.[1] This model, then, will serve as a starting point or "scelethon" for the planning system, in that it will define certain dimensions about a planning system and identify certain characteristics that seem to be more or less universally applicable. In subsequent chapters we shall discuss how to build on the framework developed here in order to achieve a more focussed, or tailormade planning system with capabilities that match the specific needs of a given company.

The conceptual scheme for planning to be advanced in this chapter is based on the premise that a planning process should have an explicit focus in terms of indicating which executives should be involved in what aspects of the planning tasks, as well as when these various planning tasks should be dealt with. Thus, we shall propose a conceptual model for corporate planning which provides a vehicle for communication, information handling, interaction, iteration and decision consensus among the various managers of a corporation. This is done by employing a "division of labor" among managers at several organizational levels for different aspects of strategic responsibility. Also, there will be several stages of focus that we shall introduce in order to allow the planning system to possess the desired adaptation, integration and post-facto learning capabilities. Let us in this chapter first discuss the concept of levels of strategy; then the concept of stages in the planning process; and finally the information handling characteristics of the planning process These represent the three basic dimensions in the conceptual scheme, the three "backbone"

elements of corporate planning. When it comes to discussing each of these
three elements, however, we shall find it useful to first introduct the
particular concept as such for then to discuss how this can be applied or
interpreted in real corporate settings.[2]

2 - 2. Three Levels of Strategic Planning· The Concepts

If we consider a typical divisionalized corporation we find that it
typically will be engaged in several different businesses, each being
carried out by a general management unit, called the division management.
The corporate headquarters will attempt to provide a useful overall corporate
setting by creating a meaningful balance between the divisions. Within each
division there will be specialized departments that perform the various
functional tasks, such as marketing, manufacturing and R&D. The strategic
tasks of each of these three major management groups will be different;
each group will be faced with key strategic decisions that in their own way
will be critical for the success of the company; however, the strategic
variables in focus will naturally not be the same.

At the corporate level the primary strategic task will be to develop a
favorable portfolio strategy for the diverse business activities by providing
a balanced set of "legs" for the company to stand on -- balance between
growth and profits opportunities, degree of economic and political risk, and
so on.[3] The concerns at the corporate level will be expressed primarily in
terms of effects on strategic resource·flows to and from the various businesses,
providing a strategy for improving the quality of the portfolio A central
issue to be dealt with here is to determine from what business sources
excess strategic resources should be taken and to which businesses these excess
resources should go Or, in other words, which of tne company's businesses seem

provide the best basis for growth and which of the businesses might be required to curtail their growth. The former would typically receive a net influx of strategic resources, while the latter would be giving up some of its generated resources. The strategic resource that most typically will be at the center of focus in a portfolio strategy analysis is of course the pattern of funds flows.

A key issue here is to determine the riskiness of the portfolio. How much do the various businesses interrelate? Are they subjected to largely the same or different business cycle patterns? To what extent are they relying on the same type of competition? These and other questions can be raised and analyzed at the corporate level in order to come up with a portfolio strategy and plan. In Chapter Three we shall examine approaches for analyzing the corporate portfolio strategy planning need, at this stage it will suffice to acknowledge the nature of the strategic planning task at the corporate level, what should be the balance between one's businesses, where should one expand and where should one contract; where should excess funds go and where should these funds come from?

The next level of strategy will be at the division level. Here the strategic task is to determine how the particular business can succeed. The variables in focus here are how to improve the competitive position of one's own business, how to concentrate on future developments of the business within segments that seem more attractive, and how to develop business activities that are complementary to other activities already pursued, such as utilization of plant, equipment or sales organization. We shall denote the strategic planning task at the division level as the business strategy development task.

It is important to stress the difference between the corporate portfolio strategizing task and the divisions' business strategizing tasks. The former, having delegated the operating business responsibility to the various divisions, deals with how to contribute to the success of the company by putting emphasis on what seems to be a reasonable pattern of businesses. The latter deals with how to succeed with a given business.

Most businesses will have more than one product or one market, and so we may want to consider the division's business strategy as a portfolio of products and/or markets, i.e., another portfolio strategy analogous to the corporate portfolio strategy. Often the product/market elements within a division are called "Strategic Business Units" or "SBU"s. This is however not a realistic analog for the following two reasons.

In the corporate portfolio the elements will be businesses that are more or less self-contained and independent of the other businesses. Thus, a particular division can be sold without much effect on the other businesses' operations. Within a division or business, though, various products and/or markets will be interdependent, since they will be largely supported by the same functional organization. Thus, if one product and/or market is sold or closed down, the functions will feel the effect immediately in terms of utilization of their freed-up functional capacities.

Secondly, just as the corporate management interacts downward in the organization pyramid with a series of general or division managers, each representing a business, so each of the managers interacts downward in the organization with a series of functional managers, and SBU managers, none of whom however is a full-blown manager. Thus, the division manager is the lowest general manager in the organization, his "portfolio" of products and/or markets represents tradeoffs within his business, a strategic task distinctly different from the corporate level's task of developing a sound portfolio of autonomous businesses. As we shall see in the next chapter, entirely different analytical techniques will be employed in assessing the corporate strategic portfolio position than with each division's product/market strategic business "portfolio" position.

We have already alluded to the third level of strategic tasks, namely those faced by the various functional managers (such as marketing, manufacturing or R & D), or by the SBU managers within a business. Here the task is to contribute to the strategic success of the business by focusing on the particular strategic variables in the domain of a particular function-, product- or market-manager. However, the key to strategic success here is widespread cooperation and coordination; functional strategic plans generally do not make much contribution to business success in isolation, only as part of interfunctional strategic programs will the functions typically be able to enhance the general success of the business. For instance, a typical way to strengthen the position of a business might be to develop, say, a new product. This will require the close cooperation between the various functional departments; the strategizing task is to plan the cross-functional program. To start out with strong functional plans, on the other hand, would probably easily lead to the formulation of actual "barriers" to the implementation of strategic programs. There are many examples of strategic programs falling "by the wayside" because they cannot be reconciled to fit with each of the functional plans and the strong vested interests typically behind these by the functional departments.

We have now identified three levels of strategies and strategic planning in the firm. It should be a requirement that a corporate planning system be hierarchical in the sense that it reflect the distinctive division of labor in strategy formulation, implementation and planning that is implied by this. At the corporate level the strategic focus should be to develop an overall portfolio strategy which should reflect a desired risk/return balance between the various businesses that the firm is in. This is the strategic management task of the C.E.O. par excellence. At the division level, in contrast, the task will be to focus on how to succeed relative to one's competition within the particular business at hand. The division manager should be the one closest to understanding the intricacies of this business. The division of labor among the managers within the firm thus calls for each division manager to be responsible for the strategic success of his own business, within the context of the corporate portfolio strategy. At the functional or SBU level within a division the various managers will bring their specialized skills to bear on aspects of the planning of strategic programs that typically will have to be developed with inputs from several of these sources, again a division of labor - specialized excellence being provided as a complement to the division manager's general management role.

We shall claim that this three-level hierarchy of strategies is relevant in most corporate settings. In some corporate settings where one is engaged in one business only, typically smaller companies, there will only be two levels of strategy in that the portfolio level disappears. Such situations can be handled more or less analogous to a division's business planning and should not be the cause for further discussion as such. In other corporate settings, however, particularly when we are dealing with large, complex organizationl settings, we might be led to believe tnat

there should be more than three levels of strategy. In the next section
we shall discuss several examples to illustrate whether a recognition of
more than three strategic levels might be appropriate. As we shall see
this will rarely be the case.

3. Three Levels of Strategic Planning   Implementational Considerations

In this section we shall discuss whether there are instances when
it would be appropriate to have more than three levels of strategy in the
corporate planning system. Towards the end of this section we shall also
briefly touch upon the instances where the strategic levels get "truncated"
to two. We shall discuss three types of settings when one might assume
that there should be more than three levels of strategy. One is the so-
called group structure, typically within very large and/or highly diversified companies. Does this call for a group plan and a group strategy,
i.e., a separate strategic level between the corporate portfolio and the
divisions' business strategic levels? A second type of setting refers to
the role of the so-called SBUs within a division, as already touched upon.
Does this call for an SBU planning task below the divisional business
planning and distinct from the (cross-)functional programming? A third
setting occurs when we have a so-called matrix structure, such as can
commonly be found in multinational corporations. Does the "adding of,
say, a geographical area dimension" imply an additional strategic level?

Starting with the so-called group phenomenon, we shall claim that the group
rarely or never represents a fourth strategic level that is generically
different from corporate portfolio strategizing or divisional business
strategizing, but that the group's planning efforts invariably can be
seen as part of one of the other two. In instances in which group planning can be seen as an extension of corporate portfolio planning we typically have a highly diversified company where it would be difficult for

the C.E.O. to interact directly with each operating division, none the least due to sheer lack of time. So instead the C.E.O. creates groups where a group vice president interacts with a smaller and manageable set of divisions, on behalf of the C.E.O. and the corporate level. It is important to recognize that the group thereby handles a part of the corporate portfolio and not a group portfolio of its own; the strategic problem is not to develop a series of partial group strategic plans reflecting a balanced tradeoff between the expansion patterns for the groups' businesses. This would imply that each group would have to define its own businesses for expansion as well as for funds generating independently of the other groups, without being familiar with the growth and funds generation opportunities elsewhere in the company As a consequence there is a danger that some groups will be expanding businesses that might be less favorable to the company as a whole than other growth opportunities in other groups. Similarly, some businesses that have been designated to provide funds within a group might not be the most advantageous sources of funds when seen in an overall corporate context Also, a group portfolio strategy might be less amenable to encompassing selected risky investments, given that such a risk would have to be "absorbed" by a smaller number of businesses than if seen as part of the entire corporate portfolio Thus, group strategies are likely to result in suboptimal resource allocation decisions, which would also in most likelihood result in too conservative a corporate portfolio strategy. Hence, is not an answer to propose that the corporate strategic portfolio can be developed as a portfolio of groups; these are already too aggregated. Strategic portfolio tradeoffs must be made from a corporate viewpoint, and must be based on the complete set of businesses as "building blocks," not partial subsets

By means of the following example we shall explore some potential problems with perceiving a fourth level of planning in connection with a group structure. A company with 2.0 billion dollars in annual sales had been reorganized into three groups some years ago. Two of these groups were considerably larger than the third, one being involved in pulp and paper manufacturing activities, including heavy emphasis on end-use conversion through eight different divisions, the other being involved in various metals-processing manufacturing activities, again spanning a fairly wide spectrum of activities through nine divisions. The third division was within a diverse area of emerging growth opportunities, primarily based on plastics, many of the businesses of its four divisions having originally developed as offsprings from the activity bases of the old businesses. The senior management was primarily motivated by the attempt to ease their operations-related time-loads by instituting the three groups. A number of unforeseen issues did however surface when the corporate planning system was modified to reflect the new organizational structure. First, the group managements were more or less asked to take over as "stand-ins" large parts of the roles previously held by corporate management in the planning process. To free up corporate management's time was exactly one of the main reasons for delegating portions of the planning responsibility The group managements responded to this task by instituting group staffs on their own in order to facilitate the execution of their "semicorporate" planning tasks. The problem that soon arose was what should be the role of each group management in strategic resource allocation, should this be addressed by each group as the new group structure set-up implied or should at least the

major resource allocation decisions be referred to corporate management?
The company "experimented" with both approaches, neither yielding satisfactory
results. In the former case three group portfolios were emerging, as a
result of considerable efforts by the group managements to develop portfolios
that were reasonably balanced risk/return-wise as well as funds accumulation/
funds utilization-wise. Thus, the senior management at the corporate level
was no longer able to see directly what was the overall pattern of business
strategy tradeoffs, instead they were faced with deciding on resource
allocation tradeoffs between three groups. Given that each group aimed at
presenting a relatively balanced portfolio there were de facto not much of
a substantive role left to corporate management in the resource allocation
process, top management's potentially most effective tool for strategic
change. As mentioned, the alternative approach tried was to have corporate
management jointly involved with group management on the major resource
allocation decisions. Here, too, however, corporate management was
suffering from not having the entire business portfolio pattern clearly at
hand; ad hoc and sporadic corporate involvement could not be a substitute
for a systematic corporate attempt at taking each resource allocation
within the context of the overall strategic portfolio pattern that the
senior management would want to drive at. In Chapter 6 we shall consider further
the subject of operational solutions to prevent the groups from becoming
"strategic filters".

In other instances a group may contain a set of "divisions" in a highly
related set of businesses. This may have come about by a series of
acquisitions of a number of smaller firms within more or less the same
business, as proliferations into related business lines and/or as geographical
extensions. What often becomes apparent here is that each division cannot

develop a business strategy independent of the other divisions. On the contrary, by not coordinating the strategies of the divisions a major competitive advantage might be wasted -- typically the very rationale for carrying out the acquisitions in the first place The result is a lot of overlap, competition with oneself, and so on. In instances like this the group itself is indeed one business. As such it should carry out the business strategizing and planning; whether or not the divisions should be kept depends on what would be a rational way of organizing the functional, product and market activities within the business. To allow each of the divisions to develop its own business plans and have the group create a higher level business plan does not make sense; again we have only three strategic levels of planning.

An example of this problem could be found in a European-based company which was in the cement business as well as in several segments of the building materials businesses. The company had been formed through the merger of two previously independent companies each with their major business emphasis on cement. However, each company also brought into the merger several building materials businesses. Both firms were into sheets for roofing -- but utilizing competing production technologies They had also been competing within the market for prefabricated concrete elements and blocks; however, the production technologies were even more different and each had well established brand names in the market-place Finally, each company had several ready-mix concrete plants, some of which depended heavily on delivery to some of the element manufacturers that depended on a process where concrete was a major ingredient. This "myriad" of companies were all maintained as independent divisions after the merger, except for the ready-mix concrete plants, which formed a new division. Coordination among the companies was to be achieved by having all building materials based divisions reporting to a building materials group. What happened when the plans from the divisions emerged was that they revealed competitive strategizing patterns which would have potentially strong negative impact on other divisions within the group. The most extreme examples of this were when the plan by the ready-mix concrete division proposed to launch its own element and block production based on an excessively concrete-intensive production process, and when the element division which based its production on a small fraction of concrete raw material only proposed a new plant which due to economies-of-scales production efficiencies combined with an intensivated retailer rebate marketing program would enable the division to capture a significant market share increase (but, alas, mostly at the expense of other divisions within "the group!") What was needed in this instance was to consider the "group" as the focal point for the development of a building materials business strategy and to treat roofing materials, elements and blocks, and ready-mix concrete as product lines within this business.

The example just discussed lead us to consider the second area where we might be lead to questions whether we are dealing with four levels of strategy when. As we shall see, however, there are in fact only three distinct strategic levels here too. The problem to be discussed deals with now to consider the strategizing task <u>within</u> a division when the division consists of several SBUs We have already touched upon this before, but a more extensive discussion is warranted The SBU should be seen as the "building block" of the strategizing task within a division For each SBU the task should be to develop a pattern for success within this particular product/market segment. An important aspect of this is the establishing of the funds flow patterns that follow as a consequence of each SBU's development pattern. For the division, then, a "portfolio" pattern of the funds flows of the SBUs will be developed. However, the task of defining the development of SBU strategies should however be seen as one part of a division's overall business strategizing task, calling for additional divisional planning steps to modify the "first cut" divisional funds-flow "portfolio" pattern. The reason for this stems from the typical interdependence between SBUs within a division, as we have already noted. This gives rise to an additional element of divisional strategizing, namely to develop a consolidation attractiveness dimension which reconciles the strategic roles of each SBU within the division. Of paramount importance in this respect will be the facilitation of sharing of resources where possible, most notable production but also R & D, distribution and marketing. Also important will be to take advantage of counterseasonal patterns, pursue vertical integration opportunities, utilize barriers to entry opportunities represented by already established good-will positions (such as a trade-name), existing service and distribution channels, and so on. Thus, given that a business strategy consists of a consolidated set of SBU product/market strategy inputs it is the totality of these elements that constitute a division's business strategy. It is consequently normally not productive to consider the individual SBU elements of such an overall business strategy as a separate strategic level,

because this might create a tendency to partition a business strategy into
units that might be perceived as more separable then they in fact are.

To illustrate the difficulty that might occur when allowing SBU-
strategizing to fragment a divisional business strategy let us discuss
two examples, which both will illustrate that we are still dealing with
the three original generic strategic levels despite the appearance of
several more levels on the organization charts. The first example relates
to a company which is in several areas of the cosmetics and toiletries
business, and with annual sales of approximately 1.0 Billion dollars
The company is organized into four "divisions," one being the "dental
products division." The dental product division consists of two "groups"
the "toothbrush group" and the "tooth-paste group." Each of the two
groups have their separate product development activities, and production
facilities. Marketing and distribution is also largely independent for
the two groups. Within each group there are three product lines, each
headed by a product manager and each aimed at different market segments.
The potential for confusion as to what would be the relevant strategizing
elements is amplified in this example due to the particular use of organization unit labels which is not consistent with the ones adopted in
this book. According to our terminology the company would have a corporate
portfolio strategy that consists of the corporate level and the four "divisions," each of these in fact being a group. The business strategizing
task should be carried out by the "groups," tooth-paste and tooth-brush
being the two entirely separate businesses. The three product lines within each of these divisions would be to consider as SBUs. These cannot be
dealt with as independent strategic entities, in order to come up with one
integrated, non-fragmented path of direction, these should be seen as planning elements within their respective divisions' business strategizing task.

Within each of the toothpaste and toothbrush divisions SBU managers and functional units will cooperate to develop (predominantly) cross-functional strategic programs to "put muscle behind" the execution of the divisional strategies. In this example, we see that what might at first appear as five strategic levels in fact easily can be reconciled into the three standard hierarchical strategic categories. Needless to say, if we choose not to consider the strategizing hierarchy in such a consolidated form but instead base the planning task on the more extensive five-level structure there will be serious dangers of both a suboptimal portfolio strategy as well as too fragmented business strategies. We also see that we should be aware of the different usage of organizational labels from company to company, underscoring the need to focus on the generic differences among the components of the organization chart; where in the organizational hierarchy is in fact a particular strategic task carried out?

Let us as a second example consider the formal structure of a high technology oriented company with annual sales of around 200 million dollars and a record of rapid growth. The lowest level at which this company requires strategic planning is the "business element," defined as a business system which involves a single product line or a particular service capability being supplied to satisfy the needs of a single market segment. The company has 101 separate business elements. Considerable effort goes into developing an appropriate delineation of what seems to be a useful business element, keeping not only a logical product/market delineation in mind, but also attempting to keep the SBUs at reasonable size, not too small to be unable to "afford" a professional management "overhead," not too large to be unwieldy to manage A separate manager, then, is responsible for each of these business elements. Above the business element

level are 27 divisions. Each division, headed by a division vice president
is responsible for a "family" of business elements These business elements were related to each other in the sense that they were sharing a
large portion of the division's functional capabilities, notably manufacturing, research and development. Often the business elements of a
particular division were serving relatively related markets, but this
did not always have to be the case. Thus, in some instances business elements might draw on a common marketing functional capability, in other instances not The divisions are parts of seven groups, each headed by a
group vice president. However, one of these seven groups were different
from the others, in that it consisted of one division only, however, this
division being considerably larger than the others.

The strategizing task is carried out as follows: Each of the business element
agers were charged with developing a strategy for their SBU. Considerable
effort went into this, and a standardized and quite elaborate format was
followed. Each division manager developed a strategy for his division by
consolidating his SBU strategies. The groups then developed their strategies by consolidating its divisions' strategies, and, finally, a corporate
strategy was developed as an aggregation of the groups. Two types of problems became apparent. First, by splitting the business strategizing task
into two by focussing on SBU strategies and division strategies resulted in too
much fragmentation. An overly proliferated pattern of disjoint
or at best loosely connected business activities resulted. Secondly, by
splitting the portfolio strategizing task into two by focussing on group
strategies and a corporate strategy the portfolio strategy became an amalgam
of several balanced group mini-portfolio strategies, thus preventing senior
management from properly considering the entire span of strategic options.

From our discussion of the four examples thus far we see that the creation of additional levels of strategy rarely will be warranted. Basically neither the corporate portfolio strategy nor the divisional business strategy should as a rule be divided up to create additional strategic levels.

Let us now move to a third, and after more complex area where one frequently sees a call for additional strategic levels of planning. This relates to the international activities of companies. A lot of unsatisfactory strategic treatment of the international operations seems to exist. We shall point out three areas of concern, none of them calling for the creation of an additional level of strategy, as we shall see.

The first issue relates to the question of whether the international activities are part of any of the existing businesses. If so, the international activities should be treated as part of the business plan of the domestic division, unrealistic business plans will emerge if a global business planning point of view is not considered. If, on the other hand, an international activity is not part of any of the other businesses but is a business on its own, then we have a business which should be treated as a division on its own. Typically, a business in a foreign country might be run this way, particularly within consumer products businesses, even though similar types of products might be marketed in other parts of the world; strategically there is business independence.

In many situations, however, there might be some degree of interdependence as some independence, so that it is impossible to get a clearcut judgment as to whether a particular foreign operation should be seen as a separate business division or as part of a worldwide business division domestically based.

What we might be faced with here is a so-called <u>matrix</u> worldwide business planning setting. Take, for instance, a worldwide product division business which is part of a corporation in which it coexists with several other worldwide product division businesses. For each of the worldwide businesses it might be useful to be aware of and maybe even explore potentials for coordinating its appearance in a given country. However, this does not change the basic worldwide business planning strategic thrust. Take, on the other hand, a company which has several independent foreign business divisions. It will of course be important for each of them to be aware of new product developments and even to carry out some worldwide coordination of research, product development and marketing profile. Again, however, matrix planning does not call for dramatic reemphasis; the country division's business planning is still the cornerstone of a three-level strategic planning hierarchy.

Let us as a final point emphasize the <u>relevance</u> of matrix planning to help provide a proper degree of focus at the corporate portfolio level as well as at the divisional business level. In Chapter 6 we shall discuss further how to operationalize matrix planning. At the corporate portfolio planning level the various businesses will provide the major sources of inputs. However, we might also want to assess the geographic implications of a particular portfolio, so that political risks and opportunities can be assessed on an overall corporate basis. Matrix planning is useful here. At the business planning level of a worldwide business too there might be a need for matrix planning to insure that the business incorporates functions, products and countries (markets). None of these situations complicates the three-level strategic planning approach just developed.

In the Appendix to this Chapter we have illustrated some of the issues of how to define relevant strategic levels within a multinational corporation by means of an extensive, detailed example   This example is intended to further illustrate some of the complexities of reaching a meaningful strategic "division of labor" in real-life corporations.

Let us now turn to the issue of when there might be fewer than three strategic levels in the planning process. As should be clear from our previous discussion, when a company consists of what is essentially only one business there will be no strategic portfolio level, as there is no possibility to develop a tradeoff strategy with other businesses within the company, then. Thus, a single-business firm is facing a strategic planning task which essentially is analogous to the business planning task of divisions of a diversified firm. Consequently, there will be only two strategic planning levels in such a single business company.

Although the size of a company typically tends to be correlated with its degree of diversity, this is not a general rule. There are several large companies that essentially are in one business, or at least are entirely dominated by one business. Examples can be found within the energy industry, the metals-processing industry and within the transportation industry, among others. Among such large single-business firms there is often a tendency to label a functional department as a "division" and to make the department manager a "division head" For instance, we might have a smelting division, a rolling mill division and a sales division within an integrated steel company. The use of the word division in this context does of course not give rise to a divisionalized portfolio strategy We are still faced with a two-level strategic planning task.

We have now completed our discussion of the hierarchical strategy
dimension of our conceptual scheme for planning As we have seen, there are
conceptually three "generic" levels of strategy and strategic planning·
corporate portfolio planning, divisional business planning and (inter-)
functional programming. We do not find more than these three distinct
generic strategic levels even though the actual organization chart might
indicate several additional levels In a single-business company only two
of the strategic levels will be present. By now, however, it should be
clear that a typical real-life and evolving organization might provide an
extremely complex setting for the development of an overall corporate strategy. The requirement that a planning system should have to be logically
clear and specific in terms of the strategic division of labor among organizational subunits within the organizational hierarchy is frequently
not easily met in practice; it is often difficult to get a clear picture
of the three levels of strategy and who are responsible for what aspects.
Our conceptual scheme for planning will as one of its major premises be
based on an utilization of the "division of labor" that this sharpened
strategic focus provides. Thus, the three strategic levels distinction
is critical in our planning scheme.

Let us now turn to a discussion of the other dimension of our conceptual planning scheme, namely what seems to be a relevant set of stages,
or steps, or planning cycles, for identification of strategic options, for
narrowing down these options, and for monitoring progress towards strategy-
fulfillment.

2 - 4. Stages of the Planning Process

We shall propose a total of five "stages" for identifying environmental opportunities and/or threats, for narrowing down our strategic
options in such a way that they recognize our own strengths and/or weaknesses and for monitoring progress towards the chosen strategic options,
namely "objectives-setting," "strategic programming," "budgeting," "monitoring" and "linking to managerial incentives." We shall discuss each of
these five stages in turn, in terms of their specific individual purposes
as well as their interrelationships.

4-1. Stage One - Objectives-Setting

The first stage, objectives-setting, serves primarily to identify
relevant strategic alternatives, so that the issue of "where" or in what
strategic direction the firm as a whole as well as its organizational
subunits should go can be addressed.[4] This is an extremely critical phase
of the planning process in that it should set the innovative and creative
tone that should be a major characteristic of good planning. It is at
this stage, above all, that the planning process should facilitate a clearer
outlook towards the firm's environment, a sensitivity to the environmental
opportunities and threats facing the firm. Too often the planning process
fails to create this environment-oriented, opportunistic and creative
atmosphere, but becomes a process with mechanistic, extrapolative dominance
instead. Needless to say, if the planning process should suffer from lack
of appropriate "openness" at this stage it will become exceedingly likely
that the remaining steps of the planning process will turn out to be less
useful too, handicapped by the inappropriate starting position of the
planning process. In order to facilitate the development of a creative
set of objectives we shall suggest that it might be useful to consider

four aspects of the objectives-setting stage. These are an assessment
of the opportunities and/or threats facing the corporation as well as its
various businesses, the comparison of one's own performance criteria with
available outside criteria for what seems to be "normal" performance to
be expected of comparable organizations, a delineation of assumptions and
constraints for objectives-setting, including a consideration for the
general economic outlook, the firm's financial position, as well as
social and regulatory factors, and finally, a reconciliation with the
personal aspiration and style of the C.E.O. and his key management team

The first aspect of the objectives-setting process, then, is to
assess the rationale for the strategic direction of the firm and its
businesses by assessing how to take advantage of environmental opportunities and threats   This should take place ooth at the corporate and at the
divisional business levels. The divisional task to search for new opportunities and threats within its business will typically have three aspects. First, a systematic assessment should be made of potential developments with regard to the attractiveness of the business, for instance,
which segments of the business seem to have the best growth potential,
and which segments seem prone to slacken off in the future. Secondly,
assessment should be made with regard to the development of one's own
business' competitive strength; for instance, what moves might be likely
from present and potential competitors, given their strengths and weaknesses relative to one's own. Thirdly, the risks of a fundamental break-
through of some sort should be considered, such as an entirely new process for making a product, radical shifts in consumer behavior or sudden
raw material shortages, this might entirely change the nature of the
business. We are of course on very soft ground here, scenario-building
and technological forecasting may be useful tools, but these are typically

among the most "arty" aspect of planning. Again, however, the purpose is
to assess the sensitivity of "robustness" of the degree of attractiveness
and safety implied by the strategic position of the business   It should
be pointed out that the strategic position assessment must be precise
and specific in terms of the markets and products as well as the concepts
for carrying out business. One should avoid defining business strategy
at such a high level of abstraction that it becomes meaningless, an issue
to be discussed further in Chapter Three.

One company attempted to have its businesses address the issue of
operationalizing their long-term performance aspirations by having each of
them attempting to formulate a picture of where their business would be at
a given point in time in the future, in this instance ten years out   The
businesses were asked to attempt to focus on the opportunities and threats
that they see on their business horizon, and to explicitly attempt to
disregard one's own internal strengths and/or weaknesses   It was pointed
out to the divisions that the natural tendency might be to do just the
opposite, an example of "mental extrapolation" into the future based on
one's present business situation. The danger of this, it was pointed out,
would be to develop a picture of the future of the business which would
be based on the more or less wishful assumption that future opportunities
and/or threats would be based on extensions of the present. Having attempted to take a "context-free" look at the future in terms of the opportunities and/or threats seen, the division was then asked to assess
what broad areas of change this might call for in order to make the necessary reorientation of one's internal strengths and weaknesses. In this
instance, one division, which happened to be in a particular segment of
the computer-manufacturing business, identified a need to substantially

strengthen its own technological base in the semiconductor area, which was seen as critical for going after emerging opportunities within an emerging segment of the minicomputer business. A rapid move was determined to be essential in order to build up a niche vis a vis one's percieved competition, in order to "tool up" for a more aggressive performance within this niche in the market that the division had identified   In parenthesis, the division proposed an acquisition which was subsequently approved and consummated. Needless to say, this type of acquisitions was merely a move to develop a better product line position within an existing business, faster than through internal development and in response to the more aggressive performance expectations established   This should not be confused with the role for acquisitions as a way of taking advantage of opportunities and avoiding treats for the corporate level portfolio, an issue that we shall now discuss.

The corporate level task of assessing opportunities and threats should include as assessment of the general "climate" for the availability of new businesses for the company to acquire, or, probably in rarer instances, for new internal business growth opportunities for the corporate level to develop into a full-blown new division. Part of this corporate alternative business opportunity availability assessment procedure also involves assessing the potential for divestiture of a given business. It will of course be quite rare that an acquisition or a divestiture actually takes place, but the purpose of this planning activity is to carry out a systematic assessment of the opportunities of this kind on a more or less continuous basis in order to heighten the alertness of where the company realistically might be able to go in terms of "upgrading" the portfolio of businesses   This should underscore that there should be realistic assessment of potential threat to each existing business too,

and that they have to repeatedly "earn their place" as part of the corporate portfolio, given the emerging pattern of opportunities facing the
company at different points in time. The notion that some "core" business should be expected to be treated as part of the company forever
should be resisted -- hence, the ongoing assessment of divestiture potentials. The overall result of this aspect of the objectives-setting
process is of course that expectations about what should be realistic
opportunities and/or threats at the corporate portfolio level can be appropriately developed.

Many companies fall into the "trap" of developing their notion of what
should be a reasonable set of long-term performance expectations for their
company based to a large extent on an "intellectual extrapolation" of the
firm's performance of the past. Instead, a less inhibited assessment of
what seem to be reasonable long-term opportunities and/or threats should
lead to the firm's overall performance expectation. To keep a close eye on
what performance aspirations other companies seem to be aiming at is useful
in this respect. We shall discuss this as part of our second general
issue about the objectives-setting stage.

Let us now turn to the second major aspect of objectives-setting,
namely the desirability of comparing a company's own tentative criteria
for objectives performance with available outside performance criteria
that comparable corporations and/or businesses seem to be pursuing. A
first step for the corporation as a whole might be to compare itself with
the performance of selected other companies deemed by management to be
relatively equal to one's own company in terms of such businesses as size
and types of business involvements Comparative performance data can be
found in such listings as Fortune's 500, Forbes Annual Report on American
Industry, or stock market reports This should signal whether the

performance of the company as a whole seems reasonably up to par, or whether it is outstanding, alternatively lagging behind. This should give corporate management an indication as to the success of the company's adaptive attempts as a whole and whether or not there seems to be an imminent need to strengthen the efforts to adapt to the environment.

For each of the particular business divisions a similar evaluation of one's performance can now also be made by making use of the so-called PIMS data bank. Currently over 1200 "businesses" are contained in the data base, a "business" being defined in terms of an operating unit selling a distinctive set of products to a distinctive market and with a clearly identifiable set of competitors, i.e what we have denoted an SBU. A multiple regression model is used to diagnose strategies at the SBU level, indicating what would be a normal ROI for an SBU in a particular strategic position (in terms of its market share position, growth, and so on). Thus, a division can "compare" its own SBUs performance record against the norm, again leading to potential identification of businesses that might be under pressure to improve on its adaptation posture to the environment.

The process of making acquisitions and/or divestitures might also shed important and useful light on the company own performance criteria. To illustrate the positive effects of an ongoing acquisition/divestiture assessment on the establishment of realistic and operationally useful performance expectations as part of the planning process, one highly diversified company with annual sales of approximately two billion dollars might serve as an example. This company receives an average of 12 acquisition leads per week (some of which being relatively preliminary, others considerably more detailed). A separate group within the corporate planning department make the first screening-type analysis and recommendations on this. Relatively few leads will of course be followed up further, but the corporate planning department's acquisition group plays a central role in providing the continued analytical support here too. The results from this activity are that a healthy notion of what might be a realistic set of alternatives for modifying the present business portfolio with its three groups and 52 divisions gets surfaced. The constant exposure to external business opportunities and what seem to be reasonable patterns of performance among these have heightened senior management's ability to articulate and express what they feel are reasonable strategic performance standards for its own business divisions Being able to draw on this external "data-base" further seems to have increased corporate management's credibility with its divisions when it comes to communicating and discussing its performance expectations with them. In order to achieve this useful effect on the corporate planning process, then, a key feature seems to be that the acquisition analysis support function is resting entirely with the corporate planning group so that this learning effect can be instilled into the planning process. The commonly found corporate practice of having a separate corporate acquisition group is less likely to be able to provide this positive effect In parenthesis, such detached groups might also face the prob of not fully comprehending the performance needs of the corporate portfolio pattern and the specific directions towards which the portfolio should change. Acquisitions that are strategically detached from the portfolio strategy might be the not too uncommon result.

A third major aspect of the objectives-setting phase is to make more explicit and to communicate a set of underlying assumptions and constraints relevant to what will be a feasible corporate strategy. These have at least four aspects. First, the general economic outlook should be considered as a factor that might have a dampening or a stimulating effect on the firm's objectives-setting in general. Expectations about the long-term developments of the general economic climate traditionally pay an important role in modifying corporations' objectives. Relatively recently developed new sources of information for the firm to use in this respect are economic forecastic models such as the DRI model, the Wharton model or the Chase Econometrics model.[5] These model services might give forecasts of narrower business segments too, of particular relevance to specific divisions.

A second class of constraints would be to state common assumptions with regard to such items as interest rate, social security expenditure rates, tax rates, currency rates, internal overhead charges, and so on. The purpose here is to see that plans can be developed on the basis of common assumptions, so that they can be compared and discussed on the basis of substantive strategic issues of concern, not bogged down in questions relating to the premises for the plans.

Thirdly, the financial constraints that the firm faces should be made more explicit. This relates to the unused new financing capacity that the company possesses, the cost of raising new capital and the rate of dividend payouts that is being attempted. It also relates to the firm's decision with respect to relative emphasis on pursuing growth versus ROI, the former typically being a more long-term oriented type of goal while the latter typically being more short-term oriented in nature. An "optimal" desired growth path can be envisioned based on these factors. It is of course impossible to determine exactly the most advantageous path of expansion based on the amount of funds one should borrow. What is essential, however, is to communicate a realistic picture of the financial situation, so that strategies can be developed consistently with the financial goals and on a sound basis, not on overly optimistic or pessimistic grounds In Chapter Three we shall discuss an approach for a strategic audit of a firm's financial position, in order to see what particular needs for planning a given financial position might imply.

Finally, there might be a number of other non-financial constraints that could be important for the development of realistic plans, such as issues relating to social factors, political factors, business ethics, government regulations for setting safety standards, pollution, energy conservation, and so on These factors will probably become relatively more important in the years to come. Thus far many of these constraints have been seen as negative intrusions by the public sector into the strategic management of corporations. It is probably a competitive advantage for those companies that see these constraints in a positive sense, attempting to build their strategies to neutralize the constraints as much as possible. This is again back to the basic challenge of the objectives-setting task, namely to adapt to environmental opportunities.

A large multinational corporation headquartered in France was encountering a lot of problems during the corporate-divisional interface on reviewing divisional objectives. Many of these problems stemmed from lack of corporate-wide awareness of several types of common assumptions Invariably it took several meetings to clear up the confusion stemming from this resulting lack of compatibility between the various divisions' proposed objectives. After the corporate planning department issued a set of common

planning assumptions much of this confusion disappeared and there was a
better basis for discussion of what might be substantive matters of
disagreement. The corporate planning assumptions document contained the
following elements

- a corporate creed, stating in broad terms what type of company
  it was striving to be. This creed was partly based on the
  results from a survey about how several levels of management
  were seeing their company.

- a set of principles with regard to modes of ethically acceptable
  business conduct and social responsibility.

- a set of definitions of terms Some of these were verbal,
  while others indicated uniform ways of measuring quantitative
  phenomenae (such as how to measure relative market share).

- a set of economic assumptions from the corporate economist's
  office which indicated what discount rates to use in net
  percent value calculations, what annual percentage increase
  rate to use for items such as wages and energy, and which
  currency exchange rates to make use of. The corporate
  economist's assessments were revised every year, and was
  reviewed and approved by the chief executive officer.

The fourth and final class of issues with respect to the objectives-
setting process relates to the role of the C.E.O. and his key line managers.
The objectives-setting stage provides a venicle for the C.E O and the division managers to be explicit about their aspirations for their organization
What is the nature of the risk they are willing to take for their organizational climate in the company in terms of what seems to be a minimum

tolerable performance expectation? How can we be more explicit about what
is an acceptable organizational notion of what seem to be preferred directions to go?

For instance, when we contrast a well established firm within a
relatively mature business, say, a cement manufacturing company with a
relatively new, extremely rapidly growing company within an emerging high-
technology business area, we might probably (at least implicitly) find
significant differences in the managements' aspirations· by tradition
relatively little willingness to take new risks, say, by diversifying into
new business areas in the first case versus much more of a readiness to go
after new emerging strategic opportunities in the latter, acceptance of
relatively comfortable and less challenging performance levels versus strive
for even more rapid growth and increase in profits ambitions. This
aspirations-related aspect of a firm's organizational climate is highly
relevant for striking a realistic and useful planning direction. Undoubtedly,
we are here dealing with important constraints in terms of setting realistic
aspirations for what is the relevant potential for strategic change
Recognizing this explicitly in the planning process does of course not mean
that planning does not have a mission to attempt to improve lackluster
aspirations. Rather, it implies that one should attempt to be reasonably
explicit about the realistic potential for change in strategic thinking.
The pervasive influence of a C E.O. in particular, who might happen to be
an extremely strong-willed individual who sees obstacles as challenges and
enjoys pursuing unorthodox opportunities, is probably an extremely influential
determinant of the choice of objectives

Before concluding our discussion of the objectives-setting stage, let us briefly discuss the distinctions between two notions that have become established in the terminology of planning, namely what do we mean with a goal versus an objective? Objectives, in the terminology of this book, are more general statements about a direction where the firm intends to go, without stating specific targets to be reached by particular points in time. A goal, on the other hand, is much more specific, indicating where one intends to be at a given point in time. A goal thus is an operational transformation of an objective, typically a general objective often gets transformed into several specific goals.

It is important not to let semantics block one's use of the goals and objectives notions. First, it should be noticed that some persons use the words interchangeably, or some label the more general direction-setting expression as a "goal" and the more specific targets an "objective", exactly contrary to the use of the words that we have proposed above. Every organization should of course be entirely free to use the labels it chooses; however it should be consistent in its use of the two words. A more important objection about the use of the two words, however, is the fact that they tend to dichotomize when we are dealing with one decision-making process in which the emphasis should be on the transformation from general to specific. Thus, we are dealing with an objectives/goals-setting process in which we emphasize both general and specific elements. The objectives/goals-setting stage is thus one step, not two. The output from this step will be a set of objectives, transformed into more specific goals, specific enough in terms of non-financial as well as financial detail to provide an operational basis and focus for the subsequent organizational effort of developing strategic programs for "how to" achieve the objectives and goals. The strategic programming task will be discussed in the next section. Another indication of the degree of specificity needed at the present stage is that subsequently we must be able to measure progress towards the goals, one of the intents of the monitoring stage.

In summary, the objectives-setting stage serves a very important purpose in the planning process in that it facilitates a creative, imaginative adaptive focus on environmental opportunities and threats. Unless this step of identifying and doing a first sorting of the major relevant strategic options is appropriately executed the entire rest of the planning process is likely to more or less resemble an extrapolative exercise. There will of course be a large element of intuitive managerial talent behind the setting of imaginative objectives. However, we have recommended that it is useful to pay specific attention to the following four classes of issues when developing objectives: a thorough assessment of the opportunities and/or threats facing the company and each of its businesses, the establishment of outside and relatively objective criteria for assessing the company's and its divisions' levels of performance, the delineation of various classes of constraints that need to be observed when developing objectives, and, finally, an explicit recognition of the pervasive influence of the C.E.O. on whether the objectives will be marked by excellence or mediocrity.

4-2. Strategic Programming

The second stage of the planning process relates to the development of strategic programs for achieving the chosen objectives, -- or we have decided during the previous objectives-setting step "where" we intended to go; now the issue is the "how" to get there execution of the strategic programming process takes place primarily at the functional levels within each of

the existing business divisions   The intent and emphasis is on developing
long-term programs for achieving internal growth   A separate, corporate level
set of programs might deal with acquisition and/or divestitures and/or new
business development that fall outside the charters of the existing businesses; we shall discuss this after having gone through three aspects of
internal growth programming   We shall first discuss what seem to be some
of the basic characteristics of strategic programming, both in general as
well as more specifically for four different types of strategic programs
that we have identified.   Then we shall discuss the need for evaluating the
match between the sense of direction actually provided by a particular strategic program and the strategic goals that the program is intended to help
fulfill.   The final aspect of our discussion of strategic programming at the
functional levels within the businesses shall deal with the need to utilize
one's specialized functional human resources in such programs where this
scarce resource which is so critical in the strategic programming context
can be utilized as meaningfully as possible

As a first aspect of strategic programming at the functional levels
within the businesses of the firm, we shall stress that the strategic programming process poses intellectual challenges, calling for imagination,
skill and professionalism.   Strategic programs cannot be heavily based on
past experience; they are unique, and the challenge is to attack unstructured problems in an imaginative way.   Typically strategic programs are
interfunctional in their nature, requiring coordinated inputs from different
functions, such as R & D, manufacturing, distribution and marketing   The
strategic programming activity also typically goes on all year around, it
is a continuous process.   Informal elements of communication and interaction
are particularly important, above all at the initiating stages.   The

annually recurring corporate planning process adds to the strategic programming process in such a way that it requires that the "status" of the
programs be written down once a year, thereby providing an explicitness
or "inventory" as to the status of the various strategic programs in process
at that point in time.

Given that there typically will be a large, diverse and unique set
of strategic programs for any company at a given point in time, it is
difficult to give useful general examples. However, the program activities
seem to fall into the following broad areas.[6]

a) Existing revenue programs. One example of this might be the
   development of a set of marketing programs for the existing
   product line. Typically, this will imply a heavy involvement
   by the marketing department in working out the basic concepts
   of the program, such as advertising theme and selling approach.
   However, other functional departments, such as production and/or
   distribution also typically will be involved in order to
   facilitate the availability of the products at the right place
   and time. Another example might be the development of an
   improved product, which might be perceived as necessary by the
   marketing department but which might involve the research and
   development functions as well as production too. In both
   instances the necessary functional skills need to be mobilized
   to meet the requirements of the particular program. Cooperation
   among the functional specialists is essential. Although maybe
   a too strong generalization this type of strategic programs
   tends to focus on how to modify and improve on one's products
   or services in an effort to adapt to emerging environmental
   pressures, such as pursuing new opportunities or responding to

threats. Thus, these programs are primarily aimed at improving
the effectiveness of existing SBU strategies

b) New revenue programs One example of this might be the planning
and development of new products within the general business area
of a division. Here typically there will be a need for the
involvement of a broader set of functional skills than often
might be the case in existing revenue program developments
Also, given that the uncertainty typically will be higher with
such a program, making it difficult to specify the exact nature
of each function's involvement, it becomes particularly important
that such programs get "managed" on such a basis that a cross-
functional and project-focused emphasis can be maintained. We
shall discuss aspects of how to operationalize this later, and
see the critical importance of a program focus particularly when
it comes to taking decisions with regard to major changes in its
direction, discontinuation or scaling up. In general we might
say that this strategic program type too is centered around
adopting to environmental opportunities and/or threats by developing new products and/or services, often for new market niches
Thus, the thrust of these strategic programs tends to be to develop new, effective SBU strategies.

c) Efficiency improvement programs. One example of this might be
a program to "streamline" the production/distribution process,
so that the production runs become more economical and that
inventories might be trimmed as well. This might not only
involve the production and distribution department but might also
require engineering inputs in redesigning the product line,
marketing's inputs in harmonizing the new program with their

produced more cheaply, and so on. The general thrust of this type of programs will typically be around the integrative aspects of planning. The focus is on improving processes rather than developing new products; to provide more efficient strategies not only for each SBU but also for exploiting economies due to interdependencies among SBUs.

d) Support programs. Some programs might involve the development of better administrative support routines, such as an improved management information system. While, say, the data-processing department might take a lead in the development of this, other administrative support functions as well as the business generating functions will typically also be involved In general these strategic programs are intended for improving the "organizational climate" for being better able to develop the adaptive and/or integrative programs that directly affect the organization's competitive position. Most of the support programs tend to be integrative in nature.

A second aspect of the strategic programming process relates to the need to evaluate strategic programs to emphasize how well a particular program seems to contribute towards a particular goal. This is often a difficult task. There is often a natural tendency for each function to develop standards for judging the success and appropriateness of a strategic program which tend to be based largely on criteria associated with each function, and not on less partial cross-functional success criteria R&D, for instance, might focus on the extent to which the program has been successfull in providing answers to some critical, but previously unknown technical properties; manufacturing might emphasize the choice of a program alternative that minimizes the constraints of production. None of these

concerns, however, emphasizes the overall strategic fit as such. A program might represent truly innovative research breakthroughs without
contributing towards the development of a new product for a particular
market niche as hoped for. The market potential may in fact be entirely
lacking. Similarly, a production expansion program might make sense from
a production efficiency point of view, although the market for the expanded production might be lacking. To complement the often partial
roles of the functional managers, it is important that the division manager apply his general management viewpoint to the evaluation of strategic
program alternatives. It will be one of his key tasks to make a proper
selection of program alternatives in such a way that the business proceeds as intended towards the stated objectives

     The assurance of strategic focus of the strategic programming activities
is not easy to achieve. We shall discuss approaches to this later in the
book; however, a rather involved example to illustrate the nature of the
task might be beneficial to discuss at this stage We shall therefore see
how the pharmaceutical division of a highly diversified company, heavily
dependent on its R&D function, approaches this. For such a business
which will be heavily R&D-intensive relative to businesses in most other
industries it seems paramount that major decisions taken within the R&D
function's domain are resolved consistent with the pharmaceuticals business strategy. It is particularly necessary to integrate R&D planning
closely with other functions so that the programs fit in the overall business plan, in order that the strategic thrust of R&D will provide the necessary inputs for the implementation of the strategic programs of the
business and also to enable the degree of risk-taking within R&D to be
consistent with the risk-taking posture of the objectives of the pharmaceutical business as a whole.

As a program of developing a new drug proceeds through the stages of gradual completion -- ideas-feasibility check - development - pilot stage - semicommercial stage - commercial stage -- two critical issues emerge

- should we do this program all together -- does it have the desired strategic potential?

- is the likelihood of commercial success high enough so that we might continue investing in the strategic program?

The dilemma of the latter decision, i.e., of whether to continue with a program or not, stems largely from the agonizing judgment that has to be made with regards to whether the added costs incurred can be expected to yield enough progress towards reducing the risk of commericial failure. Trade-off considerations of this kind will be central to the strategic programming process.

In order to assess the strategic impact of a new program, the pharmaceutical company raises three classes of questions as part of its strategic programming process:

1. Does the contemplated program contribute towards establishing for division a business segment that it would be good to be in?

2. How does the thrust of the strategic program impact the intended outputs, i.e., how is it expected to lead to modified or new products that fit in our own business activities?

3. Does the division have its own functional capabilities to solve the programming issues at hand, above all the technical R&D capabilities?

Before attempting to answer any of these three issues the division management attempts to assess the important implicit technical/scientific risks of strategic programs. A formal list of assessment factors should be developed for this. Elsewise it is easy to "exclude" ths scientific

research staff's inputs from the overall assessment of the program. In
terms of assessing the general business goodness properties of a program
we might ask the following questions (the division should of course already
know the answers to the below questions for its business segments already
in existence):

i. Is the commercial sales potential significant or quite limited?

ii. What is the potential annual growth rate?

iii. What is the risk of "surprise factor obsolescence?" In case of
various negative developments for the product do we have
alternative ways of making potential commercial use of the project?
For instance, a modification which had been positioned within the
relatively more mature local anesthetics segment turned out to
have useful application as a medication to restore heart arrhythmia,
a relatively faster growing market.

iv What is our protective research-base position vis a vis
competitors? How fast might competitors react? What would be
the strength of a patent position? What is the degree of
"exclusivity" of knowledge about the technology? (Alternatively,
is the technology widely shared?) For instance, patents and
specialized know-how has given one pharmaceutical corporation a
virtual monopoly within the light tranquilizer market   With the
expiration of the patents, however, it is questionable whether
this dominance can be maintained. A patent position does, however,
not seem to yield the same protection in all countries, in some

countries, notably, there is little reinforcement to prevent copying. Issues of these kinds will be important for assessing the contribution of an R&D effort to establish a strategic position.

v.   What are the opportunities to have a major restructuring impact on competition and on the whole industry? The advent of the digital and semiconductor-technologies, for instance, had profound impacts on the competitive balance within the watch industry and the calculator industry, indeed these industries are entirely different in nature today (competitors, marketing outlets, prices, ...).

vi. What special environmental factors might be significant in judging the goodness of the program, such as ecology, energy, political or geographical issues, and above all, tighter than normal governmental safety procedures for new drug testing?

Addressing now the nature of the potential strategic fit of the program with the present businesses we might ask the following set of questions:

i.   How much capital is needed? Is the magnitude of the capital requirement so large that we most likely will be unable to carry out the project? Another question relating to capital needs would be whether the investment needed is large enough to provide a barrier to entry protection from other countries. A third related issue is to assess the patterns of the expected negative and positive funds flows associated with the strategic programs, so that the magnitude of the balance between the negative and positive funds flows can be judged during various stages of the program's development.

ii.   Do we have the in-house marketing capabilities for relatively
      immediate commercialization of the product, or would it take time
      to develop the relevant marketing capabilities through establishing
      new market niches?

iii. Do we have the necessary manufacturing capabilities, or do we
      need to develop these?

iv.   Would there be potentials for raw materials shortages, and in
      case, would there be substitutability potentials?

v.   Is there a "champion" for the project in the organization? It
      seems important that there is a credible person in the organization
      who believes in and "pushes" the project. This point is probably
      a critical one for an organization's ability to actually "deliver"
      innovative, operational new product outputs, but it may also pose
      a dilemma. The vested interest that the champion might develop
      in the program might jeopardize his judgment when it comes to
      decisions calling for significant changes in the program's status,
      abandonment decisions in particular A formalized strategic
      review approach such as the one we have just discussed is probably
      particularly important to reduce indecisiveness with regards to
      "pet" programs.

The relative importance of each of the above factors would obviously
not be the same; at the pharmaceutical division business attractiveness
factors 1, 2, 3 and 4 and specific fit factors 1 and 2 are particularly
critical.

We might draw a two-dimensional chart which summarizes the "portfolio"
of strategic programs in terms of the attractiveness of the output states
that the programs are intended to lead towards, as well as in terms of
strategic fit with one's existing functional capabilities and skills, as

is done in Exhibit 2-1.

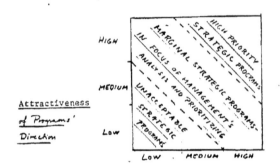

Attractiveness
of Programs'
Direction

Exhibit 2-1. R & D Projects' Strategic Postures

As will be seen from this we would expect strategic programs that measure
high on both dimensions to contribute positively towards the implementation
of strategies of business segments that we would attempt to give high priority to, while at the other extreme we would expect a program which measures low on both dimensions to be part of an unattractive strategy that
we would not pursue. The difficult strategic choices, then, come for the
in-between cases, which need to be managed selectively and which should
receive particular attention during the programming process.

We shall now return to the third major aspect of strategic programming,
namely that for a strategic programming effort to be successful it will
have to be executed in such a way that it takes advantage of the particular
strengths that the functional organizational units possess. Since organizational
capabilities, involving "investment" in human resources, can be difficult to
build up over a short period of time, it is important not to undertake
strategic programs which require functional skills that are weak or

strength, it will be advantageous to pursue strategic programs that utilize
this skill. A useful tool for checking whether the strategic programs are
consistent with the organization's strengths is to develop a functional
strength profile, which consists of assessing one's own strength within
each function relative to one's major competitor (or, if one cannot
meaningfully identify one major competitor, relative to the competition in
general within the business). Besides serving the purpose of providing a
better match between the strategic programming activities and the
organization's own strengths and weaknesses, such a profile might also
provide the basis for a key functional executive development plan for
improving one's programming strengths in the long run. Finally, a business might want to acquire another company instead of embarking on the
often time-consuming task of developing a particular set of functional
skill factors internally In such instances, it is particularly important
that one's own competence profile and the one of the candidate for acquisition complement each other so that one can obtain strengths not
presently presented.

Exhibit 2-2 illustrates how such a competence curve was looking in
the pharmaceutical firm that we have discussed earlier. This company

a very strong base in its research capabilities. However, the "bottlenecks"

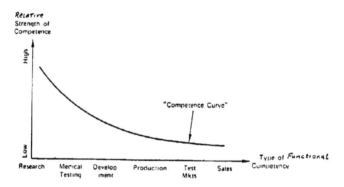

Exhibit 2-2. "Competence curve." Illustrating relative strength of
functional departments' capabilities.

for getting new products into commercial success was typically the
marketing-related functions   This finally led to several changes in some
of the company's strategic programs, most notably that the development of
several new drug programs were pursued through joint ventures with companies
with stronger marketing organizations, and that licensing was scaled up.

     The relative competence strength of each function as plotted on the
vertical axis of Exhibit 2-2 can of course not be measured in precise
ordinal terms   What is useful, however, is even a relatively crude assessment
of how each function's capabilities, strengths and weaknesses, seem to
compare with those of a few of the firm's relevant major competitors   This
will in turn highlight which of the functions are strong or weak relative to
one's competition.

Having now completed our discussion of strategic programming at the functional level, emphasizing the corss-functional nature of the process, that it should be carried out with a clear strategic context in mind, and that major differences in functional capabilities should be recognized in order to utilize slack from strengths and avoid bottlenecks from weaknesses, we shall shift emphasis and discuss the strategic programming task at the corpora level. In this respect, it is important to distinguish between acquisitions whic are alternatives to internal growth strategic programs of a business, as just discussed, and acquisitions/divestitures of businesses to change the strategic portfolio balance. While the former is the primary responsibility of an existing business division itself resulting from an analysis showing that this is an easier way of attaining the business' objectives than through internal development, corporate acquisitions/divestitures require a different kind of strategic programming activity. Typically, this is the major corporate level strategic programming activity. Others might be corporate level exploratory R&D to provide "seed" to the divisions for new products for the future, as well as strategic programs to improve aspects of the firm's administrative systems. This programming activity is often somewhat more standardized than what is typical for programming within the divisions. For instance, a corporate staff group may be chartered with the tasks of securing potential acquisition candidates, of analyzing their effects on the overall business portfolio pattern, particularly the overall financial and risk situation, as well as negotiating. Other corporate groups might look for new venture opportunities and "nurture" those programs decided upon through its first stages of development through a corporate internal new ventures "division". As soon as the new product has been firmly established the typical intent is to transform it into an ordinary business division. A third type of corporate strategic programming activity might be various central research activities which are deemed to be in a highly exploratory stage and would therefore not be touched by the divisions or which might be so risky that no single division might want to undertake the program. The output of these activities is also expected ultimately to have a major effect on the company's business portfolio through establishing the basis for new business divisions. It is important that these activities are seen as a part of the overall planning process as strategic programming to implement intended portfolio strategy changes.

We have seen several examples of problems being created in the strategic programming phase when the clear distinction is being relaxed between the interfunctional programming activities that are so critical as part of the implementation of a business strategy versus strategic programming activities that are part of corporate portfolio strategy development In particular there seems to be a danger that corporate programming activities might hamper programming within the businesses One company, for instance, was very active in its attempts to grow through acquisitions, this activity being spearheaded by the C.E.O. himself Several of the acquisitions were within business areas that were overlapping or very close to some of its present divisions. When these acquisitions subsequently were "handed over" to the divisions, this did not only cause the expected resentment stemming from the division managements' lack of participation in what was indeed a strategic program for their business. Also, however, the division's present programs needed complete overhaul now that a previous competitor suddenly would have to be integrated in the business Another company carried out central research which was subsequently handed over to existing divisions. Not only was there strong divisional resentment because it had to "pay" for an increasing share of the research activity as a project "progressed". A more fundamental problem of course was the poor strategic fit of the centrally developed programs with the business strategies. Central research, on the one hand, typically did not have a close enough understanding of and feeling for the business. The business on the other hand put the blame on central research whenever one of their products was in some sort of competitive trouble. In general, extreme care should be taken whenever a significant share of the strategic programming activity is carried out outside the divisions, notably at the corporate level. In such case, a clear portfolio focus of intended impact must be demonstrated to be the rationale for the corporate programming activity in each case.

We have now completed our discussion of the second stage of the planning process, namely the development of strategic programs for operationalizing the implementation of the broader strategic directions decided upon during the preceding objectives-setting stage. A successful strategic programming effort is of course critical for the development of a useful overall planning approach - even the most brilliant perceptions about strategic direction become rather useless unless they can be followed up by an imaginative implementation effort. To successfully facilitate strategic progress along an intended path of direction will typically be a long-term effort. Consequently, most strategic programs will be laying out the pattern of implementation over a period of several years. It follows that the degree of detail of program specification cannot possible be too overly abundant. However, for the near-term portion of the strategic programs a more specific elaboration of the strategic programs is often useful, in order to establish a relatively clear pattern of activities to be carried out, say, over the next year by a wide number of organizational subgroups, and in order to specify the nature of various executives' responsibilities and what to be held accountable for. This is the purpose of the third stage in the planning process, the budgeting cycle, to be discussed in the next section.

4-3. Budgeting

The budgeting stage, also called the action program stage, is the
third step in the corporate planning process   As pointed out this stage is
closely related to the strategic programming stage: After a set of strategic
programs has been decided on, a more detailed set of action programs will
have to be established for the next year. As such, the budgeting stage is
merely the "tip of the iceberg" reflecting a detailed operations activity
pattern for next year which should be consistent with the longer-term
strategic programs. The purpose of the budgeting stage then is above all
to establish a pattern of activities for the near-term execution of the
strategic programs, in terms of assigning specific tasks to various organizational units and groups of management, and in terms of allocating the
necessary financial resources to the carrying out of the envisioned patterns of activities. As such the budgeting cycle serves the purpose of
facilitating coordination and integration above all, i.e. facilitating
that the strategy implementation activities are carried out in an efficient manner.[7]

It is important to see budgeting as the culmination of the strategic
planning process. Unless there is a clear and logical relationship between
objectives-setting, strategic programming and budgeting, the decision-making
purpose which should be the aim of the corporate planning activity will be
sacrificed. The three stages of the process discussed so far can be seen
as attempting to identify the strategic options and to "narrow down" these
options through eliminating alternatives gradually, thereby focusing on
analysis of the remaining alternatives   This can be seen from Exhibit 2-3

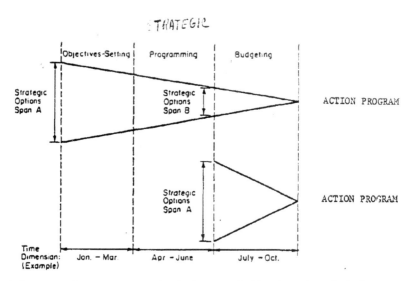

Exhibit 2-3. Narrowing Down Strategic Options Gradually through each Cycle Versus no de facto Narrowing Down Before Budgeting.[8]

It can also be seen from Exhibit 2-3 that by <u>not</u> adhering to the strategic decision-making purpose by allowing for a gradual 'narrowing down" during the objectives-setting and strategic programming stages, virtually the same set of strategic options faced by the firm during the objectives-setting stage will have to be faced by the firm and decided upon during the budgeting stage, strategic options span A versus strategic options span B in the case of prior narrowing down. Thus, an exceptionally high "capacity" for strategic decision making will be called for duing a short period of time. More likely, the quality of strategic decision-making will suffer, either because of less in-depth analysis of all relevant alternatives, or because several alternatives might not have been identified at all. Thus, "Action Program I" of Exhibit 2-3 is likely to be of a better quality than "Action Program II."

It should be noticed that while it is essential that some "narrowing down" is done during the objectives-setting and strategic programming stages so that the budgeting process can be carried out within a relatively well defined context, it is not possible to provide general guidelines about precisely how much the strategic choices can be narrowed down prior to budgeting This will vary from company to company depending above all on the degree of complexity and uncertainty associated with the company's businesses Within relatively stable businesses relatively more rapid narrowing down can take place early in the process, thus providing for a budgeting process which will be more *focussed* and concerned with less alternatives than in the case of more complex and uncertain businesses. We shall return to this issue of systems tailormaking in Chapter Five.

Maybe the most important role of the budget is to provide a "blueprint" for the actions that each group of the organization will be expected to carry out during the coming near-term time period. Each piece of these actions should of course be coordinated so that they add up to an overall integrated action-plan for the company. This overall action plan should be the "tip of the iceberg" of the company's particular strategic strive The process of developing the budget, then, will bear the burden of ensuring that the bits and pieces of each organizational fit together appropriately.

It is further critical that the budget is structured in such a way that it provides for relatively unambiguous "blueprints" for what each organizational unit will be expected to be accountable for carrying out during the period to come. This is probably relatively straightforward when it comes to the corporate and divisional level managers, but probably much less clear at the functional level. Given the establishing of the prior strategic emphasis on cross-functional program focus, the budgets should, however, complement the strategic programs by restating the short-term program consequences along functional dimensions. This gives us a unique and flexible tool for effective determination of each organizational unit's role in developing the near-term actions to be carried out, for performance tracking and control. In Exhibit 2-4 we have illustrated this two-dimensional emphasis which often is useful in achieving both a useful cross-functional strategic programming focus as well as a budgeting focus that unambiguously spells out the action program tasks of each function.

Although the two-dimensional inter-relationship that is indicated in Exhibit 2-4 would be the normal in most organizational settings, there are some organizations where the emphasis might be placed almost solely on the program dimension or on the functional dimension. We shall indicate examples of two extremes when the one or the other of the dimensions is absent.

STRATEGIC PROGRAMS	Organization Unit				Total
	Research	Develop-ment	. . .	Market-ing	
PROGRAM 1					
2	→I PROGRAMING			→	→
.					
.					
.			II Budgeting		
n					
Total					

Exhibit 2-4:   The Strategic Programming/Budgeting Sequence

One extreme would be a business that is virtually in its entirety in an exploratory or embryonic stage of development and which has thus not yet emerged at a commercialized stage. In such a setting the business activity can appropriately be described as one of persevering a set of critical developmental programs, and management are attached to these programs, their tasks are based on a temporary program organization. No permanent functional departments as such are yet developed. The budget in this case would merely be more detailed specifications of the strategic programs indicating the near-term actions to follow for the temporary organization. Examples of this might be large new business developments, such as for instance an oil company's attempts to develop synthetic fuels from a coal liquification process.

At the other end of the spectrum, we might conceive of an extremely stable and well established business where next to no new business strategic program is bound to occur. All strategic programs associated with the existing business tend to be efficiency developments and are affecting one function in particular, due to the well defined and understood way of carrying out business. In this instance both strategic programs and budgets will be developed by the functional departments. Examples of this might be found within the integrated oil industry, the steel industry or the utilities industry. We might view these industries as extremely stable in their way of carrying out their business. Thus, the nature of the strategic program/budget interface will change as we go from a temporary organization (cross-functional dominance of programming and budgeting) through the "normal" business cases (cross-functional programming; functional budgeting) to highly stable business settings (functional dominance of both programming and budgeting).

The budgeting process is a critical stage as part of the overall integrated strategic planning systems approach taken in this book in that we shall have to consider the overall completeness and balance of design. However, beyond discussing budgeting to the extent necessary for the overall systems understanding, it is outside the scope of this book to give a detailed discussion of the many aspects of the budgeting process _per se_ Let us therefore turn to the remaining two stages of the corporate planning process, which deal with monitoring of actual performance and linking strategic performance to the incentive system. A valid question, maybe, is to ask why also these two functions should be seen as parts of the integrated corporate planning system. This will be clear, however, after we have briefly described the two next stages

4-4. Monitoring

The monitoring stage is intended for measurement of progress towards fulfillment of the strategies decided on during the three previous stages. The measurement of progress should take place for the output of _each_ of the three previous stages, i.e., progress towards objectives-fulfillment, towards strategic programs fulfillment, and towards the fulfillment of the operating budget. At the present stage, we shall raise and briefly discuss the types of monitoring tasks we might face, the types of measurements we might employ and what types of corrective actions might result[9] In Chapters Four and Five, aspects of this discussion shall be followed up more thoroughly.

There are three types of actions that can be taken to measure actual performance relative to a standard (a plan) and observing a particular deviation One is to take corrective action in time to ameliorate a problem while the implementation of a strategy is still taking place, the strategic goals might still be reached, particularly if necessary corrective modifications are taken in time. We shall call this a __steering control__ approach. A second result of measuring deviation from plan is to decide to withdraw from the particular strategy or to continue further. Instead of abandoning a strategy we might also have the opposite situation that we are monitoring a particular economic and/or competitive position before committing significant resources to initiate a particular strategic move. We shall call this an anticipative go – no go control approach. Finally, we might be faced with a situation where there is little we can do __post facto__ in terms of modifying or abandoning a strategy as a result of discrepancy between actual and planned. However, a valuable benefit in many such instances is the __learning__ that takes place in analyzing what went wrong: What was unreasonable in our assumptions? How did we misinterpret competitive forces in the environment? Which of our own skills did not hold as assumed?

We want to monitor the progress towards the fulfillment of the objectives agreed upon during the objectives-setting stage for the reason that this gives us the most direct and explicit picture of whether we indeed progress as intended towards our objectives. A critical part of this monitoring task will be to focus on particular environmental factors. Of the three types of control just discussed (steering control, go – no control and learning control), steering control is clearly the most attractive given that we might have an opportunity to modify our approach before the task has been completed, i.e., we might still have a chance of reaching the goal originally intended and we might be able to save resources which otherwise would have been wasted by taking us in an unintended direction. When it comes to objectives-monitoring, steering control might be particularly useful. Here we are monitoring progress towards a goal that typically will be several years out

in the time horizon before attainment   Thus, we might have time and
flexibility to act if we monitor progress towards this phenomenon   Since
we are dealing with issues that will be of critical magnitude for the firm,
the payoff from this type of performance monitoring might be high.

In attempting to measure progress towards a particular objective, we
should take an approach which is tailormade to the particular circumstance
at hand. This might imply that we make use of measurements that are not
expressed in dollars, but in some physical phenomenon, or as an index   In
performance measures of most kinds there will be a tradeoff between the
degree of relevance of the measure we choose for reflecting changes in the
phenomenon we want to monitor, and the degree of objectivity that we can
attach to the preciseness of the measure   While more traditional dollar
variables are easier to measure objectively, they are not necessarily
relevant to measure progress towards a long-term strategic goal.

Failure to fulfill a particular goal might be due to unreasonable
assumptions at the outset which will call for subsequent modification of
the goal, or it might be due to the organization's lack of ability to
implement satisfactory strategic programs. We have to measure progress of
each of the strategic programs to determine whether lack of program
fulfillment is a problem, and if so, in which strategic program and what
particular problem. There is another important reason for measuring progress
towards strategic programs. As already discussed, a strategic program is
unique, it is "one of a kind". Thus, it follows that we need temporary
performance monitoring systems for each program, in contrast to the monitoring
of the major objectives and goals which typically will not change dramatically
in general nature over time, although changes in emphasis might occur more

frequently. For such temporary phenomena it is particularly important to measure progress towards a completion schedule. A set of "milestones" will have to be achieved within certain time limits and at specified cost At particular intervals the strategic program's viability will be reassessed and a decision made whether to proceed, modify or discontinue. Such progress monitoring is important for a strategic program, given its temporary nature and the interfunctional, project nature of the management groups involved.

Monitoring of performance relative to the budget is of course a well established procedure in many corporations. Performance measurements at this stage offer a unique opportunity to track short-term progress fulfillment, and our measures are relatively more precise than our measurement of objectives and program fulfillment. It is useful to get this information, even though a relatively larger share of it will have to be reacted to as learning control. In fact learning control will be dominant for progress monitoring at this stage, in contrast to the go - no go control dominant in the strategic programming stage and the steering control of the objectives-setting stage.

There is however an important modification of the monitoring approach to be made when interpreting short-term performance progress. There might be opportunities to trade off long-term strategic progress against short-term progress, unless the budget-monitoring system specifically also measures changes in the strategic position, so that short-term performance can be interpreted relative to the changes that have taken place. If not, a business might for instance boost its short-term results by "trading off" against long-term market share through making cuts in its advertising and/or product development expenditures.

Let us now turn to the related issue of motivating management based
on how well they perform relative to objectives, strategic programs and
budgets. The feasibility of and basis for performance incentives have of
course been established through setting long- to short-term standards for
performance during stages one through three and monitoring performance
through stage four.

4-5. Managerial Incentives

The concept of corporate planning rests upon the premise that managers
are motivated and willing to work together towards a long-term strategic
advantageous position for the firm. For this to be possible, there must be
at least some degree of congruence between the personal goals of each
individual key manager and the corporation's goals Clearly, given that the
key managers themselves are instrumental in the formulation of objectives
and goals as well as strategic programs, the personal beliefs and business
judgments of the management team will to a large extent be congruent with
the firm's. However, an individual's objectives might to some extent differ
from the firm's, and there might also be organizational subgroups that have
different goals. A particularly difficult problem where there might be goal
incongruence is the difference in time horizon between the corporate strategy
and the individual manager's goals. Because of pressures to show a short-term
individual track record to establish oneself for promotions and job autonomy,
the individual manager might tend to overemphasize short-term "window dressing",
and "sharp elbow" individualism, and consequently see the budget as relatively
more important to him than objectives and strategic programs fulfillment
Frequent job transfers make this an even more plausible mode of managerial

behavior· one only has a limited amount of time to "prove" oneself before
being transferred; the risk of being "caught" for executing strategically
unsound but in the shorter term "interesting" decisions is lessened, given
that the particular manager does not get "stuck" with the decision for a
long period of time thereafter; the accountability of a manager for strategic
management is lessened. Ironically enough, management incentive schemes
as we find them in many companies today tend to reinforce short-term
behavior in that bonuses primarily tend to be linked to the annual performance.[10]

Our approach is that the incentives that are under the discretion of
the company should be administered in such a way that they ameliorate some
of the goal incongruence just discussed. Hence, management incentives are
an integral stage of the corporate planning system.

We shall employ a notion of incentives which is broader than
managerial bonus payments. In fact we shall identify three classes of
managerial incentives: monetary rewards, non-monetary rewards and individual
feedback. Monetary rewards might be bonuses or stock options. The value of
stock options to a large extent will depend on fluctuations in the stock
market, so we do not favor this incentive payment form since the manager's
fortune can be significantly changed due to factors entirely outside his
control.

Non-monetary incentives can be of several types, and are probably
going to be increasingly important, given a growing sense of professionalism
among management as well as an emerging trend in personal marginal taxation.
It is therefore important that these often highly effective discretionary
items be incorporated into the managerial incentive scheme. Such incentives
might be job promotions and job assignments This is a highly "political"

process in most corporations, at least when it comes to promotions above certain managerial levels   To some extent the promotion process can be depoliticized and tied to some sort of formal assessment of how well a manager has performed, a fairer and more professional approach. Another related non-monetary incentive would be the degree of discretion that a manager is given for managing his operation, say his business. Managers who perform better should expect to enjoy more freedom in designing and executing their strategies, with fewer modifications imposed during the planning review process. Assuming that it would not jeopardize the corporate portfolio strategy, the more successful managers might be given more discretion over funds management and receive more investment funds as well, in recognition of senior management's confidence in the successful divisions' strategies and programs.

Thirdly, behavioral incentives will consist of individual praise, feedback review, and criticism given to each manager   A systematic review with each manager of his strategic as well as operating performance might be an important motivating device in the hands of an inspiring leader   Similarly, praise and occasionally some criticism during planning - and/or monitoring - review meetings might be effective.

The key of course is that the incentives must be tied to performance as reflected in the achievement of objectives, strategic programs and budgets. While managerial incentives as just discussed are old and well established in most companies they may not have been executed in the context of the strategic planning system   Hence, not only might an opportunity to create a more realistic emphasis on planning be lost, but, worse, the non-coordinated incentives might actually reinforce non-strategic managerial behavior

This concludes our discussion of the different stages of the planning process. The major purpose of emphasizing a set of distinctive stages has been to strengthen the focus of the various planning activities, so that it becomes clear "when one is doing what." Specifically we have emphasized the need to orderly identify <u>and</u> narrow down strategic options, to achieve <u>both</u> adaptation as well as integration, through the execution of an objectives-setting stage, a strategic programming stage and a budgeting stage. We have also stressed the needs for two follow-up stages in order to reinforce the strategic direction set during the first three stages, namely monitoring and incentivating. This focus on five specific stages for setting strategic direction constitutes the second major dimension of our conceptual scheme for corporate planning.

2 - 5. A "Three by Five" Information Model of Corporate Planning

We have by now identified two of the three major dimensions of our corporate planning conceptual scheme - three levels of strategies and five dimensions of identifying, narrowing down and monitoring strategic options. The third dimension of the conceptual scheme, which is to be discussed in this section, emphasizes that there is an important information - and communication-flow aspect of the planning process that needs specific attention.[11] This will identify a pattern of interaction and iteration among the various managers responsible for the various levels of strategy, all of whom contributing towards the development of one overall plan for the company as a whole, internally consistent among its parts but allowing for the restatement of what are the plans for the various organizational sub-units as part of this. Exhibit 2-5 gives a flow-chart model which indicates how the various levels and stages discussed thus far can be put together. The model specifies a logical sequence of steps that should be carried out in order to make the process "come alive" within a corporation. We shall briefly discuss each step, following the numbering within the circles of Exhibit 2-5. It should be noted, however, that the meaningful implementation of these steps may not always be straightforward, for two reasons. Partly this is due to the fact that we are dealing with a behavioral process, as already stated above. This means that a description, step-by-step, of the logical path through the process is likely to be far too simplistic as a guideline for describing how this behavioral process actually may take place. Even though the discussion of the sequence of steps in this section therefore probably smacks somewhat of being too "mechanistic" it is however a useful starting point for describing the planning process. Subsequently through the book we shall see how this

behavioral process is dominated by feedbacks, negotiation meetings, revisions, and so on. In addition to the fundamental need to recognize that
we are dealing with the implementation of a behavioral decision-making
process, there are also a number of other implementation problems, typically stemming from misconceptions about "technical" aspects of the planning process. In Chapter Four we shall discuss the most common of these
implementation issues.

- Step 1: The C.E.O. states his long-term "aspirations" for the company,
  in terms of tentative and relatively general long-term objectives and stating his key assumptions behind the objectives
  (such as, for instance, general economic trends and resource
  constraints on the company). Comparison with the performance
  patterns of other companies relatively similar to his own
  might play an important role in shaping the C.E.O.'s aspirations. Also, of course, the C.E.O. will draw on any experience in the company with planning in the past as well as
  the past performance records.

- Step 2: Each division defines his business charter in terms of identifying the "border lines" for the product/market/services
  his division is in, and in terms of providing a general rationale
  for why one should be in this business based on its long-term
  expected attractiveness. He also proposes a set of division
  goals in terms of competitive strength position to be generally
  aimed at, and elaborates on the rationale and assumptions behind
  these. The center of the division manager's emphasis in all
  this is on the environment he is facing, a creative and opportunistic "digestion" of the opportunities and threats he sees.
  He finally proposes a tentative resource requirement estimate

in accordance with the strategic positioning proposed for the business. (It should be noticed that in Chapter Three we shall discuss in detail a way of stating the strategic position of a business in terms of its competitive strength and the attractiveness of its business. We shall see then that the strategic positioning of the business is likely to have strong implications on whether the business will be expected to become a net funds user or a net contributor of funds).

- Step 3. The C.E.O. approves the division objectives and strategies. The approval of each division's statements must be assessed within the context of the overall portfolio pattern that emerges from the overall set of divisional inputs, as well as from potential acquisition opportunities that might exist. He then summarizes the output of the objectives-setting cycle by stating the corporate portfolio strategy as well as specific but tentative corporate and divisional goals, which will serve as the focus for the next cycle.

- Step 4 The C.E.O. initiates the strategic programming cycle with a call for divisions programs to be focussed on how to achieve the divisional goals.

- Step 5: Each division manager will state for his functional organization the division's strategy, general objectives and specific goals, i.e. the division's expected strategic role within the overall strategic pattern developed in the previous cycle. He will then ask his functional organization for alternative strategic programs for "how to get there."

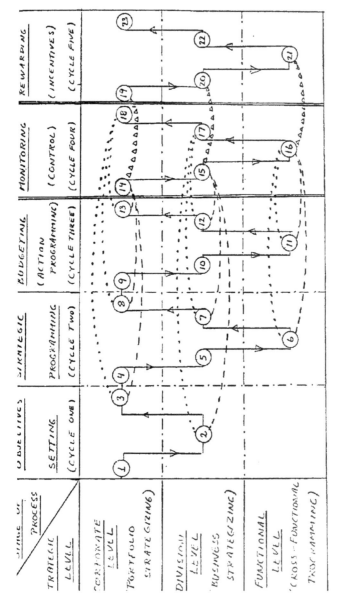

Exhibit 2-5: A Conceptual Model of the Steps in the Information Flow of the Strategic Planning Process.

Legend: — The basic information/communication flow; solid line.
— The tracking of actual vs. planned performance; broken line.
— The corrective actions and modifications of plans; dotted line.
— The comparison of actual vs. planned performance for incentives; triangle line.

- Step 6: The functions will identify strategic program alternatives, typically in close crossfunctional cooperation. The alternatives may be new ones, such as the development of a new product, or reassessment of existing ones, such as continuing with a mature product. Program alternatives will be analyzed and the best ones will be recommended to the division general manager. Typically the task of carrying out this step tends to be extremely time-consuming and is normally going on all year around. However, at the time when this stage of the planning process is reached each year the "status" of the ongoing strategic programming activities should be summarized.

- Step 7: The division manager should at this point make a selection among strategic program alternatives, attempting to come up with a strategic program "package" that fulfills the intended objectives and goals for the division. This strategic program package, including the expected associated funds flow characteristics, will then be recommended to the C.E.O.

- Step 8: The C.E O. will evaluate each divisional program package input within the overall portfolio context that emerges. He will then make tentative resource allocations to these long-term divisional strategic programs, based on their merits in the overall strategic portfolio context, and "competing" not only with each other internally but also against the allocation of funds for acquisitions. Thus, it is primarily at this stage that the major thrust of the C.E.O 's power to influence the long-term direction of the firm might be applied. This resource allocation pattern marks the culmination of the strategic programming cycle of the planning process.

- Step 9· The C.E.O. will start out the budgeting cycle by calling for divisional budgets to reflect the near-term actions to be carried out as part of the longer term strategic thrust.

- Step 10· The division managers will communicate the division goals and strategic program "package" to its functional organization the way it had emerged from the previous strategic programming cycle, and call for functional or departmental budgets.

- Step 11: The functional departments will develop and submit for approval their budgets, reflecting their near-term involvement in the execution of the various strategic programs. The strategic programming - budgeting sequence at the functional level, as indicated in Step 6 together with the present step, thus follows the two-dimensional format discussed in Section 4-3 and illustrated in Exhibit 2-4.

- Step 12: The division manager will corrdinate, review and approve the functional budgets and submit his emerging division budget for corporate approval.

- Step 13 The C.E.O. will approve the emerging corporate budget which reflects the near-term actions to implement the portfolio strategy. This final resource allocation culminates the budgeting planning cycle. It should be noted that tne information flow has a segment of discontinuity after this step. The first thirteen steps of the information flow, encompassing the three first cycles of the planning process, have been focussed around developing a prior set of plans, culminating with the completion of Step 13. The remaining steps of the information flow, on the other nand, encompassing tne monitoring and reward cycles, are focussed around aspects of posterior comparisons

of actual performance with the performance that had been
planned.

- Step 14: The C.E O. states the overall monitoring tasks, to track actual
performance against the near-term goals, against the achievement
of the strategic programs and against the fulfillment of the
objectives, i.e. against the outputs of planning cycles three,
two, and one. He assigns to each of the divisions the task
of monitoring their own performance in progressing towards the
fulfillment of their objectives, strategic programs and budgets. Also he assigns to his own office the task of monitoring
the progress towards portfolio strategy fulfillment. As part
of this, the C.E.O. establishes limits of deviations for actual
performance against each of the objectives, strategic program
and budget standards, attempting to assess when a modification
of one or more aspects of the portfolio strategy is needed,
either as a result of a deviation induced by one of the internal divisions or because of environmental changes.

- Step 15 The division manager states the monitoring tasks for his own
organization, and assigns to his functional managers and to
managers specifically appointed to run specific strategic
programs the tasks of monitoring progress towards budgets and
strategic programs. The division manager also assigns to his
own office the monitoring of progress towards his business'
strategy fulfillment. Further, he develops standards for
when deviations should lead to modification(s) in one or more
aspects of his business strategy, either as a result of deviations in strategic program fulfillment, functional budget
fulfillment, or changes in key environmental factors affecting

the business.

- Step 16: The functional managers monitor progress against their budgets. Similarly, progress against the strategic programs is being monitored, by a functional manager if the program involves his department primarily, or by a manager assigned to the task if the program is more heavily crossfunctional in nature. Significant deviations are being reported to division management, together with analysis and suggestions for how to react, if at all. Less significant deviations are being responded to by the functional or strategic program managers directly. It should be noted that the monitoring or control cycle consists of two distinctive but interrelated types of tasks, the tracking of actual performance to be compared with the established standards from the plans, and the execution of corrective actions resulting in modification of the plans. In Exhibit 2-5 this has been indicated by lightly broken lines for the tracking relationships and with dotted lines for the corrective action relationships respectively.

- Step 17: The various monitoring inputs from the different aspects of the fulfillment of the strategic programs, functional budgets as well as pertinent changes in the key environmental factors, are being reconciled in terms of the emerging effects on the progress of this business as a whole, progress towards the fulfillment of the business' strategic objectives, towards its strategic programs and towards its budget. The emerging pattern of progress and deviations is being reacted to in terms of initiation of ameliorating actions and revision of plans; however, particularly serious deviations are being communicated to the corporate management.

- Step 18   The C.E.O. monitors progress towards the long-term portfolio
objectives, towards the overall portfolio of strategic programs
and towards near term budgets, partly as the result of the
performance inputs he is receiving from his division, and
partly based on the inputs received from his own office's
monitoring, particularly of key environmental factors. The
monitoring at this level too is likely to lead to corrective
actions if necessary and possible, the initiation of such
actions depending on the degree of magnitude of the decision
as well as the extent to which a decision might have reper-
cussion on the execution of other strategic elements within
the overall portfolio, i.e. whether or not a particular organizational level possesses the discretionary power to act.
The monitoring cycle does not culminate at a particular point
in time, but is an on-going process until next year's revised
monitoring targets are being established through the carrying
out of planning cycles one to three again.

- Step 19· The fifth cycle, rewarding or incentivating, also represents
a discontinuity in the overall information flow process from
cycle four. However, this cycle is nevertheless closely related with the other four. It emerges with the C.E.O.'s involvement in setting personal achievement goals with his division managers, with regard to their expected contribution
to the success of the fulfillment of objectives, strategic
programs and near-term budgets. This draws directly on the
planned outputs of Cycle One (Step 3), Cycle Two (Step 8), and
Cycle Three (Step 13), and reflects the accountability that

the C.E.O. is assigning to the division managers for their performance.

- Step 20. The division managers set personal achievement goals with their functional managers and strategic program managers, reflecting their expected contribution towards the fulfill- ment of longer-term strategic programs as well as nearer-term budgets (consistent with the planned outputs of Steps 7 and 12).

- Step 21: The functional managers and strategic program report to their division manager the nature of their actual contribution towards their agreed upon personal targets. This draws upon the information already revealed during the tracking of actual vs. planned performance during Cycle Four.

- Step 22. The division managers report to the C.E O. the nature of their actual contribution towards their agreed upon personal targets. This also will be based on the performance tracking information gathered during the monitoring stage.

- Step 23: The C.E.O. disburses incentives to the various levels of man- agers based on actual versus intended performance in accordance with the prior and posterior information provided during the previous 22 steps of the planning process. Incentives might be monetary as well as nonmonetary.

This concludes the sequence of steps to be carried out in our pro- posed conceptual scheme for corporate planning, encompassing the devel- oping of a set of plans that feature both adaptive as well as integrative strengths, are being monitored in terms of how well they are actually being fulfilled, and are being tied to the performance of specific man- agers in terms of what these should be held accountable for and receive incentives for accordingly. Although the steps may seem straightforward

enough most companies will typically have considerable difficulties in
actually making such a "way of strategically managing the company" work.
Most of the remainder of this book, in fact, will discuss how to operationalize the model. At this point, however, it is important to stress
again that this model is a behavioral one, its general distinctive char-
arteristics thus being that it is a communication flow model, it is interactive, it is iterative. At this point it is useful to discuss each
of these three characteristics more specifically.

The task of developing an operational set of coordinated strategic
plans for a large, complex corporation is certainly not a trivial one,
given that a large number of interrelated elements of plans will have to
be created. The complexity of the task of developing plans is particularly
high when we are faced with a highly diversified corporation, where each
business plan will have to fit within the overall corporate portfolio
strategy context. In order for this to become feasible it is typically
necessary to develop tight time schedules for what should be developed and
reviewed by whom within the corporation. The communication system specifies this, as indicated by the flow chart (or "snake") of Exhibit 2-5, it
is a system with a high degree of interdependence and typically little
slack; it is therefore necessary for each unit within the organization to
adhere strictly to communciation patterns and time schedules

The system is interactive. This is a reflection of the intent to
develop a system which enables the release of the creativity, skills and
insight of individual people across the organization by means of a clear
"division of labor" among managers. This interactive mode follows a
highly formalized pattern of "top-down"/"bottom-up" interfaces within
the organization. This two-way process goes on at each of the five

stages of the process, when it comes to objectives-setting, strategic programming, budgeting, monitoring as well as incentivating. Although it therefore will be essential with a two-way interaction at each stage, the actual balance between the top-down and bottom-up influences may of course change between the cycles, and it will normally also be different from one firm to another   In Chapter Five we shall discuss this.

The system is also iterative, although this may not be directly apparent from Exhibit 2-5, except for the corrective actions that are being initiated as part of the monitoring stage and which may lead to modifications in objectives, strategic programs and/or budgets. However, with the need to develop complex, coordinated planning outputs at each stage of the planning process, a lot of trial and error will normally have to take place before a finalized set of plans can be reached. There are two aspects of this. First, during each stage a gradual, coordinated commitment across the organization's strategic hierarchy is the output objectives, strategic programs or budgets. Particularly when the planning system is new and/or during periods of major and rapid changes the tentative plans can go "up and down" several times before a "consensus" is reached with respect to the outputs of a particular planning cycle that can be "signed off" by senior management. These iterations are inevitable, although they might represent a time-consuming and perhaps frustrating set of meetings and revisions. This is a necessary and unavoidable part of planning which underscores a major characteristic of the process. planning involves rigorous, detailed and time-consuming work for all, the plans are only as good as their weakest part. In Exhibit 2-6 we have indicated that there typically might be five different kinds of "iterative loops" of this kind with the planning process

(Encircled numbers 1 through 5 in Exhibit 2-6):

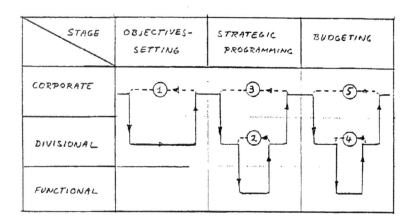

Exhibit 2-6: Iterative Loops in the Strategic Planning Process

- loop 1: When the C.E.O. receives the divisional inputs indicating the
potentials for where the businesses might be going he may
have to reconcile the emerging portfolio picture with his
initial tentative objectives. As a result we may ask one or
more of the divisions to revise their inputs, and he might
change his original tentative objectives as well. One or
more iterations may be necessary before the loop is closed.

- loop 2: During the division manager's strategic programming package
consolidation he may frequently go back to the functional
departments and request revisions in particular programs,
in order to facilitate a better overall match of the individual programs into a more coherent package from the business viewpoint.

- loop 3   When the C.E.O. receives the portfolio of divisional strategic
           program inputs he may have to cycle one or more of these back
           for revisions, so that the portfolio strategy becomes as de-
           sired.

- loop 4: During the budgeting cycle a division manager may have to
           recycle the functional budget proposals so that the overall
           budget might attain the desired strategic properties, i.e.
           become a near-term reflection of the longer term strategic
           program thrust.

- loop 5: Similarly the C.E.O. might want to call for revisions in one
           or more of the divisional budgets so that the final overall
           fit is achieved.

The other aspect of iteration relates to revisions that have to be
made to a completed stage of the planning process because subsequent
analysis at later stages indicates that the decisions taken during the
previous stage were not all that plausible in retrospect.   These "major"
iterations may be necessary as a result of entirely unforeseen
circumstances. In most instances, however, these iterations might have
dysfunctional effects and should therefore by kept to a minimum. The
reason is that corporate planning as a decision-making process implies
that the organization's members should be expected to commit themselves
to particular directions and courses of action by the end of each stage.
If it is widely accepted that one can "get away" from these commitments,
then an unrealistic and easily too much of a "blue sky" atmosphere for
planning might be created. Needless to say, too, additional and less
useful planning is created through this kind of iteration   It should
be stressed that these "major" iterations refer to modifications of
prior stages before the overall set of action programs or budgets

have been completed, i.e. iterations affecting two or more of Cycles 1
to 3. These undesirable revisions should not be confused with the desirable revisions of Cycles 1, 2 or 3 resulting from actions taken in
the monitoring stage.

2 - 6. Summary

In this chapter we have developed a conceptual model for corporate
planning. This conceptual scheme is based on three general sets of premises. First, it acknowledges that there is an opportunity for "division
of labor" among the various levels of management in an organization, so
that three distinctive levels of strategy can be developed, with the
corporate management to be held primarily accountable for the portfolio
strategizing task, with division management to focus on business strategizing, and the specialized functional management groups to cooperate
on developing strategic programs. We have attempted to demonstrate in
our discussion the significant benefits that might accrue to an organization by having an explicit structure in the division of labor to carry
out the strategic tasks. This will provide for specialization, but within an overall corporate context.

The second premise that the conceptual scheme rests on is that the
planning task must accomplish a multifaceted set of purposes, much broader
than we maybe traditionally have been recognizing. Specifically, relevant
opportunities must be identified and "narrowing down" choices must be made
to arrive at a "best" set of coordinated action programs for the company.
This underscores an issue that we have been stressing, namely that planning is a decision-taking process. In line with this it is also necessary
to see monitoring and incentivating as part of the planning process. We
have suggested that a systematic and sequential shift of focus from one

key activity to another is useful to facilitate the development of full-bodied plans, which might encompass both adaptive as well as integrative qualities instead of being partial. A useful set of cycles are objectives-setting, strategic programming, budgeting, monitoring, and incentivating.

A final premise of the conceptual scheme is the acknowledgment of the behavioral nature of planning, that it is a framework for interaction among human talents Thus, the planning process should be seen as an information process, and above all should facilitate innovative and creative managerial behavior. To facilitate this the planning scheme that has been developed incorporates explicit patterns of interaction, sets out clear sets of agendas for "when to discuss what," assigns explicit patterns of accountability to the various managers and incentivates those managers that contribute towards the firm's strategic success.

Why is it necessary with such an elaborate conceptual scheme for planning? We shall briefly suggest two interrelated reasons at this point; however, as our discussion proceeds several other reasons will emerge. First, given that we are proposing that the task of planning should be approached by means of <u>process-model</u> for planning it becomes essential that the overall logic and rationale of the process is made explicit and understandable to a relatively wide number of managers. In order to do a good job, both in terms of understanding and motivation, within the much narrower part of the planning process model that he normally will see, it is essential that he has a clear feel for the overall approach. Only an explicit process-oriented conceptual corporate planning scheme can facilitate this Related to this is our second rationale for the necessity of a conceptual scheme Given the many facets that planning consists of it is unreasonable to expect that all aspects of planning shall be equally well elaborated and operationalized at once.

However, developing a firm's planning system gradually requires a keen understanding of how the various elements that are being developed fit into an overall scheme, almost like attaching bits and pieces to a schelethon Many companies, unfortunately, lose track of this, and consequently, end up with several modules for aspects of planning that cannot be reconciled. Consequently, even though considerable efforts have gone into planning, these efforts do not lead to a pattern of evolution towards an overall integrated planning system.

Our conceptual scheme is a general model which should apply to any multidivisional company, and also to any single-business firm in a modified version by eliminating the portfolio strategic level. It is clear that the conceptual model as outlined here represents only a first "cut" at installing a corporate planning system Further modification is needed to tailor-make the system to respond to the planning needs dictated by the firm's situational setting, we shall discuss this in Chapters Four and Five Therefore, before seeing how we might build certain desired capabilities into the model we need to discuss how to undertake an analysis of a particular firm's situational setting, in order to better identify a firm's particular planning needs. The subject of the next chapter will deal with this, particularly the identification of what needs a firm might have for planning, stemming from the strategic setting that the firm finds itself in

Appendix: An Example of a Complex Hierarchical Organizational Structure

The following example is intended to illustrate the complexity of identifying the relevant levels of strategies in a complex, diversified, multinational organization. The example is intended to underscore the need for careful analysis of a firm's formal organization structure in order to determine the "division of labor" for strategy-development within a company.

The company was a Swedish-based industrial company, working mainly in the fields of pharmaceuticals and chemical products, on a worldwide basis, with world sales of approximately 250 million dollars. The company had five autonomous divisions: pharmaceuticals, industrial anticorrosion chemical specialties, chemical-based consumer products, agricultural feed products, and fish protein products. The company had started out and established itself primarily within the pharmaceutical field, the other divisions were still relatively small and the results of internal diversification efforts seen from Exhibit 2-7. As can be seen from this, the pharmaceutical division, which accounts for seventy percent of sales and most of the profits, is exhibited in considerably more detail than the other four divisions. Within the pharmaceutical division itself there seem to be a number of "divisions," namely five "product companies" which are responsible for the development of their own product lines, most of these being larger than any of the nonpharmaceutical divisions. Also, there seem to be a number of "market companies" responsible for selling in the various geographical territories around the world. An initial issue stemming from the organizational structure is the potential dysfunctional effect that the extremely skewed size distribution of business divisions might have on strategy development. In terms of developing an

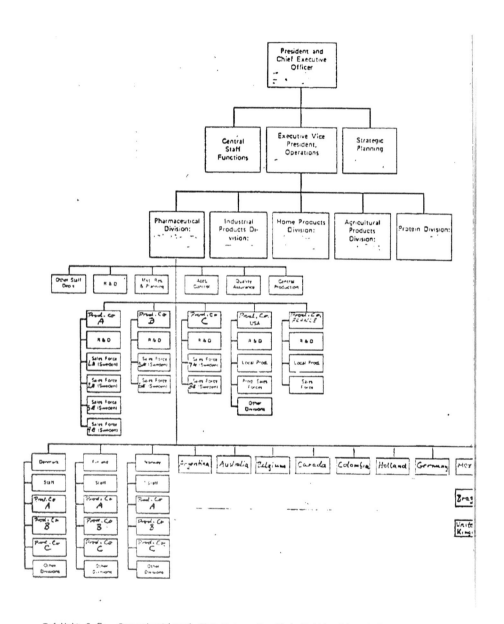

Exhibit 2-7: Organizational Structure, Swedish Multinational Company

overall company strategy based on the businesses as strategic unit "building
blocks" the present organizational set-up is potentially less useful, in
that the smaller divisions might detract from the attention of senior management as to where the true portfolio tradeoffs and choices should be,
above all between various segments of the pharmaceutical area. By adding
relatively small, unfamiliar and potentially problem-ridden businesses to
a company's portfolio there might easily develop a problem of "overloading"
of the strategic system in that senior management get distracted in too
many directions and fails to pay sufficient attention to critical strategic
portfolio issues concerning the core businesses. Thus, it seems to be a
definite advantage for effective portfolio strategizing that the size distribution among business divisions is relatively even.

A second organizational issue relates to the way the pharmaceutical
sector is built up in structure. We are dealing with a remarkably complex
structure with at least five major different key substructures·

a) In Sweden we have a "divisionalized" type of organizational structure,
    with each of the three Swedish product companies operating their own
    "business", with their own R&D capabilities and independent marketing
    and distribution forces. This implies a considerable duplication of
    efforts -- with three R&D organizations and eight sales force
    organizations in Sweden. Presumably the activity levels of the
    product companies is high enough to justify the costs of duplication.
    There is considerable benefits from having relatively simple and
    easily identifiable strategic units like these, not the least because
    people typically can better associate themself with such strategic
    settings. There are, however, also potential difficulties that a
    product company might develop strategies that might "hurt" the other

product companies and thereby potentially hurt the company as a whole, by adopting marketing campaigns that might create bad-will for the others, by focusing on the same customers and thereby causing customer "fatigue", by competing for the same personnel resources, and so on. This problem becomes even more difficult due to a high potential for increasing overlap between the three product companies business segments, stemming primarily from the difficulty of keeping the outputs from pharmaceutical R&D efforts to develop within the interest areas of each product company, not touching upon other product companies' sphere of involvement. It should thus be a planning task to provide strategic coordination across the pharmaceutical businesses in Sweden, i.e integration planning.

b) Within the rest of the Nordic countries (Norway, Denmark, Finland) each of the product companies have their own marketing and sales organizations. However, all of these (together with the sales organizations of the non-pharmaceutical divisions) are part of a geographical area company. We thus seem to have a sort of matrix organization with the product dimension being the dominating or "leading" one and the area dimension being supplemental or "grown" Presumably, then, we might expect that the product organizations should be primarily involved in integration planning. However, we would expect the area dimension to be primarily involved in adaptation planning. Thus, the area viewpoint should be in the center of focus when developing the inputs from these countries to the overall pharmaceutical sector strategy Thus, the issue would be to focus on the strategic opportunities of each country so that the relative involvement can be determined on the basis of relative country

attractiveness, and not by merely adding up the strategic inputs
of each of the product line organizations per country. Hence, the
planning system should facilitate the availability of country-wide
inputs as a vehicle for adapting to environmental opportunities
and/or threats.

c) Within the rest of the world there is a total of 10 marketing
companies that carry out marketing and sales in a given country of
all the product companies under a common corporate "label"; none
of the product companies have separate sales forces What we seem
to have here is a different form of a matrix structure, this time
with the area dimension as "leading" and the product dimension as
"grown". Thus, the integration planning tasks should be heavily
focused around the area; the adaptation planning task, however,
should be more heavily focused around the product/business
dimension -- which products/businesses are potentially the most
attractive in the years to come given our own strengths and the
general business attractiveness trends in this area? Thus, the
planning system should provide these inputs about long-term product
opportunities from the areas worldwide into the objectives-setting
of the pharmaceutical sector.

d) The product companies outside Sweden, namely U.S.A. and France,
form yet another strategic set-up. These organizational units are
both chartered with the function of R&D in order to develop their
own products within defined business segments (analogous to the
Swedish product companies) as well as to market the products of
the other product companies in the U S.A. and France respectively
(analogous to the 10 marketing companies). Thus, a dual and
particularly complex planning role seems to exist for these two
organizations. Ore is to provide the same planning inputs as an

product/business opportunities in U S.A. and France, so that the
pharmaceutical sector can take the potentials of these important
markets into account when the sector's overall objectives are
formulated. Secondly, there is a planning need to be carried out
with respect to the direction of the particular product/business
segment of the organization, analogous to the planning tasks of
the three Swedish product companies. The organization will have
an important need for area opportunity inputs from the 10 marketing
companies as well as from the Swedish and other Nordic countries to
develop meaningful plans for this In general a clearcut distinction
will have to be drawn with regard to the two above planning tasks,
so that the overall pharmaceutical sector's global strategy will
not suffer from unclarity with regard to the R&D/product roles of
U.S.A. and France as well as with regard to the market opportunities
in U.S.A. and France for the other (Swedish) pharmaceutical products
and R&D.

e) Outside of Sweden the four non-pharmaceutical divisions seem to rely
    on the pharmaceutical division's organizational resources. A major
    argument for this is that the size of the other divisions is still
    so small that they cannot afford the "investment" in developing
    their own separate international organizations. The problem with
    this, however, is that a lack of realism might develop as to what
    should be the true strategic opportunities worldwide. Similarly,
    the accountability for successful strategic fulfillment might
    easily get diluted.

In summary, then, we see that corporate portfolio planning task involves developing an emerging balance between the pharmaceutical division and the other four divisions - where should the emphasis be? However, it also seems clear that the portfolio strategizing task in this instance is both much simpler and probably also relatively less important than the task of developing a business plan within the pharmaceutical division. Here the issue is that the five product companies represent different SBUs. Thus, a good pharmaceutical division business plan will have to be based partly on planning inputs from the SBUs and partly on an approach which builds on the interrelationships between the SBUs   When it comes to the third level of planning, namely the development of predominantly cross-functional strategic programs, this will also be relatively complicated given the extensive duplication of functional capabilities, particularly when it comes to R & D. The setting of this example should illustrate the enormous difficulty of developing a meaningful hierarchy of strategic tasks in a highly complex organizational, multinational and with matrix structures Two additional issues of relevance for the discussion in this book emerge from this. How can a company's planning system indeed provide the necessary support that is needed to develop such complex strategies? Secondly, is it really appropriate and necessary with such a complex, fragmented and multi-hierarchical organizational structure given the considerable risks that will be implied from lack of strategic focus and high costs in the forms of overheads, duplication and communication? We shall discuss each of these issues, in Chapters Four and Six respectively.

Footnotes - Chapter Two

1. The conceptual scheme to be presented is an extension of Vancil, R. F.
    and P. Lorange, "Strategic Planning in Diversified Companies", <u>Harvard</u>
    <u>Business Review</u>, Jan.-Feb., 1975. Several authors have presented
    conceptual frameworks for corporate planning; see, for instance,
    Gilmore, Frank F. and Brandenberg, R. G., "Anatomy of Corporate
    Planning", <u>Harvard Business Review</u>, Nov.-Dec., 1962, Stewart, Robert F.
    <u>A Framework for Business Planning</u>, Report No. 162, Long Range Planning
    Service, Stanford Research Institute, Menlo Park, 1962, Anthony,
    Robert N., <u>Planning and Control Systems: A Framework for Analysis</u>,
    Division of Research, Harvard Business School, Boston, 1965, Humble,
    John W., "Corporate Planning and Management by Objectives", <u>Long Range</u>
    <u>Planning</u>, June, 1969, Steiner, George A., <u>Top Management Planning</u>,
    MacMillan, New York, 1969, Ackoff, Russel L., <u>A Concept of Corporate</u>
    <u>Planning</u>, Wiley-Interscience, New York, 1970, Ringbakk, K. A., "The
    Corporate Planning Life Cycle - An International Point of View", <u>Long</u>
    <u>Range Planning</u>, September, 1972, Cohen, Kalman J. and Richard M. Cyest,
    "Strategy: Formulation, Implementation and Monitoring", <u>Journal of</u>
    <u>Business</u>, Vol. 46, July, 1973, Malm, Allan T., <u>Strategic Planning</u>
    <u>Systems: A Framework for Analysis and Design</u>, Student Litteratur,
    Lund (Sweden), 1975, Hax, Arnoldo C. and Nicolas S. Majluf, "Towards
    the Formalization of Strategic Planning - A Conceptual Approach",
    Technical Report No. 2, Sloan School of Management, M.I.T., Cambridge,
    1977, Steiner, George A. and John B. Miner, <u>Management Policy and</u>
    <u>Strategy</u>, MacMillan, New York, 1977, and Taylor, Bernard and John R.

Sparkes, editors, <u>Corporate Strategy and Planning</u>, Wiley (Halsted Press)
New York, 1977. For a good discussion of the role of <u>formal</u> systems in
planning, see Steiner, George A., "Comprehensive Managerial Planning",
in McGuire, Joseph (editor), <u>Contemporary Management: Issues and
Viewpoints</u>, Prentice-Hall, Englewood Cliffs, 1974.

2. We shall not do an extensive survey of the planning literature in this
    book. Several planning literature surveys exist; see, for instance,
    Hussey, David E., <u>Corporate Planning: Theory and Practice</u>, Pergamon
    Press, New York, 1974, Hofer, Charles W., "Research on Strategic
    Planning: A Survey of Past Studies and Suggestions for Future Efforts",
    <u>Journal of Economics and Business</u>, Summer, 1976, Steiner, George A.
    and John B. Miner, <u>Management Policy and Strategy</u>, MacMillan, New York,
    1977, and Lorange, Peter, "Formal Planning Systems: Their Role in
    Strategy Formulation and Implementation", in Hofer, Charles W. and
    Dan Schendel, editors, <u>Strategic Management: A New View on Business
    Policy and Planning</u>, Little-Brown & Co., Boston, 1978. For those who
    wish to be referred to case studies on corporate planning practices,
    see, for instance, Baynes, P., <u>Case Studies in Corporate Planning</u>,
    Society for Long-Range Planning, Bath, 1973, and Lorange, Peter and
    Richard F. Vancil, <u>Strategic Planning Systems</u>, Prentice-Hall, Englewood
    Cliffs, 1977.

3. For a discussion of portfolio strategy analysis, see Ziemer, D. R.
    and P. D. Maycock, "A Framework for Strategic Analysis", <u>Long Range
    Planning</u>, Vol. 6, June 1973.

4. There exist several excellent literature discussions on the relevant
    aspects of objectives-setting; see, for instance, Simon, H. A., "On
    the Concept of Organizational Goal", Administrative Science Quarterly,
    June, 1964, Aguilar, F. J., Scanning the Business Environment, MacMillan
    New York, 1967, Andrews, Kenneth R., The Concept of Corporate Strategy,
    Dow Jones-Irving, Homewood, 1971, Guth, William D., "Formulating
    Organizational Objectives and Strategy: A Systematic Approach",
    Journal of Business Policy, Autumn, 1971, Denning, Basil W., "Strategic
    Environmental Appraisal," Long Range Planning, March 1973, Rhenman
    Eric, Organization Theory for Long-Range Planning, Wiley-Interscience,
    New York, 1973, Bowman, Edward H., "Epistemology, Corporate Strategy,
    and Academe", Sloan Management Review, Winter, 1974, Paine, Frank T.
    and William Naumes, Strategy and Policy Formation: An Integrative
    Approach, Saunders, Philadelphia, 1974, Latham, G. P. and Yukel, G. A.,
    "Review of Research on the Application of Goal Setting in Organizations",
    Academy of Management Journal, December, 1975, Vancil, Richard F.,
    "Strategy Formulation in Complex Organizations", Sloan Management
    Review, Winter, 1976, Quinn, James Brian, "Strategic Goals: Process
    and Politics", Sloan Management Review, Fall, 1977, and Tosi, H. J.,
    Rizzo, J. R., and Carroll, S. J., "Setting Goals by Management by
    Objectives", California Management Review, Summer, 1977.

5. Data Resources Institute (DRI) provides a well-known service of
    industry-specific as well as larger sector econometric models. Another
    well-known model is the Wharton econometric model. See McCarty, M. D.,
    "The Wharton Quarterly Econometric Forecasting Model, Mark III",

Wharton School of Finance and Commerce, Philadelphia, 1974, and Duggal, V. D., L. R. Klein and M. D. McCarty, "The Wharton Model Mark III: A Modern IS-LM Construct", International Economic Review, October, 1974. See also Pindyck, Robert S. and David L. Rubinfield, Econometric Models and Economic Forecasts, McGraw-Hill, New York, 1976, Ch. 12.

6. See Vancil, Richard F., "Better Management of Corporate Development", Harvard Business Review, Sep.-Oct., 1972.

7. The following articles and books discuss in more detail issues brought up in section 2-4-3: Sihler, William H., "Towards Better Management Control Systems", California Management Review, Vol. 10, No. 3, 1971, Mockler, Robert J., The Management Control Process, Appleton-Century-Crofts, New York, 1972, Pyhrr, Peter A., Zero-Base Budgeting, Wiley-Interscience, New York, 1973, Newman, William H., Constructive Control, Prentice-Hall, Englewood Cliffs, 1975, Bales, C. F., "Strategic Control: The President's Paradox", Business Horizons, August, 1977, Carter, E. E. "Designing the Capital Budgeting Process", in Nystrom, Paul C. and William H. Starbuck, editors, Prescriptive Models of Organizations, North-Holland Publishing Co., Amsterdam, 1977, and Stonich, Paul J., Zero-Base Planning and Budgeting, Dow Jones-Irwin, Homewood, 1977.

8. See Lorange, Peter and Richard F. Vancil, "How to Design a Strategic Planning System", Harvard Business Review, Sept.-Oct., 1976, Exhibit 2.

9. See footnote 7 for a number of references pertinent to monitoring. See also Child, John, "Strategies of Control and Organization Behavior",

Administrative Science Quarterly, Vol. 18, 1973, and Lorange, Peter and Michael S. Scott Morton, "A Framework for Management Control Systems", Sloan Management Review, Fall, 1974.

10. See Porter, Lyman W., Edward E. Lawler III and J. Richard Hackman, Behavior in Organizations, McGraw-Hill, New York, 1975, Steers, Richard M. and Lyman W. Porter, Motivation and Work Behavior, McGraw-Hill, New York, 1975, Murthy, K. R. S., Corporate Strategy and Top Executive Compensation, Harvard University Press, Cambridge, 1977, and Tosi, H. J., Rizzo, J. R., and Carroll, S. J., "Setting Goals by Management by Objectives", California Management Review, Summer, 1977.

11. For discussions of several aspects of the planning process as a basis for communication, interaction and conflict-resolution, see Delbecq, Andre L., "The Management of Decision Making Within the Firm: Three Strategies for Three Types of Decision Making", Academy of Management Journal, December, 1967, Melcher, Arlyn J., "Towards a Theory of Organization Communication: Consideration in Channel Selection", Journal of the Academy of Management, March, 1967, Arrow, K. J., The Limits of Organization, Norton, New York, 1974, Hinnings, C. R., Hickson, D. J., Pennings, J. M. and Schneck, R. E., "Structural Conditions of Intraorganizational Power", Administrative Science Quarterly, Vol. 19, No. 1, 1974, Vroom, Victor H. and Arthur G. Jago, "Decision Making as a Social Process: Normative and Descriptive Models of Leader Behavior, Decision Sciences, Vol. 5, No. 4, 1974, Arrow, K. J., "Vertical Integration and Communication", The Bell Journal of Economics,

Spring, 1975, and Hunger, J. and Stern, C., "An Assessment of the
Functionality of the Superordinate Goal in Reducing Conflict", Academy
of Management Journal, December, 1976.

CHAPTER THREE

Auditing the Company's Strategic Positions Determining Planning Needs.

3-1. Introduction

Before any step can be taken in terms of attempting to implement a
strategic planning system along the conceptual lines presented in Chapter
Two, it will be necessary to develop a clear picture of where the company
and its parts stand in terms of strategic position as of today. The
situational setting of the firm, its strategic position, will be a major
factor in establishing the needs for planning that a particular firm will
have. The purpose of this chapter is to propose a framework for assessing
the types of needs a company will have for planning. Only after having
established a relatively clear picture of what capabilities the planning
system should be able to provide will we be in a position that we can
tailormake a planning system in such a way that it might be able to meet
these needs, by "building" the desired capabilities into the conceptual
planning scheme. It is thus an essential step to carry out a strategic
audit of the firm's situational setting, as a prerequisite to a tailormade
approach for implementing a strategic planning system. This chapter
explores approaches to strategic audits and planning needs analyses.

A necessary first step in the strategic audit-planning needs analysis
will be to identify what are the "building blocks" of the planning system --
which are the divisions (from a strategic relevance point of view), what
is the nature of the corporate portfolio strategizing task, and so on.
We shall approach this by first operationalizing the concept of a Strategic
Business Unit (SBU) as the smallest general management denominator and
business strategizing "building block" for the planning system. We shall

then propose an analytical approach for assessing the strategic position of
an SBU, in terms of its market snare and the growth of the business it is
in. This is, however, based on the relevance of two phenomenae that
provide the basis for the SBU strategy analysis, tne experience curve and
the product life-cycle concepts We shall have to discuss when these
premises seem to be relevant as well as identifying the situational settings
where they seem less relevant. The SBU analysis will culminate with the
identification of the adaptation- and integration-related planning needs
stemming from the strategic posture identified.

Having discussed how to assess the strategic posture and planning
needs of one SBU we shall then approach the issue of how to consolidate
this into an analysis of a cluster of several SBU's, typically what one
will be faced with to establish the planning needs at the division level
of the firm. A shift in focus will then follow, in that the corporate
level strategic portfolio position and planning needs of the firm also will
be assessed We shall discuss two basic aspects of this First, we shall
address relevant ways of assessing tne nature of the financial performance
pressures that the firm as a whole is under. Prominent factors in this
respect will be profitability and stability in earnings patterns. Secondly,
we shall analyze the nature of structural pressures that the firm might be
facing, such as being in exceedingly unattractive business segments or
seeing one's competitors making innovative corporate moves to restructure
their business mix. Chief among the tools to assess this phenomenon will
be funds flow analvsis and comparative portfolio analvsis of oneself versus
key competitors. At this point we shall also find it useful to address
the issue of how to assess the companv's overall exposure to environmental

risks and the different needs for planning that arise from different environmental exposures. We shall conclude this chapter with a brief discussion of practical guidelines for how to organize the strategic auditing and planning need assessment tasks, including indicating which executives should be involved. In an Appendix, we shall provide an example of how one highly diversified company approaches the task of developing an index of strategic fit within its corporate portfolio for each of its 40 divisions, based on an assessment of the situational strategic positioning of each division.

3-2. The Strategic Business Unit (SBU) Concept

In order to analyze the strategic position of a business, such as a division of a diversified company, it is useful to adopt as a "unit of measurement" or "building block" the concept of Strategic Business Unit (SBU), which we have already briefly discussed in Chapter Two A Strategic Business Unit can be defined as the smallest organizational unit that performs an identifiable general management business task, i e., the creation of a specific and distinct product or service that serves a well-defined market, distinguishable from and relatively independent from other product/market combinations.[1]

There are several important implications of this definition of an SBU that need to be raised in order to operationalize this concept. First, the definition of an SBU assumes that one is able to define and formulate "in writing" an operational mission for the entity. Particularly important in this context is the need to actually be able to identify a well-defined market, and also to come up with a clear perception of who are one's

competitors. This will have to be specific and far-reaching Secondly,
it will be critically important that the particular definition of an SBU
actually allows management to better conceive of and focus on a set of
truly unique potentials and risks that characterize this business. These
opportunity and/or threat factors should have a high level of visibility
and ought to be clearly identified. Thus, the definition task is a
creative one, calling for an imaginative delineation of an SBU along
dimensions which are likely to be critical for the development of a
successful competitive strategy. Thirdly, the common thread of products
and/or services that run through the SBU entity must be clearly identified.
Thus, the definition of the SBU must not represent such a high level of
abstraction that it will become more or less meaningless. Finally, we
probably will have to be reconciled to the fact that although the task to
come up with a useful definition of an SBU and to develop a clearly
delineated and useful pattern of SBU's is a critical requirement for
strategic management, this task is a difficult one which probably will
have to be classified more as an art than an exact science This is an
important recognition, in that it should allow management to approach the
SBU definition task in a creative and imaginative manner, without being
frustrated by the predictable lack of success they might be likely to
experience in applying too stringent and inflexible criteria to the task.

   Let us provide a set of questions that might serve as a first
checklist for whether we have a reasonable delineation of an SBU, in that
if any of the questions below will have to be answered in negative terms,
then we might have a problem with this particular SBU delineation.

a) Does the SBU enjoy a strategic independence from other SBU's
    which is operational, in the sense that it is feasible to
    develop a competitive strategy for a particular SBU, relatively
    independently of other SBU's? Another way of phrasing this
    question is to determine the extent to which the competitive
    strength of the SBU is based on other SBU's or not, and whether
    an assessment of the attractiveness of the business can be done
    independently of the other businesses or not. This last
    question can normally not be answered affirmatively unless the
    SBU has control over its own raw materials sources as well as
    its own finished products markets. If however an SBU does not
    have full control over its sources and/or markets, then there
    is at least a requirement that there should be separability of
    cost and/or revenue-patterns among the SBU's, by means of a
    transfer pricing scheme Needless to say, the criterion of
    "pseudo-independence" between SBU's by means of transfer
    pricing schemes has to be done carefully, it is often difficult
    managerial judgment to draw the line beyond which the
    arbitrariness of forced independence becomes so great that it
    would be more natural and beneficial to combine these units
    into one larger SBU, pursuing one larger strategy

    It should be stressed that although an SBU normally should
    enjoy independence from other SBU's when it comes to being
    able to pursue its own competitive strategy in a discretionary
    manner, as just discussed, this does not necessarily imply

that each SBU should be organized so that it possesses its own functional departments. Functional departments might be shared by all or some of the SBU's within a division, as a way of performing a functional task more efficiently The functional department might report directly to the division management, or to, say, the SBU which is drawing most extensively of this particular function.

b) If the product or service that is being created by the SBU hypothetically was withdrawn from the marketplace, then a key question is whether or not the company would be out of the competition within this general area of business. If not, we have an indication that the SBU might not be strategically independent of other SBU's, and we need to assess the degree to which strategic relationshps to other SBU's exist.

c) Is the corporate and/or the divisional management's intent pseudo or real when it comes to the dealing with an SBU? An important premise for the rationale of establishing SBU's is the potential to benefit from a "division of labor" among managers within the firm's organizational hierarchy when it comes to focusing on various strategic tasks, as discussed in Chapter Two. A manager responsible for an SBU should be able to be "closer to the competitive scene" than anyone else in the company, and should have sufficient discretionary leverage to act on the basis of this to secure an advantage for the firm. However, a typical phenomenon among managers is that they

prefer a decentralization mode of operation down to their own
level in the organization but centralization at the levels
below oneself. Hence, it is often difficult to practice the
"hands-off" management style that is needed in order to make
the SBU concept work.

d) Does the company have adequate management skills and talent to
allow for the operational functioning of SBU's as vehicles for
defining and implementing strategies? This may often be the
most critical issue. An important issue in this respect is
probably the type of experience the company has been having
with regards to traditional responsibility centers   There are
typically three types of responsibility centers relevant to the
decentralized management of the line activities of a firm, cost
centers, profit centers and investment centers. (The so-called
revenue center can be seen as a "hybrid" between a profit center
and a cost center. A discretionary expense center is primarily
relevant in connection with staff department activities.) The
sequence of the listing of these is important in that it
signifies an increasing degree of decentralization and autonomy
to be enjoyed by the management responsible for the performance
of the responsibility center, the cost center, with discretionary
responsibility for inputs only (costs, expenses), the profit
center, with discretionary responsibility for inputs and outputs
(revenue), the investment center, with discretionary responsibility
for inputs, outputs and investment base (size of investment that

has created a given net output)   We might consider an SBU as
a logical extension of the investment center, in the sense that
responsibility for long-term performance has been delegated to
the management of the responsibility center, in addition to
short term performance responsibility. We might apply a
conceived measure of long-term ROI (or residual income) to be
optimized by the SBU. In order to do this the SBU's management
must develop and implement a long-term strategy which encompasses
the development of the long-term competitive strength of the SBU,
its strategic base. Thus, an SBU may be more appropriately
relabeled a "strategy center", will have discretionary
responsibility for inputs, outputs, investment base and
"strategic base".

In an evolutionary sense, the step from managing an investment center
to the one of managing an SBU is probably a relatively natural and short
one. Thus, a strong investment center tradition is probably an advantage
when attempting to develop a decentralized strategic mode of operation.
However, the change from a short-term performance fulfillment orientation
to a long-term strategic orientation can certainly nevertheless be a
formidable problem. Particularly critical is the change in the responsibility
center manager's style from being heavily into the short-term, firefighting,
"stick-and-carrot game" to having to go through an orderly planning process
of identifying and narrowing down long-term strategic options. The switch
in managerial style is of course even higher when one attempts to evolve
into such a strategic mode of operation from a less "full-blown" traditional

mode of decentralized operation, such as attempting to go from a profit center or particularly a cost center mode of operation to an SBU. Such a monumental change in management style seems to be what was called for in the cases of some of the major integrated oil companies when these "broke themselves up" into strategy centers. (Gulf Oil Corporation for instance was reorganized into seven strategy-centers, Sun Oil Company (now Sun Company) was reorganized into 14 SBU's.) To restructure into a pattern of SBU's is therefore particularly difficult in instances where there is an "evolutionary jump" bypassing one or more of the evolutionary sequence of stages in the responsibility center chain It might be a real issue whether an organization in fact will be able to mobilize the necessary managerial competences for this switch in mode of operation overnight.

A second and related issue involves the degree of past stability in organizational structure as well as maturity of managerial communication patterns within the organization. If there have been a number of recent reorganizations and/or structure changes due to, say, acquisitions, and/or if for instance the management succession rate has been high, then it might be more difficult to create a meaningful SBU structure. An essential reason for the SBU concept as its role as a building block. the focus of strategizing for competitive business success. In order to do this, however, it assumes that management in fact are familiar with their businesses in a quite intimate way.

We see then that the issue of identifying a reasonable set of SBU's is not an easy one, and because it calls for a considerable degree of managerial judgment, this task typically causes concern among management attempting to undertake a business position strategic assessment the first time. Experience, however, shows that the task typically does not turn out to be as difficult as anticipated -- for three reasons. First, when starting out with the assumption that one's present product-market grouping is going to be the basis for the analysis unless compelling reasons for doing otherwise are given, the task becomes more one of modifying, rather than creating a new structure from zero. Secondly, as we start applying to our SBU's the question of what is the market share of the SBU relative to other SBU's, we might come up with answers that indicate that our definition of SBU's is unreasonable. For instance, if we can quite readily identify what might seem to be several market shares, each for different "sub-segments" of the business, then we might have applied a too aggregated SBU definition. Or, alternatively, if the market share is 100% or close to this, then we should be particularly suspicious about whether a too narrow definition has been made of what would be a relevant market segment for the SBU. Thirdly, when we employ the concept of market growth to the SBU's and we find that they seem to fall remarkably close together into a pattern which reflects a sound/steady growth, and with a few SBU's receiving the embryonic-high growth label on the one hand or the mature or decline label on the other hand, then we have an indication that we might have grouped our SBU's into too large units. Conversely, if there is no dominance of normal growth SBU's on the middle of the scale we might have applied a too fragmented SBU grouping. (In the next section we shall discuss why the concepts of market share and market growth should be included in our analysis, and we shall define market share and market growth then.)

3-3. The Concepts of the Experience Curve and the Product Life Cycle as Premises for SBU Strategic Analysis

Having established the concept of SBU's as our unit of business strategic analysis, we shall now develop a way of analyzing the strategic position of such an SBU It turns out that it often will be useful to assess the SBU in terms of the degree of competitive strength that it represents as well as the degree to which the SBU is positioned within an attractive business segment. Market share and business growth rate are often useful proxies for determining such a strategic position. Before we launch our discussion of how to carry out this type of analysis, however, it is necessary to examine the rationale behind the approach. This rests on two premises -- the so-called experience curve and the product life-cycle concepts. We shall discuss each of these in turn.

The first premise relates to the so-called experience curve concept.[2] This stems from the learning-curve phenomenon of work-and-motion study engineering, which states that when repeating a production task several times, such as for instance building a new airplane, experience in building the first plane will make it easier to build the second plane, and so on. The cost per plane is therefore expected to go down as a function of the number of planes built, due to the labor costs saved per plane as a result of learning. Similarly, there might be savings due to better utilization of materials, more advantageous purchasing and less overhead burden per plane when the number of units produced goes up, all reflected in lower production costs per plane. The consequence of the learning curve effect which causes lower costs per unit produced is that it is likely to be a competitive advantage to be able to produce a higher volume of units than one's competitors

Although traditionally developed in the context of job-shop manufacturing settings one might expect that there will be learning-curve effects at work when it comes to continuous process oriented industries too. In such settings, however, it might probably be more the technological advantages associated with modern and large capital equipment that provide the competitive advantage rather than the learning effects experienced by the labor force. Thus, the more capital intensive the industry, the less important will typically the learning curve effect be. Instead, plant size and sophistication of equipment might provide an alternative competitive advantage for those who are able to invest the equipment with the largest scale economies

The concept of learning curve effects has been extended to also apply to many of the managerial and support functions that are carried out within a firm   This is based on the assumption that a management team which consists of experienced executives and is well coordinated will probably do a job faster and better than a recently assembled team of less experienced executives. Marketing expertise, for instance, is probably one of several managerial factors that will be accumulated with experience. The marketing organization which enjoys the larger volume of business will be in a position to potentially accumulate relevant insights and experience to a larger extent than a smaller competitor. Thus, it will be in a better position in terms of "marketing value added" per unit produced. Given this broader and extended application of the learning curve concept it has become common to denote this as the learning curve phenomenon.

There might, however, be several limitations on the learning curve phenomenon. As already discussed   it should be clear that the absolute magnitude of a positive learning curve effect is likely to decrease as volume goes up, after some level of activity there is probably little more to be gained in learning curve effects. Thus, when two competitors have reached this level of size there is probably no longer a very significant competitive advantage to be the larger one Further, the strengths of learning curve effects will also differ from industry to industry. It is probably higher in labor-intensive industries, and in industries which to a large extent rely on job-shop, product-related manufacturing. The durability of the learning curve advantages is also an unknown, the effect is certainly not permanent. One reason is due to factors such as job rotations, hence, this is another reason for management to attempt to cut down on unnecessary job rotations. Another is that there might be necessary with major job task modifications that in many ways can be compared with starting the learning curve anew. Thus, for companies that are in industry settings that are encountering a rapid rate of change, such as frequent technological modifications within areas of the electronics industry, then positive learning curve effects will be harder to obtain on a more permanent basis.

A final problem with applying the learning curve concept would be within extractive industries where a natural resource is being depleted to the extent that further production requires that one go after reserves that are more difficult and expensive to reach than the older reserves. Thus, cost per unit might jump _up_ as production increases We can probably readily find examples of this within the oil and gas exploration industry — it may for instance become necessary to carry out more expensive deep-water offshore exploration, or in the uranium industry -- it may become necessary

to erect deeper mine shafts to reach the only available unexplored deposits
There will of course be opportunities for positive learning curve effects
to counteract the negative effect just discussed in these instances too, at
each new "stage" of more expensive exploration there will be a learning
curve effect, say, from drilling holes more efficiently from an offshore
semi-submersible rig.

Despite the many questions that can be raised about the exact nature
of the learning curve effect, it seems however clear that in general high
market share and volume will yield at least some competitive advantage.
Thus, the market share position relative to one's competitors is normally a
significant aspect of the strategic audit of a business. Different planning
needs will be created depending on the relative market share position   If
an SBU enjoys a high share, then the task will be to plan so that the
learning curve effects can in fact be achieved; they do not come automatically'
If in a low market share, the task will be to plan so as to ameliorate some
of the potentially negative effects from not having the same learning curve
potential as one's competitor-high efficiency, for instance, by specialization
on segments that can provide some basis for learning curve effects "in the
small"

Let us now turn to the question of the empirical relevance of the
experience curve premise as a relevant element in our strategic audit
analysis of a business unit. There is a strong accumulated empirical
evidence that suggests a positive relationship between market share and
profitability, i.e., that profits are a function of market share, due to
experience curve effects [3] The studies further indicate that several other
factors too are important in predicting the economic performance of a

business, but that market share is clearly the most significant   It is
beyond our purpose to review and discuss these research findings in detail
here. However, one large-scale empirical attempt at determining the critical
strategic factors that influence the economic performance of a business needs
to be discussed, the so-called PIMS project (profit impacts of marketing
strategies) that is being carried out at the Strategic Planning Institute,
a non-profit institution. Three reasons justify a brief discussion of PIMS
at this point, namely the remarkable detail, scope and ambitiousness of the
project, the real-life strategic decision-making orientation of its design,
and the wide-spread impact and use that the results from PIMS have had on
actual corporate planning practices.[4]

Over 1,200 businesses (SBU's) from more than 100 companies are in the
PIMS data base. The mission of the project has been to isolate those
variables that determine ROI, approaching this by means of a multiple
regression model which contains 37 independent variables and predicts 80%
of the criterion variable. These 37 independent variables have been listed
into nine factor groups, which we shall list in terms of order of impact
upon ROI.

1. Investment intensity

2. Productivity

3. Market position

4. Growth of served market

5. Quality of product/service

6. Innovation and differentiation, when supported by market share

7. Vertical integration, when markets are stable, not growing or
    growing very rapidly

8. Cost push influence

9. **Current strategic thrust**; the direction of change of the variables.

A company might make use of the PIMS data base as a vehicle for shedding light on what should be a "normal" ROI for a business within a particular industry and with a given set of situational characteristics. This might provide useful inputs, say, for the setting of top-down expectations for various SBU's. The model might also be used as a vehicle for searching for how to improve a particular SBU's strategic position.

While the PIMS approach sheds considerable empirical light on the importance of an SBU's strategic position as the determinant of performance, and while also it might be used by a particular company as one specific tool in its planning process, there are also several limitations with the approach. Some of these limitations refer to methodological constraints of the study; it is however outside the scope of this book to discuss these nere. Other limitations refer to the ways the data should be used in the planning process, however, and these merit brief mentioning The major danger is to develop an overly mechanistic, extrapolative approach to strategy formulation as a result of the use of the data. It should be stressed that the data are historical and also that they do not measure the quality of strategic insight on behalf of management. It is therefore important not to allow the data to become more or less an unescapable "law" for how one's business should do. Positive, creative thinking focused around opportunities and threats can facilitate strategic success of the future, not extrapolations of the past. Another danger, albeit much smaller, is the strong emphasis on ROI as the criterion for judging the success of an SBU strategy Not only might it be

that other financial variables such as net cash flow are more relevant as
indicators of the creation of strategic values. More importantly, strategic
performance should probably be judged in terms of variables that emphasize
longer term effects in addition to near-term ROI.

There is an additional important general implementation issue which
relates not only to the use of PIMS but to a vast number of tools and
techniques that might be used in business strategizing, referring to how
to appropriately position such tools as _elements_ of the overall planning
process. We shall however delay the discussion of this until the end of
our discussion of strategic position analysis of SBU's later in this chapter.
Instead we shall return to the other phenomenon, in addition to the learning
curve concept, which is a premise for our SBU strategic position analysis

The second premise for our SBU strategic audit analysis relates to
the so-called product life-cycle concept [5] This is based on the observation
that products tend to follow a life-cycle pattern of evolution over time.
Consider for instance the following product life-cycle scenario A product
might be starting as not much more than a set of untried ideas that will
have to be refined to go through a first "embryonic" stage of commercialization, say, with heavy emphasis on getting a better focus for what the
market niche might be, through marketing, ironing out production problems,
and so on Having succeeded through this first stage (most product ideas
probably don't), the product, if well conceived, might enter into a period
of growth. The emphasis during this growth stage will probably be more on
trying to get the product produced and distributed in order to respond to
an unsaturated demand for this product idea, attempting to reap benefits
from the fact that the prices can probably still be maintained at a

reasonably comfortable level. A major concern of course will be to attempt to reach the market ahead of one's competitors. As a probably inevitable more or less gradual saturation of the market demand for the product is approaching, another life-cycle stage is being reached, the mature stage The concern here might typically be more to make the product available at a lower price, to emphasize learning-curve effects and process improvements, attempting to take advantage of efficiency programs in order to come up with a competitive product so that one's own margins can be kept. After some time again, however, another period of decline in the demand for the product might set in due to obsolescence in the face of new product developments The emphasis during such a decline stage will probably often shift towards "orchestrating" a reasonable retreat, getting as much cash as possible out of the project before it dies out entirely.

From the above example we see that a product might go through several distinctive evolutionary stages as part of a life-cycle. To a large extent it will of course be a matter of taste how many distinctive generic stages one should divide a typical life-cycle into. For the purpose of our present discussion we shall find that it shall suffice with a very simple categorization between four distinctive stages· the embryonic or start-up stage; the growth stage; the leveling off or mature stage, and the decline stage.

From our description of the stages of the product life-cycle, it seems natural to examine what might be funds-flow considerations associated with this. During the embryonic and growth stages the "investments" in getting the product developed, commercialized and distributed on the market are likely to outweigh the funds generated from sales. During the later stages, however, income from sales should outweigh the more modest continued expenditures needed for keeping the product alive. The criterion for wehther a product is economically viable, then, would be the extent to which the expected accumulated inflows will be larger than the expected accumulated outflows (time-adjusted), a dilemma, of course, is due to the fact that a large share of the outflows will be committed before any significant inflow might be expected.

It should be noted that as with the learning curve concept, the life-cycle concept does not represent an "iron law". There are many products that nave continued to grow largely because management was able to manage a continued growth through innovative product modifications, marketing extensions, and so on. There are also examples of companies, however, that took the evolutionary life-cycle movements to be so inevitable that management's actions actually lead to an unnecessary shortening of the life of a product through early decline. Nevertheless, the product life-cycle position is an important and useful concept in our strategic audit analysis, typically it is an effort which is largely outside the discretionary domain of management This is of course an important contrast with the market share/learning curve position which typically to a large extent can be under the influence and discretion of management.

From our discussion this far in this section we nave seen that the two premises identified for assessing the strategic attractiveness of an SBU -- market snare position and growth rate posture -- seem to be highly interrelated. In fact, it is not possible to make a strategic audit without simultaneously assessing a SBU on botn these dimensions, as we shall now discuss.

3-4. The market share/market growth grid

The approach of assessing the strategic position of a SBU on a two-dimensional grid with relative market share and business growth as the two dimensions was spearheaded by the Boston Consulting Group (BCG) under its president Bruce Henderson. This development probably represents one of the more, if not the most significant contribution to strategic planning over the last two decades. By today this approach, or extensions of it, has come to be close to household items in the "tool-kit" of managers with business strategizing tasks, very popular and widely used [6] Exhibit 3-1 illustrates the basic BCG grid.

Before discussing the strategic implications of being positioned at various cells in the grid, let us first define the dimensions of the two axes. At the horizontal axis relative market share is normally defined as the sales of one's own SBU relative to the sales of the largest competing SBU. If this measure takes on values larger than one, then one's own SBU is the leader in this business, if, for instance, the relative market share is two, then this SBU is twice as large as its largest competitor. If the measure is taking on values less than one, then the SBU is smaller than the largest competitor, a value of one half, for instance, indicates that the SBU is half the size of the largest competitor Relative market share has of course been chosen instead of absolute market share because it gives a direct indication of one's own learning curve advantage potential relative to the competition On the vertical axis annual compound growth of the business is being measured The growth rate can be measured in several ways. For instance, in some businesses with highly erratic growth tracks, such as certain parts of the electronics components businesses, it may make sense to measure average growth over a period of several years in order to lessen the effect of such near-term fluctuations around a longer-term growth trend. Similarly, for certain businesses the growth will be highly dependent

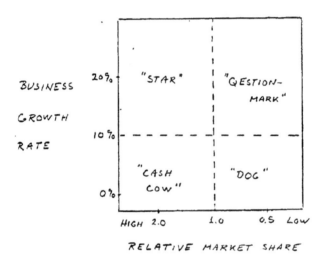

Exhibit 3-1. Strategic Position Grid for a SBU

on general movements in the economy; in such cases one might adjust the growth calculation with some sort of gross national product movements index or another index deemed meaningful as an indicator for general economic movements adjustments. It might also be that the general inflation rate should be compensated for. The key is to apply a measurement for business growth which is useful in distinguishing between SBU's that are in a high growth mode versus those which are less so in a particular business. The measurement chosen must of course be consistently applied in the analysis of all the SBU's of the firm. We shall return to the issue of defining more

operational measurements for the two dimensions of Exhibit 3-1 at the end of
this section, after having discussed the impact of the strategic positioning
of SBU's within the cells of the matrix.

Let us now discuss the strategic implication of being positioned in
each of the four cells of Exhibit 3-1. The first cell we shall discuss is
the one labeled "star". This is a very advantageous position, strategically,
in that one's own SBU is the dominant one in the market place, and also that
the business one is involved in is in a high growth area. In terms of funds
flow implications, however, there will on the one hand be a potential positive
effect from the experience curve advantage that the SBU is likely to enjoy
relative to its competitors. On the other hand, the presence in a high
growth business is likely to require considerable investment in capacity
expansion of production and/or distribution facilities. In total, while
the overall funds flow balance is likely to be more or less neutral, it is
difficult to predict whether the net position will show a small negative or
positive value.

The position marked with high market share but low growth, however,
is likely to be a net contributor of funds; the competitive experience curve
advantage of this SBU position is good and the growth rate is low, causing
the SBU to enjoy the funds flow benefits from its advantageous experience
curve position while no longer having to invest heavily in sustaining an
adequate production and/or distribution facility, now that the growth has
fallen off. SBU's in this position will typically be a "cash cow", i.e.,
provide the "backbone" of discretionary funds for continued expansion into
new product areas Typically a SBU in this position was previously in a
"star" position.

New product developments might typically be classified to fall into the high growth/low market share segment. Here the issue will be to invest in new SBU's which over time can build themselves a marketing base and become "stars". The net funds flow position is of course expected to be heavily negative -- reflecting the "investment" in future market share. One issue facing the strategists is that uncertainty might be high that such new ventures might fail, hence, we denote this cell with a "question mark".

. Let us finally consider the fourth position -- low market share and low growth. Such a position is clearly strategically undesirable for a SBU to be in; neither is the growth such that the SBU offers much of a long-term promise of potential for the future. Nor is the competitive position strong enough to provide a likely base for competitive advantages Although it is likely that the funds flow position will be approximately neutral -- neither large cash inflows nor outflows, the SBU will consume managerial resources and will easily develop into a "drag". When a SBU ends up in this "dog" position (after a long period as a "cow", hopefully) this is when we might expect that the likelihood is high that at some stage the decision must be taken not to actively pursue this particular product any longer, but gradually to phase it out or to withdraw

As already alluded to, we have several alternative paths of evolution in terms of changes of position within the strategic grid that a SBU might go through. The ideal path would be one of having a SBU start out as a "question mark", then to build it up to a "star", then to reap the benefits of having the SBU evolve into a "cash cow", for finally to allow it to taper off as a "dog", that eventually will be terminated as a business. In Exhibit 3-2 we have indicated this desired evolutionary path for a SBU with a solid

line. However, there might also be several scenarios of a SBU's evolution
that would indicate less of a success. For instance, it does not seem
uncommon that an SBU reaches the "dog" position from an initial "question
mark" position. This is an indication of a strategic failure; management
was unable to establish a solid market position for this SBU. We have
indicated this evolutionary scenario by a broken line in Exhibit 3-2.
Another less desirable but not uncommon pattern of evolution is when a
SBU reaches the "dog" position directly from a "star" position. This too
is an indication of a strategic failure; management has been unable to take
advantage of the favorable funds flow potential which would have resulted
if it had been able to maintain its market share. This is indicated by a
dotted line in the Exhibit.

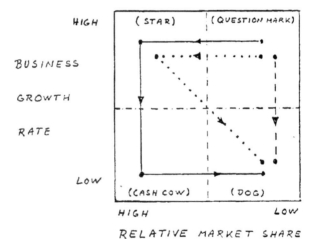

Exhibit 3-2. Evolutionary Paths for a SBU's Life-Cycle. Solid Line
Represents Desirable Path; Dotted or Broken Lines Represent less Desirable
Paths

In line with this, we can identify four major strategic alternatives
for managing a SBU within this analytical context. We might adopt a
strategy which attempts to build market share through relatively heavy
investments in strategic programs. Typically we find this for SBU's which
are in the question mark sector, but with reasonable prospects for being
moved into the star category. Secondly, we might follow a hold strategy,
which implies that enough must be invested in strategic programs to maintain
the market share. A SBU in a "star" position or a "cow" position might fall
into this category. Harvest will be a third strategic alternative for a
SBU, implying that the market share is being allowed to diminish. A SBU
in a "cow" position might be a candidate for such a strategy, but only after
it is evident that the product life-cycle position indicates a relatively
short and finite remaining usefulness Finally, a withdraw strategy might
be appropriate when a SBU offers little or no potential for further strategic
benefits A "dog" position should be a basis for candidacy for this strategy.
We might add a fifth strategic option, explore (or wait, hold), which would
apply to entirely new product developments at the preliminary pre-commercial-
ization stage, before having decided to embark on a build strategy or,
alternative, to cancel the project at this early stage.

The approach just outlined in the preceding paragraphs is conceptually
a simple and powerful one. It provides a clear picture of what is the
strategic position of a SBU, and it has an intuitively logic and sould
appeal to most executives. At this point in our discussion we need to
recall, however, that the purpose of our strategic position analysis is to
determine the needs for planning that a particular SBU will face, in terms
of adaptation as well as integration. We recall tnat only after having

determined these needs will we be able to tailormake the planning system
in such ways that it will be provided with capabilities to meet the needs
It should also be pointed out at this point that the basic SBU strategic
position analysis just discussed often might need to be modified in
important ways, now and then extensively, in order to become operational.
Thus, we need to delineate the situations in which the approach is valid
as outlined versus those situations in which modifications are necessary.
Consequently, in the next two sections we shall discuss these issues,
starting with an extention of the strategic position analysis so that the
planning needs that would follow can be deducted, and followed by a
discussion of useful avenues of modification of the basic approach.

3-5   Adaptation and integration needs of a SBU

Let us reconsider the two basic dimensions of our SBU strategic
position analysis, namely the business attractiveness factor and the
competitive strength factor, and let us for the moment assume that the
growth rate of the business and the relative market share are meaningful
surrogates for these two dimensions.   An SBU which is facing a rapid
growth rate in its industry will be confronted with a number of planning
issues which will be primarily adaptation-oriented in their nature   how
to capture a position in the market by developing more effective competitive
strategies than other companies, how to reposition oneself to new consumer
tastes, how to expand into another geographic market, and so on.   It seems
as if a major share of the planning needs of SBU's that are facing a high
industry growth grate will be predominantly adaptive.   These needs will
manifest themselves partly in terms of having to re-examine the objectives

of a SBU, given rapidly evolving new opportunities and threats. Also, however, there will be a need to develop new strategic programs as well as for making significant modifications in existing ones, in order to be able to actually implement such a rapidly evolving SBU strategy. More generally, taking advantage of a situation which offers high business attractiveness creates high adaptation planning needs.

Let us now consider the other dimension, namely relative market share. As we recall, a high relative market share might yield significant competitive advantages stemming from "experience curve effects", thus allowing the market leader to potentially enjoy lower costs per unit produced, higher margins and more flexibility in competitive pricing decisions. We also pointed out, however, that positive experience curve effects do not necessarily occur automatically. To take competitive advantage of a strong market share position, action would have to be taken to enable the experience curve effects to take place. For instance, more efficient planning of the activities of the various functions such as production, scheduling or distribution, more efficient planning of the interactions and interdependencies between the various functions, development of more raw material- and/or energy-efficient production processes, providing for improvements in quality and/or design of one's products, and so on. Thus, we see that the planning needs of a SBU which enjoys a high relative market share position manifest themselves partly as needs for making one's objectives more "robust", refined and viable, partly as needs for developing strategic programs for making increased efficiency take place. In general, we see that a strong competitive strength position will create what primarily seems to be a high need for integration planning.

At this point it is easy to extend the initial grid analysis of
strategic positioning of SBU's to incorporate the adaptive and integrative
planning needs. Given that adaptation needs will be a function of business
growth primarily and that integration needs will depend on the relative
market share position, we can easily see the combined adaptive and
integrative needs that a SBU will have when it is located in a particular
strategic position. Specifically, we have four different combinations of
planning needs for the SBU's depending on what type of SBU we are dealing
with, as illustrated in Exhibit 3-3.

HIGH	(STAR)	(QUESTION MARK)
BUSINESS	GROWTH → HIGH ADAPTATION SHARE → HIGH INTEGRATION	GROWTH → HIGH ADAPTATION SHARE → LOW INTEGRATION
GROWTH		
RATE	GROWTH → LOW ADAPTATION SHARE → HIGH INTEGRATION	GROWTH → LOW ADAPTATION SHARE → LOW INTEGRATION
LOW	(CASH COW)	(DOG)
	HIGH	LOW

RELATIVE MARKET SHARE

Exhibit 3-3. Adaptive and Integrative Planning Needs of a Strategic
Business Unit.

We see from the exhibit that a quite diverse pattern of planning is emerging.

- For a SBU which is in the "star" position we see that there is a relatively high need for both adaptation and integration planning Reflecting on this for a moment we see that it is a demanding task to strategically manage a SBU in this position.

- For a "cash-cow" type SBU there typically will be a relatively lower need for adaptation planning, but the same relatively high need for integration planning as is the case for a "star". Thus, we see that the needs focus primarily on integration, and that the task of managing a "cash cow" should be somewhat simpler than that of managing a "star", given this unidimensional need pattern

- For "question mark" SBU's we see that there will be a relatively high need for adaptation planning but a relatively low need for integration planning Again, the task to build up a new business is a unidimensional one, where a clear adaptive focus must be kept.

- Finally, for SBU's of the so-called "dog" type there will be relatively low needs for both adaptation and integration planning. This is a reflection of the relatively uninteresting strategic prospects that such a SBU setting represents for a company. Consequently there should not be a willingness to make long-term commitment to strategic developments of such a SBU. Hence, we see relatively low adaptive as well as integrative needs

It is worthwhile to notice a relatively even balance between adaptation and integration planning needs for the two SBU strategic position typologies

where there is approximate funds-flow balance -- tne "star" and "dog"
positions. The absolute level of both types of planning needs is however
much higher in the case of a "star" than a "cog" For the SBU types where
major funds-flow imbalances can be expected, however, there will be an
imbalance between the adaptive and integrative relative planning needs
the net funds-generating SBU's ("dogs") will have a relatively much higher
integration planning need than adaptation planning need, the net funds-
consuming SBU's ("question marks") will have a relatively much higher
adaptation planning need than integration planning need. In general, funds
generation creates integration planning needs, funds utilization creates
adaptation planning needs As we shall see later, this is a particularly
useful concept to utilize when it comes to portfolio level planning

It is important to notice the effects in terms of changes in the
planning needs of a SBU when the SBU evolves from one strategic state to
another Given that one important task of planning is to help facilitate
a desired evolution of a SBU's strategic posture, as indicated in Exhibit
3-2, for instance, it is important to anticipate what changes in planning
needs that such an evolutionary pattern should lead to For instance, when
investing in a SBU to attempt to influence a change in its strategic position
from a "question mark" to a "star" there will be a need, as an anticipative
move, to strengthen integration planning above all, since integration
planning needs will be expected to become relatively more important In
our experience, failure to recognize such a relative shift in needs towards
a more even balance between adaptation and integration is a major problem
in many new, initially successful SBU's With highly entrepreneurial

aptitudes, the management teams of such SBU's often find it particularly
hard to recognize or understand this change in planning needs.

Considering now a SBU which is evolving from a "star" position to
a "cash cow" position, we might anticipate a relative decrease in adaptation
needs. Again, in our experience, it is frequently a problem to have the
management team of a SBU actually realizing this shift, the result often
being that the cash-cow's funds generation task is being hampered or
"distracted" by unnecessary adaptive attempts.

It should be pointed out that for expository purposes we have intentionally created a highly dichotomized picture of how a SBU's planning
needs might change, in terms of shifts in relative emphasis between
adaptation and integration. In actual settings we are of course dealing
with gradual changes in emphasis. The key, however, is to recognize the
different planning need pressures that apply in the various strategic
positions, and to be able to clearly distinguish between shifts in the
relative need balance between adaptation and integration, and absolute.

3-6. Modifications of the SBU strategic position matrix.

Let us now turn to the issue of discussing several problems that
might arise when attempting to make use of the SBU strategic position
analysis outlined so far.[7]

The first problem to be discussed is that market share and market
growth might not always be the only useful measures for determining a
SBU's strategic position. To illustrate this we need to raise the following
fundamental question: what do we really attempt to capture by means of our
measurements of market shares and market growths? Market share is really,

as we have seen, a proxy for or an indication of the SBU's competitive
strength. Thus we need to ask whether there might be other measures of
competitive strength that could be equally or more relevant   In particular,
we might want to explore alternative measures of competitive strength in
cases where we do not expect that the learning curve phenomenon might not
fully apply. One such area might be within certain segments of high
technology industries where new products development is critical. In such
instances R&D capability, for instance, might be a more relevant measure of
competitive strength than market share. This implies that some measure
would have to be developed to assess a SBU's strength along this dimension,
relative to one's competitors. Another and related aspect of competitive
strength might be one's ability to come up with unique patent protection
in one's R&D efforts -- also a phenomenon that one would need to measure
relative to one's competitors. With a rapidly changing business environment
vis-a-vis such non-economic factors as the labor force, government relations,
etc , it becomes an important competitive strength for those firms able to
maintain good and flexible labor relations, including having located
themselves in such a way that labor costs can be kept at a competitive level
Similarly, good government relations might be a competitive advantage. This
would probably be particularly true for labor intensive and/or highly
regulated industries, such as for instance shipyards. Finally, given the
raw materials shortages that businesses now and then seem to be facing, for
instance within the energy area, it might be a competitive strength to be
able to carry out as energy efficient a business as possible. For instance,
within high energy consuming industries such as cement or the airline
business a measure of energy efficiency relative to competition might be a

highly relevant indicator of competitive strength. In total, what we see
emerging from these examples is a necessity to evaluate in each case for
a particular SBU how its competitive strength should be measured. In some
instances we may have to make use of alternative measures to market share,
in other cases we may have to develop a composite measure of competitive
strength, based on market share as well as on other measures

Let us now turn to the other dimension in the SBU strategic position
matrix, namely the growth dimension, and ask whether this is a unique proxy
for business attractiveness. Although growth used to be the "panacea",
there are presently many questions being raised as to whether this is the
only attractiveness aspect of a business Again, we might find instances
where other attractiveness factors are prominent within areas where the
underlying premise, the product life-cycle concept, does not hold. One
example of an important additional business attractiveness issue is to
attempt to avoid businesses with a heavy element of induced obsolescence.
A fairly stable and not too rapid rate of technological change is therefore
probably one increasingly important additional factor of business attractiveness. Another potentially important aspect of this is the nature of
competition itself For instance, with an industry which enjoys a more
comfortable competitive structure there is less likelihood of the competitive
pressure inducing exceedingly rapid and expensive changes into the evolution
of the product life-cycle. Barriers to entry, such as large investment
hurdles due to the cost of new plants, similarly should increase the business
attractiveness. In all these instances it is necessary to measure business
attractiveness in a different way than merely according to growth.

The examples of alternative measures of business attractiveness and competitive strength are not meant to be exhaustive. Instead they are meant to illustrate that the two dimensions need to be measured in such a way that they realistically reflect the underlying phenomena in each instance. As already alluded to, a likely development might be to devise indexes for business attractiveness and competitive strength that incorporate several factors and which employ some reasonable weighting of the factors.

Let us now bring up two more "technical" issues relating to the development of the two scales of measurement of the business growth/market share grid. The first relates to the way which is commonly proposed for measurement of relative market share, namely to measure the SBU's market share relative to the largest competitor. This measure does, however, not take into account the degree of competitive concentration within the business. For instance, in one setting we might have a business which is dominated entirely by two companies, both being approximately equal in market share and, thus, the SBU in question might be having a relative market share of approximately one. In another situation a SBU might face a handful of competitors, each being relatively equal in size, again producing a relative market share of approximately one. In a third situation a SBU might find itself within a highly fragmented industry with, say, more than 50 identifiable competitors A SBU may be one of the approximately dozen largest companies in the business, none however being significantly larger than the others. Again, the relative market share will be approximately one. Thus, in all three instances the competitive strength position appears to be the same, when in fact the basis for competition is entirely different, in the first instance we have a duopolistic

competitive setting, in the second an oligopoly, while in the third case
we are much more close to perfect competition. Consequently, it is
important to keep the <u>nature</u> of the competition in mind when interpreting
the relative market share measure, particularly when making policy decisions
such as resource allocation tradeoffs within a company which involve
comparisons between SBU's that enjoy such different competitive positions.
To be aware of this potential source of bias is usually sufficient, however,
so that qualitative modifications can be made in interpretation and evaluation.
It is usually of little benefit to modify the measure directly, say by
measuring a SBU's market share relative to the average of, say, one's three
largest competitors, or to operate with an additional competitive strength
component which measures the degree of business concentration as a function
of the <u>difference</u> between the SBU's market share relative to its largest
competitor versus relative the average of, say, the three largest competitors -- the smaller the difference the larger the degree of concentration

  Let us now raise a final issue with regards to the measurement of
the strategic position of a SBU which deals with how to come up with what
would be an appropriate growth rate level to draw the borderline between
"stars" and "cash cows" (and between question marks and dogs, as well)
It is of course important to make this distinction in such a way that a
reasonably meaningful discrimination can be made between what should be net
funds contributors versus net funds users. In practice it will of course
be impossible to come up with an exact growth rate that will constitute
such a borderline Instead, we are dealing with degrees of shifts along a
continuous vertical dimension. Thus, any SBU should be interpreted relative
to the others in terms of growth characteristic and expected funds flow

pattern   It might, however, be useful to consider a particular growth
rate range to represent the borderlines of a "band" that more or less
distinguishes the stars from the cash cows   This "band" is probably
associated with higher growth rates when it comes to service-related and/or
labor-intensive industries that do not require large follow-up investments
versus lower growth rates when it comes to capital-intensive industries
that might require massive investments on a more or less continuous basis
in order merely to maintain one's business strength position. Thus, it
seems critically important to determine for each particular industry of
concern what might be a reasonable growth rate for meaningfully distinguishing between net funds use versus net funds generation. It might, for
instance, be justified to handle a highly capital intensive integrated
aluminum producing SBU which is enjoying say only an eight percent industry
growth rate as a "star", while a low capital intensity service-oriented SBU
for specialized production of precision castings might be considered a cash
cow, even though its industry growth rate may be 25%.

The issue of interpreting what might constitute meaningful growth
rates in an industry-specific way is of course particularly important when
within a given company one is faced with making policy tradeoffs between
SBU's from entirely different industries, as exemplified in the previous
paragraph. This is, however, only one of several important considerations
that need to be paid attention to when developing a strategic assessment of
a cluster of SBU's. We shall therefore now turn to a discussion of the
aggregation of SBU's into a larger strategic picture, as we typically would
find it when a multiproduct (and multi-SBU) division develops a strategic
picture of itself.

3-7   Consolidation of Several SBU's

A division will typically have several SBU's under its discretion
The total pattern of the strategic positions of these SBU's might be
positioned on a grid as indicated in Exhibit 3-4. This will give an
indication of the overall cumulative nature of the businesses of the
division, whether it is heavily based in the "star" segment -- it is then
a typical growth division; or whether it is concentrated in the "cow"
segment -- it is then a more mature division. Most divisions will have
some SBU's in positions different from the major thrust of its business.
For instance, a predominantly mature division might have one or a few SBU's
in the "question mark" or "star" areas. This might represent an indication
of the future direction that the division wants to follow, in that funds
might be channeled from the mature SBU's and into such new developments.
The arrow in Exhibit 3-4 indicates the "natural" flow of funds within a
division that attempts to keep renewing itself. A division's pursuance of
perpetuated growth based on internally developed new SBU's is, however, a
critical strategic decision that should only be taken in the context of
overall portfolio considerations for the firm as a whole. The issue is
whether from a corporate portfolio strategy point of view it would make
sense to allocate discretionary strategic funds back into new SBU's within
the same business or somewhere else within the firm where the growth
potential might be even better, where the risk can be diminished, and so on.

When the SBU's of a division are scattered all over in terms of
strategic positionings, this might be interpreted as a lack of strategic
focus for the division   It would be hard to classify a division in terms
of whether it should be a growth division or a division chartered with

becoming a net contributor of funds within a corporate portfolio strategy. Thus, from a corporate portfolio strategy point of view a business will have strategic value only if funds eventually can become freed up for reemployment. If we assume that a company is managed in accordance with such an explicit corporate strategy, we would therefore expect that each division's plans would provide for more clearly clustered strategic focus. If, on the other hand, we assume that there is no corporate portfolio strategy concept in existence, and, instead, that the company's growth is a function of what each division is able to grow, in a more or less _laissez faire_ fashion, then we would expect the strategic positioning of a division': SBU's to be widely scattered. This latter situation is probably a quite accurate reflection of reality in many cases.

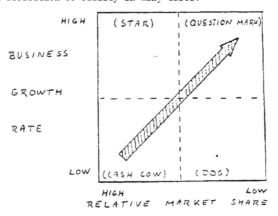

Exhibit 3-4. Transfer of Funds Among SBU's Within a Division

A critical issue will be how much funds a company will be able to actually free up from SBU's in cash-cow positions for reemployment in high

growth SBU's. It is important in this context to keep in mind that even
reasonably mature SBU's might require considerable funds to be plowed back
into its own operation in order to maintain its position This is
particularly so during periods of inflation It should also be remembered
that some funds will have to be paid out as "capital rent" to the parties
that have financed the firm -- in the forms of interests and dividends.
Thus, what emerges is a realization that there will be a <u>maximum sustainable
rate of growth</u>. To improve on this will require infusion from additional
capital from outside, one source of which might be trimming of dividend
payments.

Let us now turn to another area of concern when it comes to considering
several SBU's in context. This relates to the nature of interdependence that
might occur between the SBU's [8] A major criterion in our definition of a SBU
stressed that it be as independent as possible of the other SBU's. In many
instances, however, it is neither feasible nor desirable to make a SBU
entirely independent. First, since all SBU's are part of the same division
and since they also typically will be operating within quite related
business areas, it might be natural to pursue the question of whether it
would be advantageous in developing complementarities between the SBU's in
selected areas There might for instance be considerable savings in having
joint sales force, or in sharing manufacturing facilities Such integrative
moves might actually be essential in providing the division with a viable
position of strength in the market-place. Thus, there is a need for an
additional dimension in our strategic business assessment analysis, we need
to analyze the consolidation effect on the SBU's beyond merely assessing
whether the overall sum of the SBU's funds flow is a positive or negative

figure We shall call this the <u>consolidation dimension</u> As alluded to above, the planning reeds stemming from this dimension will primarily be of the integration type.

Several factors might go into this consolidation dimension. First, there might be other aspects to the evaluation of the cash-flow pattern from the SBU's than to focus solely on the funds generation-utilization balance. For instance, how does the cash-flow of a SBU fit in with other cash flows in terms of covariance? Common underlying cyclicality patterns would of course normally not be an advantage. The size of the cash-flow of one SBU relative to the others would be another issue Is there one main cash-flow source or is there a more even distribution among the SBU's? The latter would presumably be more advantageous because of less reliance on one source. Finally, an explicit assessment of the risk of whether there is a high likelihood or not that a particular level of planned cash-flow will accrue is necessary Such an evaluation should be carried out for the SBU in absolute terms as well as relative to the risks associated with the "reliability" of the cash-flows of the other SBU's. The issue of doing a meaningful assessment of the risk associated with a SBU's funds flow is a difficult one We shall return to this later in the chapter when we discuss the corporate portfolio strategy evaluation of the set of business divisions, at which point the "robustness" of the various funds flow components will be critical

Another set of factors that should be brought to bear on the analysis of the consolidation dimension are the so-called synergy effects. These accrue when a division's functional departments are able to serve all the SBU's, thus avoiding duplication of efforts. For instance, within the manufacturing function there might be ample opportunity for many of the activities to be carried out in a coordinated fashion within the scope of the division as a whole, in contrast to a greater degree of independent manufacturing for each SBU. It is therefore an important secondary divisional strategizing issue to facilitate a SBU pattern which will be such that an overall synergy can be developed in manufacturing. Similarly, in marketing there might also be opportunities for synergy in that joint SBU sales forces might be developed Within R&D too much synergies might be important.

During our discussion of the significance of a SBU's growth posture earlier in this chapter we have already pointed out that the life-cycle position of one SBU relative to the others will be an important element in the analysis of the business' strategic position, because of the funds flow implications from this There is however an additional problem which arises from this, and which might create integration planning needs This stems from the recognition that the strategic management tasks is likely to differ between the product life cycles, in terms of management style to be encouraged through planning, product versus process balance in the strategic programs, the nature of incentive schemes, and so on To develop a management team within a division, which might be able not only to handle the management of such a diverse set of SBU's but also to cope with changes in the balance of SBU's over time, might call for considerable planning along the management development dimension. This is yet another consolidation planning need. We shall return to how to approach this in more detail in Chapter Five, however.

It is important to recognize, however, that added size/complexity of
a division, manifested by an increase in the number of SBU's, leads to a
relative increase in integration planning needs, stemming from the
requirements of the consolidation attractiveness dimension Thus, business
diversity normally leads to relatively more integration planning.

It is also important to recognize the potential effect of organizational learning in this respect One might expect that learning will cut
down the formal work-load needed to be devoted to planning Whenever
reorganizations in a division are made, such as redefining one or more
SBU's, reassigning SBU's from one division to another, or acquiring/divesting
a SBU, then the integration planning need is likely to go up Similarly,
management job rotations, if done frequently, might increase the integration
planning need.

There are two concerns that should be raised at this point, both
relating to the fact that integration planning might have a tendency to
"suppress" adaptation planning. When the complexity of a business increases,
causing an increase in integration planning needs, then one might become
"overwhelmed" by the workload implied by the integration planning need and
pay insufficient attention to the adaptation planning needs. This seems to
be a true danger in large and complex businesses; integration planning might
easily consume so much attention that adaptation planning is likely to suffer
The typically relatively stronger formality and numbers-orientation of the
integration aspect of the planning tend to reinforce this danger

Similarly, when a division "goes down the learning curve", and its
management becomes more and more comfortable with (integration) planning, a
natural and desirable reduction of effort spent on integration planning

should follow. However, this may also be accompanied by a similar reduction in adaptation planning, i.e., a reduction of planning emphasis altogether This scenario for the "degeneration" of planning is not uncommon, particularly in mature business settings. A "false" sense of perceiving that one is mastering planning as a whole is allowed to develop because of the organization's improved abilities to be on top of the more structured integration planning aspects.

We have now completed our discussion of how to approach the assessment of the strategic positioning of those organizational units within a company which pursue its business strategies. Thereby, we have come up with a way of determining the needs for planning at the business level, both in terms of adaptation as well as integration. We saw that these planning needs in part were stemming from the positioning of each SBU on the business attractiveness-competitive strength matrix. In particular, we saw that market share position seemed primarily to influence integration planning needs, while market growth characteristics seemed to impact the adaptation needs above all. We also saw that the planning needs at the division level were partly a function of the aggregated pattern of the SBU positions in question, but also partly a function of the consolidation requirements facing the division. This latter factor would lead to integration needs, above all.

Having now completed the need assessments at the SBU/division level we shall have to pursue the need assessment at the corporate portfolio level This will be the focus of our discussion in the rest of this chapter.

3-8. Corporate Strategic Planning Need Assessment. Financial Position

We shall now turn our attention to the assessment of needs for planning
at the corporate portfolio level. In this instance, too, our approach shall
be to identify what might be critical sources of strategic pressures that
would give rise to needs for various strategic planning approaches. The
factors that will be important when it comes to identifying the needs for
planning at the portfolio level will of course be expected to be different
from the factors relevant to identifying the planning needs of a SBU or
division. In those instances we focused on the business attractiveness-,
competitive strength-, and consolidation attractiveness-positions for
determining planning needs, as we recall from our discussion in the first
part of this chapter When it comes to assessing the needs at the corporate
level we shall propose that there are two other major classes of factors
that above all will be relevant, corporate financial pressures and structural
portfolio pressures. Financial pressures as a source for creating corporate
level planning needs shall be discussed in this section. In the next section
we shall discuss the role of pressures on the corporation to change its
basic structure, creating another set of planning needs. Before proceeding
it should be noticed that these sources of pressures too will create
adaptive as well as integrative planning needs. The specific nature of
these needs will however be different.

Proceeding with our discussion of the relevance of the financial
position of a firm, a first distinction might be to determine to what extent
the financial position of the company as a whole might be characterized as
"strong" or "weak" It is of course difficult to define exactly a strong
or weak financial position, and for our purpose an exact definition is not

needed. What is needed for our purpose might however be to focus on the following two interrelated issues. First, to carry out an evaluation of what might be the financial strength of the firm relative to what would be "normal" for companies of approximately this size and pattern of diversity Unused debt capacity is probably an important element in such an assessment Equity is of course normally highly correlated with unused debt capacity, and might be used as a proxy for measuring unused debt capacity. Several more elaborate schemes for determining unused debt capacity also exist.[9]

Another important aspect for judging the financial position of the firm will be the near-term overall financial performance. This is the "first derivative" of the factor discussed in the previous paragraph in that it will impact the strength of the financial position Near-term reported corporate factors such as quarterly or yearly profits, return on investments, earnings per share and growth in sales might be important indicators of this. Also related to this will be the judgment of stability of short-term financial indicators over time.

In terms of the effects of these financial position factors in creating planning needs these will primarily have effects on integration. For instance, a weak basic financial position should create a high need for integration planning at the portfolio level. This is because the relatively tight and unfavorable unused debt capacity cannot provide a basis for a more aggressive expansion Rather, a weak financial position should call for a strong emphasis on integration planning to consolidate the present position, the reality of the financial situation does not allow for aggressive adaptive strategic moves. It is important to recognize this added need for integration that a weak overall financial position creates.

A better integrative capability is probably the best way for such a company to protect its position and to realistically utilize this competitive advantage   Unfortunately, despite a weak financial position, a few near-term successes might lead some companies to a false sense of comfort, overlooking the need for a continued aggressive integrative thrust.

Let us now turn to the near-term financial performance aspects. As indicated, these should also influence the needs for portfolio planning. If the near-term financial position is worsening, then too there is an indication that there is a growing integration planning need, there is not enough internal efficiency in the way the firm is operating   What is needed in such a situation is to improve on the basis for the internal operation.

We see from the discussion this far that the corporate financial position primarily is causing the use of integrative needs, and that many of these pressures may be relatively near term in nature   In fact, some of these effects, such as attempting to maintain a highly stable reported corporate earnings flow, might be seen by some as "anti-strategic"   In other words, there might be reason for some to interpret the corporate financial pressures as near-term deterrents to strategic planning, so that consequently the strategic planning should be designed so as to counteract these pressures, not to comply with these pressures   We do not share this view, however, for two reasons   First, we feel that the financial performance pressures at the corporate portfolio level are real, particularly as seen by the C E.O. Consequently, we should let the actual needs determine the design of the planning system   A normatively designed system diverting significantly from what the users perceive to be the relevant tasks will in

all likelihood simply not work. Secondly, we shall see that the structural
need that will be raised in the next section generally will add a more
long-term strategic focus to planning at the corporate portfolio level.
Our aim shall be to show that a balance between the recognition of the
financial and structural needs will lead to a better portfolio level planning
approach.

Before concluding this section on the financial pressures' roles in
creating more near-term integrative planning needs, let us elaborate some
more on why these pressures should be carefully observed in the context of
developing a strategic planning system.

Except for the C.E.O , all line executives within a corporation will
have a boss he is reporting to within the organizational hierarchy. Thus,
they will be accountable primarily to other executives within the firm, both
for strategic as well as near-term performance fulfillment. The C E O, on
the other hand, is not accountable to anyone within the firm itself for his
performance fulfillment. Rather he is accountable to the board of directors
and to the stockholders at large. For a number of reasons, none the least
because of lack of enough time to be sufficiently involved to be thoroughly
familiar with and comfortable with the major strategic issues, it will be
difficult for these outside parties to pass extensive judgment on the
strategic performance. Near-term financial performance, however, can more
easily be judged by an outsider. It is therefore to be expected that the
C.E.O is facing the near-term performance accountability issues relatively
stronger than his subordinates.

The most significant source of near-term external pressure for
corporate performances probably comes from the so-called financial analysts

These can catalyze considerable upward or downward momentum on a company's stock prices and can also influence the image and respectability of the company as a whole as well as its C E O A major parameter in the judgment of most financial analysts about a particular firm's performance potential will be the short-term profits picture, in terms of size, stability and growth. This parameter is particularly relevant to the owners, even though as an individual a shareholder would probably not pay much attention to this in his own strategic decision-making, as we shall see below.

Observing a personal household or a small, privately held corporation, the key financial measurement denominator will be the cash-flow position Strategic decisions are typically taken almost solely on the basis of whether the decision seems to be feasible from a cash-flow point of view. With the emergence of the large, publicly held corporations there will, however, be a need for additional financial measurement denominators, with "fluid" ownership of a company its value to an "owner" is the price for which he can sell or buy the stock Hence, it becomes important with a measurement of the value of the corporation as it seems to be at virtually any point in time The field of accounting has come up with the concept of profits for this. This can be seen an attempt at assigning a value as of the present of the company's life-time expected performance. Thus, a fraction of expenditures and depreciation charges are (arbitrarily) allocated as part of the calculation of the present profit. It follows that a major concern of senior management, in attempting to become accountable relative to the owners, will be to provide value for these as of today through showing spectacular short-term profits performance. Stated again, a short-term performance pressure on top management will be real and should be recognized as one determinant of planning needs. Given this, however, it will become exceedingly important that relatively near-term planning considerations should not be allowed to potentially blur more long-term concern about coming up with viable strategies for improving on the structure of the firm's portfolio. Thus, strategic resource allocations should be taken within a balance of short-term and long-term strategic context, and not being dictated by short-term profits pressure only. In the next section we shall discuss further the nature of these structural planning needs.

3-9. Corporate Strategic Planning Need Assessment: Structural Position.

At the outset of this section let us clarify what we mean with a firm's structural position as a source for determining the planning needs at the portfolio level of a company. With this we mean an assessment of the nature of the structure of the portfolio of business activities that the firm is in Is this a healthy portfolio structure or could it be improved? Do the funds flow projections that are the consequence of particular business portfolio mix structures yield acceptable financial results "down the road" or not? Are environmental opportunities to modify the portfolio structure being pursued, particularly where judged in terms of degrees of changes of the firm's own portfolio relative to the degree of change in the portfolio of major competitors? Is the overall risk that the company seems to be facing associated with a particular business portfolio structure, acceptable, or should top management seek to modify the structure to decrease or increase the overall corporate risk posture. In line with the above examples we shall distinguish between these different, but highly interrelated sources of pressures that will be part of the portfolio structure planning need

assessment   These are the pressures stemming from internally developed
funds flow considerations, the pressures stemming from comparative strategic
analysis, and the pressures stemming from top management's perception of the
overall corporate risk posture. We shall discuss each of the former two in
this section, while waiting with the discussion of risk until later, given
that this latter aspect will be treated in the broader context of relating
it to SBU and divisional risk position assessment in addition to portfolio-
level considerations.[10]

As a first step in the direction of judging the long-term attractiveness
of a particular corporation's portfolio structure, we shall discuss how this
can be guided by carrying out a corporate funds flow analysis, extending on
the pattern of funds flows sources and uses that we have developed from
analyzing the SBU's and the divisions. This corporate funds flow analysis
consists of developing a picture of the firm's overall funds flow pattern
stemming from its structure, as evidenced by the pattern of the various
organizational units of the firm   This enables management to judge the
funds flow implications of different strategic choices and to see whether
a particular strategic choice in fact is feasible from a funds flow point
of view. We shall find it worthwhile to discuss the use of a funds flow
analysis for the assessment of the portfolio structure in some degree of
detail, not only because the data for such analysis normally is available
or can quite readily be made so, but above all because there seems to be a
general lack of recognition of the funds flow analysis tool as an element
in the portfolio level strategic planning need analysis.

In order to provide a funds flow analysis which is capable of shedding
relevant light on the strategic properties of the portfolio structure, two

requriements must be met: the funds flows need to be broken down in such a way that they are associated with each strategic unit; and they need to be broken down into components which indicate those funds flow elements that are discretionary versus those that are committed, that is, that cannot easily be altered. This is an important step in the analysis of the company's strategic position because of its indication of what parts of evolution of the company might be feasible, highlighting such issues as how much funds get generated from operations and from which businesses, how much get used by expanding and/or diversifying the businesses, and what might be the needs for new external financing. We shall now go through an example of how the funds flow assessment might be carried out, in terms of what constitute useful steps in the analysis. This will allow us to then discuss several potential pitfalls and difficulties frequently associated with this kind of analysis.

A corporate funds flow analysis for strategic purposes might be approached as illustrated in this simplified example of a company with two existing divisions, the rapidly growing division A which is pursuing businesses that generally are located at the early stages of the product life-cycle, and division B which is growing much more slowly and finds most of its business in the more mature end of the product life-cycle. Further, one division, C, has been divested during the year, while another division, D, has been acquired. The former of these divisions was generally engaged in so mature businesses that it offered little prospect for long-term business viability; the latter division, however, finds itself involved in entirely new business areas that may or may not eventually become a significant commercial success. There are three major steps of analysis,

as indicated by the three segments of the example below: determination of
funds flows generated by existing operations, funds used in expanding the
business, and new external financing. The figures of the analysis for our
imaginary example look as follows

1. Funds generated by existing operations

    a) Sources of funds

        - Profits before taxes

Division A	20.0	
Division B	14.0	34.0

        - Depreciation

Division A	4.5	
Division B	7.5	11.0

        - Divestiture of Division C   2.0

                                                  48.0

    b) Uses of funds

        - Replacement of fixed assets

Division A	5.5	
Division B	6.5	12.0

        - Increase in working capital

Division A	7.5	
Division B	2.0	9.5

        - Taxes paid

Division A	7.0	
Division B	3.0	10.0

        - Dividends paid   4.0

                                                  35.5

Funds generated by existing operations (48.0 - 35 5) = 12.5

Alternatively calculated:

    Division A (20 + 4.5 - 5 5 - 7.5 - 7) =   4.5

    Division B (14 + 7.5 - 6.5 - 2 - 3)   =   10.0

    Divestiture, Division C   2.0

    Dividends   4.0

    Generated from existing operations   12 5

2. Funds used in expanding the business

    Fixed assets purchased, Division A   7.0

    Acquisition, Division D   15.0

    Total use of funds for expansion   22.0

      Total outflow before new external financing

      (22.0 - 12.5)   =   9.5

3. New External Financing

    a) Movement in issued equity and long term debt

        - Equity issued   1 0

        - Increase, long term debt   8.0

                                                   9.0

    b) Movement in short-term funds

        - Increase in short-term debt   .5

    Total inflow from new external financing   9.5

Interpreting these figures we can immediately see the relevance of this type of analysis for the assessment of the corporate level portfolio strategic position We see that Division A which is expanding rapidly is not generating

enough funds to cover its own expansion, corporate management has reallocated
(7.0 - 4.5) = 2.5 of corporate resources as a net investment for the continued
operation of this expansive business. Division B on the other hand has
contributed a net total of 10 0 in funds, which corporate management has
elected not to have reinvested in this mature business Instead corporate
management has invested in a new business, division D, which presumably can
provide an additional basis for corporate growth during years to come. These
modifications in the corporation's portfolio have been financed partly by
another portfolio strategy modification, namely the sale of the lackluster
performing division C and partly through external financing in order to cover
the needs beyond what was made available through the internally generated
funds. Thus, the above simple example signifies several significant changes
in the firm's portfolio: a relative increase in the emphasis on the business
of division A, a relative decrease in the emphasis of division B's business,
exit from an old business through the divestiture of division C and entry
into a new business through the acquisition of division D Further, the
unused debt capacity of the company has been reduced by 9 5, which is
significant in terms of corporate management's future flexibility in carrying
out externally financed additional portfolio modifications.

There are a number of less self-evident issues that potentially might be of significance when interpreting the structural portfolio planning pressures stemming from a corporate funds flow analysis. The first issue relates to the reasons for potential increases in the divisions' needs for working capital during periods of inflation, there will be an "automatic" increase in the need for working capital then. It is important to separate this source of pressure from the strategic consideration, i.e., from what is needed to maintain and/or expand the real level of operation of the portfolio. Inflation might have two additional effects on the interpretation of the cash-flow analysis. Fixed assets might have to be replaced at costs greater than depreciation. Also, the de facto unused debt capacity might be diminished, given that the external financing need typically will go up faster due to the inflation. Both of these might have an effect on the firm's potential for being able to as well as for wanting to restructure its portfolio. Thus, particularly in periods with heavy inflationary pressure it is important to separate inflationary impacts on the funds flow analysis from real growth impacts

There is however a more fundamental problem associated with approaching the issue of analysing the longer-term structural on a particular portfolio strategy path by means of a funds-flow analysis approach in the way just outlined. This is because the analysis is based on historical data, generated through the internal accounting process. From a strategic decision-making viewpoint we should however be more interested in expected funds flow patterns, based on long-term plannned performance of the firm. Most companies will however typically rely heavily on historical data It will therefore be necessary to develop statements of future expected funds flow consequences from various potential strategic paths that the company might pursue The starting point here should be to extrapolate what the funds flow consequences might be from continuing to pursue more or less the same portfolio strategy. Such an extrapolation might highlight the needs for structural portfolio shifts Funds flow projections of the alternative portfolio strategies then in turn will have to be made

It should be noticed that the extrapolation of funds flow activities in this instance, as just discussed, in no way conflicts with our strong advocacy for the need for an open-ended, non-extrapolative, assessment of opportunities and threats in planning. This is what needs to take place when developing actual alternative portfolio strategies. The funds flow analyses merely project an aspect of the consequences of these portfolio strategy alternatives

Let us however now turn to another way of analysing the longer-term structural pressures on a portfolio strategy, namely by direct assessment of selected critical changes in one's own portfolio relative to one's major competitors. This analysis might serve as a valuable complement to the funds flow analysis, although typically being performed less frequently on an ad hoc basis.

The major purpose of an assessment of the structural properties of a company's portfolio in the context we shall discuss here is to determine the extent to which the structure of one's own portfolio seems to change favorably or unfavorably over time relative to one's major competitors It will of course be virtually impossible to develop exact patterns of change for one's key competitors' portfolio strategies, it is equally difficult to pinpoint exact shifts in trends of changes of such portfolio directions However, even though comparative strategic portfolio structure analysis therefore will have to be relatively crude in terms of degree of specificity, the development of an approximate picture of major comparative strategic portfolio shifts should suffice to highlight whether one's own top management should be increasingly concerned with structural changes in its own portfolio.

The first step in a comparative corporate strategic analysis should be to identify a set of companies that senior management feels it would be relevant and useful to compare oneself with. If a company finds itself in predominantly one well defined business segment, the logical choice of companies will probably not be all that difficult, namely to focus on the other ones within approximately the same businesses. For many companies however, particularly when being relatively heavily diversified, it might be less easy to single out a set of companies that it will be intuitively logical to compare oneself with. In such instances one might single out companies that are felt to be relatively similar, in terms of past performance patterns, size, diversity, nature of businesses that they are in, and so on. Other companies that might be singled out for comparison might be what one's senior management considers to be particularly superbly performing firms. Maybe, firms that are generally felt to be weak performers should be included, as well. In these cases too, however, it is important that the companies are at least moderately similar in structure to one's own.

A simple approach to a comparative structural analysis might be to collect such commonly available external performance indicators as profits, sales, rank position or Fortune's 500 list, etc., preferably over a relatively broad time-span. As discussed in the previous section, such factors will typically be closely associated with what we have denoted financial pressures, and will typically be rather near-term in nature. Thus, there will still be a need for a more in-depth comparative assessment of the longer-term trends in shifts among companies' portfolios, in order to understand the pressures one's own company is facing from the long-term portfolio strategy moves of one's competitors.

As discussed the critical strategic decision facing corporate management is how to allocate its strategic resources among its various businesses. We have also pointed out that it is useful to define what should be a strategic resource in a somewhat broader way than merely focussing on capital investments. Notably, allocation patterns for discretionary expenditures as well as for assigning key personnel will also be important Thus, ideally we would want to measure comparative changes in the allocation patterns of all these factors. However, it might become exceedingly difficult to gather the necessary data for this.

We shall therefore propose that the investment intensify in strategic programs be used as the measurement device for the comparative analysis This will have two components. First, it will be useful to measure the absolute level of investment in strategic programs relative to the competitors. This would give an indication of relative investment aggressiveness among the firms Both capital investments as well as strategic expenditures should go into this figure. It might often be particularly difficult to determine the relevant strategic expenditure spendings On the other hand, in some industries the most significant fraction of the strategic expenditures might be available from public sources, such as R & D expenditures for pharmaceutical companies, advertizing expenditures for tobacco companies, or exploration expenditures for integrated oil companies. A useful way of measuring relative investment aggressiveness, or relative strategic programming emphasis, would be to calculate the total investment (capital plus strategic expenditures) as a fraction of total assets, and to see how this fraction changes over time for all the firm being studied

Secondly, it will be useful to investigate for what uses the strategic investments are being allocated for the various firms being compared. For instance, within a conglomerate which types of business seem to receive the largest investment share, and what is the fraction of investments in new business relative to existing process improvement investments. Or, for an integrated oil company, what is the fraction of investment in up-stream (exploration, production) versus downstream (refining, marketing) activities? For a tobacco company what is the fraction of investments on loww tar brands? For a multinational corporation how much is invested on strategic programs abroad relative to domestically, and so on. A way of measuring the nature of the strategic program spending pattern is to calculate the fraction of a particular type of strategic investment rel-ative to the total for the various companies studied, and to compare shifts in the strategic program patterns over time.

Having calculated the absolute investment levels for the strategic program activities as well as the strategic program decomposition spending pattern, both in terms of comparative trends over time, it might be useful to plot the emerging shifts in investment patterns. Exhibit 3-5 indicates this

Relative Investment
Aggressiveness -
Relative Strategic
Programming Emphasis

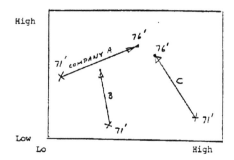

Percent Invested in a Particular Portfolio Segment Relative to Total Invested.

Exhibit 3-5: Change in Strategic Programming Investment Posture during
a 5-Year Period. X Indicates 1971 Position; . Indicates a 1976 Position.

We see from Exhibit 3-5 that Company A has dramatically increased its
relative emphasis on this business segment while Companies B and C have
decreased theirs. However, the investment aggressiveness has gone up
much more for the latter two.

This kind of analysis should be repeated for each relevant segment
into which the overall strategic programming activity has been broken
down (e.g., domestic vs. foreign; low tar vs. high tar; upstream vs. downstream). Each of the competitors' strategy when it comes to each particular aspects of their portfolio strategy might thereby be better high-
lighted. The emerging pattern of this will be to see in what direction
the various competitors seem to be going in terms of the allocation of
their strategic funds. Several important questions should be addressed
at this point. For any company one might ask whether portfolio focus
seems to become more proliferated, or whether the company is becoming more
spread (and often diluted) across a broader spectrum of directions? Is
one's own planning effort indeed resulting in a more desirable portfolio

business mix, when evaluated within the context of the competitors' moves?
Is the degree of aggressiveness in pursuing a portfolio strategy adequate
to keep up with the competition?

The emerging picture of the evolution of one's own portfolio strategy
relative to the competitors, seen as functions of the strategic spending
patterns over time, might yield another indication of the nature of the
structural portfolio pressures that a particular senior management group
is facing It should be noted that these more long-term strategic pressures
are just as real as the shorter term financial portfolio pressures that
might face senior management, as discussed in the previous section. However, it will largely be a function of a C.E.O.'s aspirations and sense
of devotion and professionalism whether he in fact will be paying sufficient attention to the structural portfolio needs. Given that there will
primarily be self-generated pressure rather than pressure from outside
which will dictate the C E.O.'s assessment of the structural needs, there
will always be a danger that the short-term financial needs might become
too dominant. In this area, above all, it appears to be a particularly
challenging role to be played for the C.E.O.'s incentive-and compensation-
scheme in order to attempt to counterbalance such an effect.

3-10. Portfolio Level Planning Needs· Synthesis

Having identified two broad classes of factors in the previous two
sections that seem to create different sets of planning needs at the corporate portfolio level, let us in this section attempt to synthesize what
the emerging combined pattern of adaptation and integration planning tasks
might be for the corporation.

We recall that the financial pressures were predominantly relative
short-term in nature and called for relatively stable, predictable financial performance. It follows that the emphasis should be on integrative

planning above all at the corporate level to facilitate this. Near-term
coordination of expenditure patterns, of trimming costs, of monitoring
inventory efficiency levels, etc. will be important at the corporate level
to achieve this. When it comes to the structural pressures, on the other
hand, we recall that these will be more long-term in nature, and these
pressures will create a need for adaptation at the corporate level, above
all. Ability to identify new long-term business opportunities, insight
to develop strategic programs to make shifts happen, foresight to reallocate
one's emphasis in time, and so on, are all critical adaptation planning
needs.[11] We see, then, that while at the corporate level integrative planning needs are primarily a function of the financial position, adaptive
planning needs will primarily be a function of the structural properties
of the firm's portfolio. We are now in the position to indicate the
mixes of adaptive and integrative planning needs that might be found at
the corporate level, as a function of different financial and structure
pressures.

In Exhibit 3-6 we have indicated how this adaptive/integrative
planning needs pattern might look at the corporate level. We see from
this exhibit that

	High		
Structure		High Adaptation	High Adaptation
Pressure		High Integration	Low Integration
		Low Adaptation	Low Adaptation
	Low	High Integration	Low Integration
		High	Low

Financial Pressure

Exhibit 3-6. The Portfolio Level Adaptation and Integration Planning Needs.

we have four different archetypes of planning needs positions, just as
what was the case in the SBU planning needs analysis discussed in the
first part of Chapter Three. Although seemingly similar at a first glance
to Exhibit 3-6, which summarizes the adaptation and integration needs
for the SBU level, the two are in fact fundamentally different. It should
be kept in mind that the two sources of planning pressure at the corporate level do indeed signify that there might be lack of stability or disequilibrium in the corporate portfolio. For instance, a financial pressure would indicate that corporate management is facing the task of modifying the portfolio so that the financial pressure might go away. Similarly, a C.E.O who is structural pressure will attempt to embark on a
set of actions which eventually might reduce this pressure Thus, what
we have when a corporation's strategic situational setting is such that
it is located in the bottom-right square of Exhibit 3-6 is an indication
that we are having a healthy portfolio. The planning emphasis will be
largely to maintain this position, and there will be litte pressure to
plan major changes. However, what we have if the company is located in
one of the three cells other than the bottom-right one is a pressure to
plan for a change in the portfolio so that the particular pressure faced
in any of these three cells might be ameliorated. Thus, any portfolio
setting which falls into any of these cells is in a state of strategic
disequilibrium.

It follows from this that there are three major types of strategic
disequilibrium at the portfolio level, and that each of these will face
different planning needs in order to evolve towards the preferred bottom-
right stable position. For a company which finds itself in the upper-
right strategic portfolio need position of Exhibit 3-6 the challenge
will be to face the needs for adaptive planning so as to "upgrade" the

structure of the corporate portfolio over the longer term, while there
"still is time," i.e. relatively little short-term financial pressures
For a company which is located in the bottom-left cell of Exhibit 3-6,
on the other hand, the need will be to plan for relatively short-term
financial improvements of the corporate portfolio The basic structure
of the portfolio, on the other hand, will be healthy and should not be
planned to be changed significantly. The third disequilibrium position
will be for a company which finds itself in the upper-left position of
Exhibit 3-6. This will indeed typically be a serious portfolio location
position, in that it indicates pressures to plan both for financial performance improvements as well as for upgrading the longer-term "health"
of the structure of the corporate portfolio. Serious corporate level
planning needs exist in this case. Contrasting this situation with the
"ideal" bottom-right stable position of Exhibit 3-6 we see that while in
the former there will be a major pressure on the corporate level to plan
for changes in the firm's portfolio, there will be little such pressure
in the latter case   Thus, while corporate level planning activities
might be expected to be intensive and result in far-reaching substantive
changes in the former case, the planning activities will probably be much
more low key and merely focussed on monitoring that the strong portfolio
position is being kept in the latter case.

We see that the corporate portfolio level's strategic planning needs
do not evolve over time in an analogous fashion to what we saw for the
planning needs of a SBU, changing in accordance with a planned sequence
of stages (question-mark, star; cash-cow, dog) For the corporate level
the needs, on the other hand, will be to maintain a stable and healthy
portfolio balance - as soon as imbalances occur the pressures will be to
restore the equilibrium Thus, while we are facing both adaptation as

integration needs for planning at both the business level as well as the
corporate level, the planning responses to these needs will be different,
reflecting the different levels of strategy we are dealing with. While
at the business level the dynamics of the business' change over time will
call for the acceptance of changes over time in the absolute levels of
planning needs both for adaptation as well as for integration and also
for the acceptance over time in the relative balance between adaptation
and integration, at the corporate level a low absolute need level for
adaptation and integration as well as an even relative balance between
adaptation and integration will always be the ideal.

We have now completed our discussion of the significance of a firm's
particular strategic setting as a determinant for the particular needs
for planning that the firm is facing, in terms of adaptation as well as
integration, at the business as well as the corporate strategic levels.
An analysis of the planning needs along these lines will serve as the
take-off point for developing a corporate planning system which will have
capabilities designed into it for adequately meeting these needs. Before
initiating our discussion of situational design of strategic planning
systems, the topic for our next three chapters, it is however necessary
that we discuss one additional issue which is important when assessing
the planning needs both at the business as well as at the corporate levels,
namely to determine the nature of the risk associated with any of these
strategic positions. This will serve as a device to magnify the importance of the needs for planning in those situations where the strategic
position is highly risky. The approach for risk assessment to be discussed
in the next section shall be emphasizing the riskiness of a strategy as
a function of its exposure to environmental factors. This applies equally
well to corporate as well as business level strategies. Hence, we shall

avoiding to doplicate the discussion by covering it as part of cotn tne
business and corporate strategy need assessment analyses

3-11. Assessment of Risk Exposure of Strategic Positions.

From a corporate strategic point of view a key issue in a strategic
audit is whether the portfolio pattern of business activities represents
a satisfactory blend in terms of exposure to environmental threats and/or
opportunities The key concern is whether the risk/return pattern deriving
from one's particular business portfolio is acceptable. Our task in this
section, thus, will be to carry out a risk/return analysis Such an
analysis must apply to the SBU level, and it must also lend itself to
aggregation into an overall picture of the portfolio risk exposure. A
major requirement must be that our analysis must be meaningful from a
senior management point of view. This seems to call for a different
analysis than classical statistical measurement of risk, in that a senior
executive must be able to relate his own perception of risk preference to
the measure. We shall propose a measure of strategic risk exposure whicn
is based on a dual set of foci it focuses on the firm's exposure to
environmental events which can be predicted with varying degrees of cer-
tainty, and it also assesses the degree of managerial flexibility that
is available in responding to a particular event. Such a predictability/
response concept is particularly useful for senior management in assessing
business as well as portfolio strategy risks, in that it closely seems to
resemble managers' cognitive structuring of their analysis of such problems [12]

A first step in such a risk assessment analysis would be for each of
the SBUs to develop a list of environmental factors that might significantly change the projected funds flows from tne SBU's and thus the likelihood of achieving the SBU strategies These factors might represent

major environmental threats to a SBU or they might represent potentially
major positive environmental developments. The emphasis should be to develop a reasonably short list of critical environmental exposure factors.
One should focus only on those factors that are judged to be truly critical. The list should be a collaboration between SBU level involved, the
division involved, and the corporate level. A SBU manager should normally
be able to identify easily the few environmental factors that represent
a potentially significant change to his business. If the division manager
has not already developed such a list for himself the question can be
raised as to whether he is "worth his salt!" This initial input from a
SBU manager will then be refined and improved on through discussions first
with the relevant division manager and then with the corporate level
Under all circumstances it will be desirable that both the SBU-, division-
corporate management be involved in the development of such a list, in
order to increase its credibility and impose a stronger sense of accountability for it.

Each of the key factors identified might turn out to be so general
that it relates to most of the business as a whole, i.e., it will affect
all the division's SBU's. However, some factors might be more specifically
related to one or a few of the SBU's. Thus, while a divison manager will
have a list of critical environmental factors which capture the exposure
of all the SBUs' which are reporting to him, this list will be shorter
than the sum of the SBU factors. However, he might have to include other
critical environmental factors that apply to his division but not to any
of the SBUs. Similarly, at the corporate level the environmental factor,
list will be less than the sum of the divisional factors, except for in
the general factors relating to the corporation as a whole that need to
be added is larger than the divisional factor duplication/reduction effort.

It will of course be impossible to identify all potentially relevant environmental factors. This is particularly so since nobody is able to outguess the future "through a crystal ball." However, given that all realize that no list of factors can ever be perfect but that a serious effort has gone into developing the list, it should not be questionable to base the analysis on what information management can perceive. Further, however, all environmental factors will not be equally important; hence a weighting of the factors might be necessary -- potentially a complicating subjective step of analysis. Let us briefly discuss each of these issues.

It is of course a critical problem to be unable to come up with a list which does not capture a significant share of the relevant factors. Even the most sophisticated and insightful management will be unable to develop a complete view of the future. However, an analysis which is based on a reasonable set of assumptions is far better than no analysis, within the area of strategic planning just as within any other area of management analysis we must utilize the information we can get and not allow ourselves to abandon analysis because we conclude that the information is incomplete.

The problem of ranking of the environmental factors should be approached as follows. First, the factors should be sorted into two subgroups· those that might have potentially positive effect and those that might have potentially negative effect on the strategic success of the business. In each of these subgroups one should identify the most important factor, if one such factor stands out, otherwise one should identify the two or three most important factors For the rest of the factors within each of the two subgroups it should be considered whether these are indeed important supporting environmental factors. If not these factors

should be abandoned from the list. The question should always be raised
whether too many factors have been included. Often this is the case,
the marginal factors on the list will not matter relatively that much after
all, compared with other factors on the list. The issue of ranking and
eliminating factors becomes particularly important as we consolidate the
factors at the divisional and at the corporate levels, in order to maintain a reasonable focus for what managers will be able to perceive on.

Having developed the lists of critical positive as well as negative
environmental factors for each SBU, division and at the corporate level,
the next question is to assess, for each factor on the lists, to what
extent, if at all, each environmental phenomenon can be predicted or
foreseen. Each SBU should develop a sense of predictability for its own
list of factors. Similarly, each division as well as the corporate level
should determine how to predict each of the factors on its list. For
prediction there are two approaches that should be explored, in combination if possible, in order to come up with a factor prediction. One
approach might be to make use of time series of historical data in order
to come up with a prediction of future developments based on past experience. This approach will almost never be perfectly applicable in that
there typically will be a lack of relevant historical data for many of the
environmental factors that are strategically significant. Also, many of
the critical phenomena would typically be expected to take place as dis-
creet unexpected events, such as crises, and can thus often not easily be
detected by analyzing trends of the past. Most critical as a potential
problem with this approach, however, might be its tendency to allow too
much emphasis on the historical trends with regards to the strengths and
weaknesses factors for developing a picture of the future. Instead, the
opportunities and/or threats should be explored relatively unconstrained

at first, for then maybe to be reconciled with the present situation and historical pattern. A second approach to assisting in the factor forecasting is to attempt to identify so-called lead indicators -- developments which relate to environmental activities that might be seen as indicators for what might happen with the factor relevant to oneself. Here too ingenuity and deductive insight is probably an important factor. Leading indicators that are too obvious typically tend to be giving warning signals too close in time to be useful. Several lead indicators might often be combined into some sort of scenario. Again, it is critical that such a scenario is not being developed through a process of "mental extrapolation," but rather as the result of a more unconstrained effort.

Despite all the rigor that one might be attempting to apply to develop forecasts for a particular environmental phenomenon, it may still well happen for some factors that few or no meaningful forecasts can be achieved. For other phenomena at least some useful forecasting support might be the result. Often to management's surprise and delight several environmental phenomena often actually lend themselves quite well to be forecasted when being subjected to hard and rigorous analysis. The emerging result of the forecasting analysis efforts is that we shall be able to get a feel for each of the environmental phenomenae in terms of whether it has a relatively high versus a relatively low degree of predictability potential associated with itself.

Let us now turn to a third step in our analysis, namely to explore what might be potential managerial response options to a particular environmental phenomenon. For each critical factor we might ask whether there is anything we can do to take advantage of a potentially positive development in the environment of, alternatively, to ameliorate a potentially negative environmental development. Thus, for each of the environmental factors a specific evaluation should be made of potential response approaches. This should allow management to come up with a better understanding of whether the firm actually can respond at all, and if so, to what extent the response can be expected to have any effect. It will probably be concluded that when it comes to some environmental factors there is little _de facto_ response potential, while for other factors there might be quite some flexibility, with several realistic response possibilities and a reasonable chance of ameliorating or, alternatively, taking advantage of an environmental event. It may turn out that for some of the environmental phenomena the degree of response potential actually might be higher than management had expected before it put systematic efforts into formal analysis of how to respond. When summarizing the efforts to determine the discretionary response potential to critical environmental factors, the factors will probably lend themselves to be ordered along a continuum in terms of degree of discretionary response potential, just as was also the case when it came to dgree of predictability.

To integrate the three assessment phases that we just have been making into an overall concept of strategic risk exposure, the predictability assessment and the discretionary response assessment for each key environmental factor relating to a SBU should be plotted on what might be termed this SBU strategic risk exposure chart. Exhibit 3-7 illustrates an example of this.

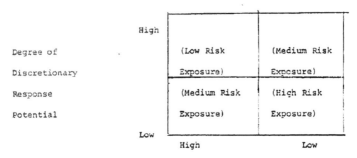

Exhibit 3-7: Positioning of the Predictability/Response Characteristics of the Major Environmental Factors that Determine a SBU Risk Exposure.

This exhibit should be interpreted as follows. On the horizontal axis we have plotted the degree of predictability from high to low. On the vertical axis we have plotted the degree of discretionary response poten- tial from low to high. Let us, for instance, assume that the most impor- tant environmental risk factor falls into the upper-left quadrant of Exhibit 3-7, so that we can predict this factor reasonably well and also enjoy a relatively high response potential. This would mean that in case an environmental factor should develop adversely there will be a fair chance that we might become aware of this development in time, thereby also being able to respond so that we can ameliorate some of the adverse effects. Assuming that the other environmental factors that might have a negative effect also generally fall within the general area of the upper left quadrant of the exhibit we might conclude that the environmental risk exposure of the strategy of this SBU is relatively low. If on the other hand our assessment locates a critical environmental factor in the lower right-hand corner of Exhibit 3-7, we are then facing a situation where we have neither much possibility to predict the development of an environmental factor nor respond to make any responsive move. In this

situation we have to conclude that the SBU is faced with a highly risky
environmental exposure. The two remaining positions at the upper-right
and lower-left areas of Exhibit 3-12 represent environmental risk exposure positions that fall in between the low- and the high-risk positions
just discussed If a key environmental factor falls within the upper
right-hand area of the chart then there will be little predictability
but still significant response potential, if in the lower left-hand area
there is high predictability but low response potential. In such a case
we can at least minimize the risk by "getting out" of the business in
time when we expect an adverse development.

To minimize environmental strategic risk exposure is of course not
an objective in itself. Risk exposure should be seen in relation to
the particular opportunity at hand; if the potential payoff of a SBU's
strategy is high then it might merit taking the risks. In order to assess
the potential of a SBU strategy we must therefore not only consider its
risk exposure but also the absolute level of the funds flow expected to
result from the strategy. This will give us a perception of the "bare
point" attractiveness of the strategy In addition to this, however, we
must also consider the potential from benefits resulting from positive
developments among our other environmental factors. Again, if the key
potential positive environmental effect is assessed to lie within the
upper left-hand corner, and the other positive environmental factors also
tend to fall within this sector, then there is a high potential for favorable gain as a result of environmental factors.

By completing each SBU element of the risk exposure analysis we
will also have the data to carry out the divisional and the corporate
portfolio environmental risk exposure analysis. From a corporate point
of view the nature of the fit in terms of risk exposure characteristics

between the divisions must be considered. One question is whether there
seems to be too much risk exposure in general, which in case might jeopardize management's view on what constitutes prudent management. An alternative question might be whether tner might be too little overall corporate risk-taking. This would mean that the company would seem unable
to reemploy generated funds in an aggressive enough way. Beyond these
critical questions about overall corporate environmental risk exposure
two less obvious issues must be raised. First, is there inconsistency in
risk-taking among the divisions? Second, what potential modifications
might be made on the portfolio strategy of a corporation in order for the
environmental risk exposure to be changed in a desired direction?

Regarding the issue of whether there is consistency in risk-taking
among tne divisions this might be explored by comparing the divisions in
terms of risk exposure relative to attractiveness of their "base plans"
and also considering the potential for gain from positive environmental
developments. It may turn out that some businesses offer far too much
risk exposure without providing a reasonable performance potential. It
may also be that the risk is very low for some businesses but that the
return potential is inadequate too The key would be to develop an intimate sense of the risk/return configuration for eacn business element
in the corporate portfolio. It will ultimately depend on senior management's attitude towards risk what risk/return level will be acceptable.
Each business should ideally fall on the "efficient" risk/return tradeoff-
line given tnis senior management's risk preference; a higher risk/return
would be too speculative to be acceptable, a lower risk/return unnecessarily
conservative The issue of achieving consistency in environmental risk
exposure among the division does consequently not imply that each division should be exposed to the same level of environmental risk out rather

that the risk/return of all the divisions should be efficient.

Regarding the issue of carrying out modifications of the portfolio
strategy in order to modify the overall environmental risk exposure
there are two considerations that should be raised. Firs, when it comes
to decisions such as acquisitions and/or divestitures as well as when
deciding on whether to significantly scale up or down some of the businesses' activity levels it is important to include in one's evaluation
as to whether this incremental portfolio change will lead to a better
risk/return fit. Secondly, it should be made explicit what kinds of modifications that should be attempted in terms of initiation of new strategic programs or even modifying the entire strategy of a business in
order to reduce its risk posture. Assessment of risk exposure and how
to improve on this should be a key element in the interaction and review
between corporate level and each of the divisions as part of the planning
process.

We have now completed the discussion of how one might approach the
issue of how to assess the nature of a strategy's exposure to environmental factors. This is an integral part of the assessment of a corporation's strategic position. Such an overall assessment of the risk
exposure is a critical ingredient for understanding what types of planning that are needed, both at the SBU and at the corporate strategic
levels.

We have now concluded our discussion of how to assess the needs for
planning, stemming from the strategic position of a firm. Before summarizing our approach, however, we shall raise one more issue in connection
with the strategic audit approach for determining planning needs, namely
to discuss what might be the key logistical considerations to observe for
when, how and by whom to do the audit. This will be discussed in the

3-12. When Should Strategic Audits of Planning Needs Be Carried Out,
       And By Whom?

The analysis of a corporation's needs for planning provides a static
view of how the company and its businesses stand in terms of strategic
strengths and weaknesses at one particular point in time[13] It is useful
for management at certain intervals to be presented with a reasonably
complete and consistently developed picture of the particular situational
setting at hand - what strategic and financial constraints there are and
what particular needs the company has for planning. It is easy to develop the argument that such a strategic assessment analysis should be
carried out before a formal corporate strategic planning system is being
installed. This will provide the necessary direction for what capabilities
to be designed into the planning system.

As a planning system starts to function after it has been properly
tailormade and installed, the system itself will provide an update of what
will be emerging new planning needs. It will consequently not be necessary
to carry out a complete new independent strategic planning need assessment
analysis on a continued basis.

It might be useful, however, to carry out ad hoc strategic position
audits of particular divisions, particularly if a particular business is
facing exceptional changes in its business climate as well as when major
strategic shifts are being contemplated, such as a major expansion or
withdrawal. In such instances, it might be useful with in-depth data on
an ad hoc basis, independently of the planning schedule. Not only will
this allow for enough detail in the data. Also, it will prevent the
holding up of the corporation's entire planning effort as a result of
almost inevitable delays that might have been caused if attempting to
provide the data for the strategic analysis of the exceptional business

setting through the ordinary planning cycle in its entirety.

When candidates are being identified for potential acquisition there is also a need for a strategic audit analysis of the new business. There will of course typically be problems gathering parts of the data in such instances, but it will typically still be possible to come up with a useful analysis. Given that the efforts involved in carrying out such a thorough acquisition analysis typically will be considerable, it might be useful to develop a step-wise analytical scheme for acquisition analysis. This might help weeding out at an early stage acquisition candidates that look relatively unpromising, so that only the potentially more attractive candidates will pass the preliminary screenings and receive a full strategic audit treatment. We shall discuss this further in Chapter Six in connection with how to avoid "overloading" the planning system.

At some intervals, however, there might be a need to repeat a full-blown strategic audit for the entire company. This may be needed as a basis for a "major overhaul" of the planning system which now and then may be necessary. We see what will be emerging new happening in many large corporations. There seems, in fact, to be a "life-cycle" for many a corporate planning system; after some years in place the present system might be abandoned and a new system installed. This might typically happen in connection with a major reorganization and/or management reshuffle. The strategic position audit is of course a useful tool at such times. One of the arguments that we shall make in this book, however, is that it would normally be more ideal to have the corporate planning system subjected to a relatively continuous process of improvement and incremental updating, thereby making it less necessary to perform frequent "major overhauls" of the planning system. Given the typically high costs of such major overhauls, not only in money terms but also in terms of the

disruption that this might cause on the managerial strategic process, we
shall argue that these typically will be considerable from a "managing
the evolution of the system approach." This issue too will be pursued
further in Chapter Six.

Who should carry out the strategic position audits? Given that a
strategic position audit might trigger a set of one-shot decisions of
potentially far-reaching consequences for the individual managers regarding
such issues as redefinition of strategic business units, relative importance of each business, etc., a central involvement in an ad hoc activity
of this kind might diminish a corporate planning executive's effectiveness
and credibility as a party in the ongoing continuous corporate planning
process. Also, the line executives too will typically have so much per-
sonally at stake that they might not be effective participants in this
process. In order not to lose credibility for the ongoing planning work
that is supposed to follow from the strategic audit, it might therefore
be useful to draw on temporary expertise from outside the main line of
the organization to carry out the strategic audit analysis - either an in-
house consultant group or outside consulting help. This might give a
better assurance of an objective audit and protect against the danger of
bias that could enter the analysis if it is carried out by managers who
are directly involved in the businesses. We shall pursue this issue further in Chapter Seven when we discuss the roles of various stakeholders
in the corporate planning process.

3-13. Summary

In this chapter we have discussed how to determine the needs for planning that different companies might have. The underlying premise for the
rationale of the approach taken in this chapter is that all companies

in fact are unique and that they therefore will have different needs
for planning. Hence, it becomes necessary to go beyond the general planning concepts that were developed in Chapter Two, namely to tailormake a
planning system to the unique needs at hand. It follows that an explicit
determination of a firm's planning needs is the first step in this direction. The purpose of this the present chapter has been to discuss how
these needs might be determined.

We have advocated a strategic position audit approach for determining
the needs for strategic planning facing the corporation. This consists
of a set of analytical steps to be carried out before developing the planning system, in order to get an adequate focus on what might be the overall
situational context for planning. This strategic position assessment approach involves assessment of a firm's strategic position at three organizational levels.

First, within each division a set of SBUs should be identified as
the "building blocks" for strategic planning. For each SBU an assessment
should be made of its position in terms of its competitive strength within the business as well as in terms of the general attractiveness of being
in this business. We concluded that a SBU's adaptation-related planning
needs would be primarily a function of the general business attractiveness
dimension, while the integration-related planning needs would be a function
of one's competitive strength, above all. In line with this a pattern of
different planning needs emerged for SBUs that were in different positions
in terms of scoring on the two just-mentioned dimensions, in terms of absolute as well as relative differences in adaptation- and integration-
planning needs A SBU in a so-called "question-mark" strategic position
would have relatively high need for adaptation and relatively low need for
integration, a "star" SBU is facing high needs for both adaptation as well

as integration; a SBU in the "cash cow" position will be having relatively high needs for integration and relatively low needs for adaptation, and, finally, a so-called "dog" will have a low need for both adaptation and integration planning. Also, given that the strategic position of a SBU typically might change over time, due to plans as well as due to evolutionary pressures, say, from being a "star" to becoming a "cash-cow," it becomes important to recognize the dynamics of changing SBU planning needs.

Secondly, the consolidation attractiveness of carrying out the related business activities of the SBUs within one division were analyzed. We pointed out that heavy consolidation challenges would lead to an increased need for integration planning, above all.

Thirdly, we proposed a corporate level planning needs analysis which also was being based on two dimensions. A financial analysis would emphasize what would be the more near-term pressures to show stable overall performance associated with a particular corporate strategic setting. This would provide a picture of the needs for integrative planning at the corporate level, above all. In addition, the corporate level assessment should include an analysis of the more longer-term structural portfolio pressures that the company is facing, as seen when extrapolating the funds flow patterns as well as when undertaking a comparative analysis of several companies' changes in portfolio structure. These longer-term structural pressure challenges would lead to increased adaptation planning needs above all at the corporate level.

In addition to the analysis of the planning needs stemming from the strategic position at the various organizational levels we also advocated the need for assessing the environmental risk associated with a strategy and outlined how such a risk/return analysis should be carried out. This attempts to relate the return potentials of a business, including those risks that are involved due to potentially unfavorable developments in the environment. The intention is to come up with an assessment of the overall pattern of business elements of the corporate portfolio which indicate whether the risk/return configuration associated with each SBU is consistent with the others and in accordance with the aptitude towards risk-taking generally acceptable to management.

Finally, we pointed out that the strategic audit analysis should be seen as an activity which is basically of an ad hoc nature. Thus, involvement in the execution of a strategic audit analysis might cause a strain on the effectiveness of managers in the ongoing corporate planning process. Therefore resource persons outside the ongoing operating line activities, such as for instance internal consultant staffs or external consultants might, be fruitfully employed for strategic audit assessments.

In the appendix to this chapter we have included an example which illustrates how one large, diversified corporation approaches the analysis of the attractiveness of its overall portfolio of businesses in order to come up with a more focussed picture of the various planning needs it is facing.

Appendix· A Portfolio Attractiveness Index: An Example.

The issue of getting an overall overview of the portfolio planning needs of one's company is maybe particularly difficult to grapple with within a highly diversified corporation, none the least because of corporate management's heavy reliance on a large number of subordinate managers' inputs to the planning process as well as on their ability to implement the plans. Given the almost impossible task for the corporate management to directly develop an in-depth feel for all of the businesses, it will be a touch task to understand tne relative attractiveness of one business versus another. One nighly diversified corporation with annual sales around 1.5 billion dollars and with more than 40 operating divisions has strengthened its attempt to comprehend its portfolio planning needs by developing an index for business attractiveness based on data collected from the planning output of each division. This is primarily intended as an aid in evaluating tne merits of each business for in turn to set better investment priorities within its portfolio of businesses. The attractiveness index was developed from a composite measure of the attractiveness of each business, based on the measurement of a total of 14 factors falling within three major areas. Five different market-related factors form a composite measure of the business' competitive strength, five factors relating to underlying aspects of the competition form a composite measure of the attractiveness of the competitive climate and, finally, a composite measure of the riskiness of the business is developed, based on four underlying risk factor measurements. A relative weighing scheme was devised, so that index value scores could be derived for each business The businesses were tnen ranked in terms of their attractiveness

The elements of the index and tne weightings of these factors were developed as follows.

1. Market attractiveness (40% weight)

   a. Market size, dollar value of overall industry sales within
      the market segments served by this strategic business unit
      of the company (15% weight).

   b. Market growth, average annual expected compound growth rate
      of sales within the market segments served (10% weight).

   c. Market maturity, an assessment of this strategic business
      unit's positioning along the product life-cycle, based on
      degree of recency of product developments, general avail-
      ability of relevant technology, degree of stability and di-
      rection of purchase patterns, and demographic/socio/economic
      trends of customer profiles (10% weight)

   d. Buyer fragmentation, an assessment based on estimating the
      total number of immediate customers who account for 50% of
      the total industry revenue within this market A high num-
      ber signifies less vulnerability to a single or a few cus-
      tomers' demands (5% weight).

   e. Frequency of purchase, an assessment of how often immediate
      customers typically buy the product. A high purchase frequency
      signifies less vulnerability exposure from potential "cuts"
      in the consumer's expenditure budget (5% weight).

2. Competitive strength (35% weight)

   a. Market concentration, the percentage of overall industry
      sales within the relevant market segment accounted for by
      the four largest competitors in the industry The higher
      concentration the better in terms of allowing the competitive

skills of a large company to bear (10% weight)

b. Relative market share; the company's market share within the
relevant market segment divided by the combined share of the
three largest competitors. (If possible, the company prefers
to measure market share in terms of physical units, rather than
in terms of dollars, because it feels that this might generally provide more reliable measures; 10% weight)

c. Consumer/customer industry franchise; an assessment of the
company's degree of established strength and recognition of
brand names within the relevant market (5% weight).

d. Technology/innovation leadership; an assessment of the company's relative standing within the relevant market, in terms
of technology leadership and product innovation

e. Quality; an assessment of the company's relative standing
within the relevant market, in terms of its products' quality.

3. Risk (25% weight)

a. Profit variability, a statistical measure of the variation
around a trend in pretax profits performance over the last
five years (10% weight).

b. Operating leverage; the ratio of total fixed costs and expenses to total variable costs -- the lower the break-even
point the better, as indicated by this ratio (5% weight)

c. Net asset intensity, the ratio of net assets employed to
revenues -- the lower the ROI the better (Notice that this
ratio, in order to provide basis for meaningful ranking between divisions, assumes that the "age distribution" of each
division's assets is relatively similar for all divisions

Elsewise, a division with relatively older assets would "automatically" receive a higher score than a division with relatively newer assets (5% weight)

d. Price leadership; an assessment of the pattern with regard to whom generally initiates price changes -- the more control by the company the better (5% weight).

The company makes use of this index to rank the attractiveness of each of its businesses. The businesses were clustered into three major groups, each with different planning needs. The highly attractive category of businesses are in need for planning which will enable them to receive corporate funds to the extent that they are able to expand and actively pursue the opportunities inherent in his business. The somewhat attractive category of businesses are in need for planning to primarily maintain their present competitive strength position, and for thus being prepared to receive corporate funds and for pursuing selected strategic programs in order to solidify its present position and to relatively improve the attractiveness position of its business. Finally, the category with what might be labelled unattractive businesses will have planning needs primarily within the area of improving their efficiency and for carrying out cost reduction strategic programs only. These businesses will also have a planning need for maintaining or improving its attractiveness as a divestiture candidate, so that it potentially might be spun off. Thereby it might provide the basis for an even larger net funds contribution than through continued operation. In total, corporate management makes use of this ranking scheme in sharpening its perception of the planning needs of each of the businesses, in interacting with the businesses and ultimately in allocating resources within what it considers a more focussed overall portfolio context. Thus, it explicitly recognizes that providing for a clearer statement of the strategic setting of each business will allow each business to focus on what should be its particular major strategic issues   Thereby the corporate management will have created a setting in which resource allocation's role as <u>the</u> tool in influencing the strategic posture that its company is in can be exploited.

Chapter Three - Footnotes

1. One of the first to emphasize product-market relationships as "building
    blocks" in a company's strategic plans was Ansoff; see Ansoff, H. Igor,
    Corporate Strategy, McGraw-Hill, New York, 1965. For a discussion of
    how to define SBU's, see Day, George S. and Allan D. Shocker,
    Identifying Competitive Product-Market Boundaries: Strategic and
    Analytical Issues, Marketing Science Institute, Cambridge, 1976, and
    Rothschild, William E., Putting it All Together, Amacom, New York,
    1976.

2. For discussions of the experience curve and its impact on business
    strategizing, see Hirschmann, W. B., "Profit from the Learning Curve",
    Harvard Business Review, Jan.-Feb., 1964, Conley, Patrick, "Experience
    Curves as a Planning Tool", IEEE Spectrum, June, 1970, Henderson,
    Bruce D., "The Experience Curve Reviewed: The Growth-Share Matrix of
    the Product Portfolio", Perspectives, Boston Consulting Group, Boston,
    1973, and Abernathy, W. J., and K. Wayne, "Limits to the Learning
    Curve", Harvard Business Review, Sept.-Oct., 1974.

3. See, for instance, Schoeffler, Sidney, Robert D. Buzzell and Donald F.
    Heany, "Impact of Strategic Planning on Profit Performance", Harvard
    Business Review, March-April, 1974, and Buzzell, Robert D., Bradley T.
    Gale and Ralph G. M. Sultan, "Market Share - A Key to Profitability",
    Harvard Business Review, Jan-Feb., 1975.

4. For a discussion of the PIMS approach, its strengths as well as limita-
    tions, see Anderson, Carl R. and Frank T. Paine, "PIMS: A Reexamination"
    Academy of Management Journal, forthcoming.

5. A vast body of literature is developed around the causes of innovation and its role as a "triggering mechanism" for product life cycle development. For a summary of the earlier literature, see Nelson, Richard R , The Rate and Direction of Inventive Activity: Economic and Social Factors, Princeton University Press, Princeton, 1962. See also, Leavitt, Theodore, "Exploit the Product Life-Cycle", Harvard Business Review, Nov.-Dec., 1965, Cox, William E., Jr., "Product Life-Cycles as Marketing Models", Journal of Business, October, 1967, Clifford, Donald K , Jr , "Managing the Product Life Cycle", European Business, July, 1969, Polli, Rolando and Victor Cook, "Validity of the Product Life Cycle", Journal of Business, October, 1969, Wells, Louis T., Jr , "The Product Life Cycle Approach", in Wells, Louis T., (editor), The Product Life Cycle and International Trade, Division of Research, Harvard Business School, Boston, 1972, and Wasson, C R , Dynamic Competitive Strategy and Product Life Cycles, Challenge Books, St. Charles, 1974

6. See Henderson, Bruce D., "The Product Portfolio", Perspectives, Boston Consulting Group, Boston, 1970, Henderson Bruce D , "Cash Traps", Perspectives, Boston Consulting Group, Boston, 1970, Gerstner, Louis V , Jr., "Can Strategic Planning Pay Off?" Business Horizons, December, 1972, Arthur D Little, Inc., "A System for Managing Diversity", Cambridge, 1974, and Hax, Arnoldo C. and Nicolas S. Majluf, "A Methodological Approach for the Developing of Strategic Planning in Diversified Corporations", Technical Report No. 3, Sloan School of Management, M.I.T , Cambridge, 1977

7. For discussions of several of the problems raised in Section 3-6, see Fruhan, William E., "Pyrrhic Victories in Fights for Market Share", _Harvard Business Review_, Sep.-Oct., 1972, Wind, Yoram and Henry J. Claycamp, "Planning Product Line Strategy: A Matrix Approach", _Journal of Marketing_, Vol. 40, No. 1, January, 1976, Day, George S., "Diagnosing the Product Portfolio", _Journal of Marketing_, Vol. 41, No. 2, April, 1977, and Hammermesh, R. G., M. J. Anderson, Jr., and J. E. Harris, "Strategies for Low Market Share Businesses", _Harvard Business Review_, May-June, 1978.

8. See Lorange, Peter, "Divisional Planning: Setting Effective Direction" _Sloan Management Review_, Fall, 1975.

9. See, for instance, Donaldson, Gordon, _Strategy for Financial Mobility_, Division of Research, Harvard Business School, Boston, 1969, Marris Robin C., "An Introduction to Theories of Corporate Growth", in Marris, R. C. and A. Wood, _The Corporate Economy: Growth, Competition and Innovative Potential_, MacMillan, New York, 1971.

10. For several works that might be interpreted so as to underscore the existence of a set of structural planning needs, see Baumol, William J. _Business Behavior, Value and Growth_, Harcourt, Brace and World, New York, 1967, Marris, Robin C., _The Economic Theory of Managerial Capitalism_, MacMillan, New York, 1968, Steiner, George A., _Top Management Planning_, MacMillan, New York, 1969, and Leibenstein, Harvey, _Beyond Economic Man: A New Foundation for Microeconomics_, Harvard University Press, Cambridge, 1976.

11. See Stevenson, Howard H., "Defining Corporate Strengths and Weaknesses", Sloan Management Review, Spring, 1976.

12. For several articles and books relevant in operationalizing the concept of environmental risk exposure discussed in Section 3-11, see Aguilar, F. J., Scanning the Business Environment, MacMillan, New York 1967, Duncan, R. B., "Characteristics of Organizational Environments and Perceived Environmental Uncertainty", Administrative Science Quarterly, Vol. 17, 1972, Denning, Basil W., "Strategic Environmental Appraisal", Long Range Planning, March, 1973, Rhenman, Eric, Organization Theory for Long-Range Planning, Wiley-Interscience, New York, 1973, Downey, H. K., D. Hellriegel and J. W. Slocum, Jr., "Environmental Uncertainty: The Construct and its Application", Administrative Science Quarterly, Vol. 20, 1975, Downey, H. K. and J. W. Slocum, Jr., "Uncertainty Measures, Research, and Sources of Variation", Academy of Management Journal, Vol. 18, 1975, and Metcalfe, Les and Will McQuillan, "Managing Turbulence", in Nystrom, Paul C. and William H. Starbuck, editors, Prescriptive Models of Organizations, North-Holland Publishing Co., Amsterdam, 1977.

13. Analogous ideas to the one of carrying out a strategic systems audit have been suggested by Ferguson ("strategic concept audit") and by Smith ("strategic information profiles"); see Ferguson, Charles R., Measuring Corporate Strategy, Dow Jones-Irwing, Homewood, 1974, and Smith, Theodore A., Dynamic Business Strategy: The Art of Planning for Success, McGraw-Hill, New York, 1977.

CHAPTER FOUR

Implementation of Corporate Planning Systems: General Pitfalls and Problems.

4-1. Introduction.

In this chapter as well as in the following two chapters we shall address the issue of implementing effective corporate planning systems. We recall that a general conceptual scheme for corporate planning was developed in Chapter Two. It was stressed, however, that in order to become useful when implemented in actual corporate settings, it would be necessary to modify the general conceptual planning scheme in such a way that capabilities were built into the system in correspondence with the particular planning needs that a given firm would have. Accordingly, in Chapter Three we discussed how to determine a firm's planning needs, stemming from its strategic situational setting. The general thrust of the task of implementing a corporate planning system, then, will be to tailormake the system in such a way that it will be capable of meeting the needs identified. However, this turns out to be such a complex task that we shall find it useful to break the discussion of it down into three. As a first implementation step we shall discuss in this chapter a number of more general pitfalls and problems that we have found to be typical when attempting to install a corporate planning system of the conceptual type developed in Chapter Two.[1] This represents an important first step towards implementation, in that it will facilitate the eliminations of problems that elsewise would have become obstacles during the subsequent sharpening of the focus for the planning system's capabilities This will allow us in Chapter Five to discuss how to tailormake the system to meet the pressing needs for planning for a given corporate setting. In Chapter Six our discussion of implementation shall culminate with focussing on a third aspect of the process, namely on how to manage the evolution of the planning system so

that it might continue to be of usefulness over time as a firm's needs
for planning might be changing.

We shall address fourteen commonly found general implementation
problems and issues in this chapter, and discuss them as they relate to
the implementation of each of the five cycles of the conceptual scheme
for planning developed in Chapter Two.

4-2. Pitfalls and problems during the objectives-setting stage.

There are five types of potential implementation problems and pitfalls
that we have found to be particularly pertinent to the initial cycle of
the corporate planning process - the objectives-setting stage. These
are the need for the C.E.O.'s full involvement, the assessment of new opportunities in the business environment by the divisions; the nature of
the portfolio approach towards corporate review of inputs from the rest
of the organization; the informal nature of the involvement by the specialized functional departments at this stage, and the need for a feedback/
iterative mechanism for re-examining and revising parts of the planning
outputs so that overall consistency might be reached among the many elements that will constitute the output of the objectives-setting cycle
We shall discuss each of these issues in turn.

1. The C.E.O. should initiate the process.

When it comes to the first issue, the nature of the C.E.O.'s involvement, it is particularly important that top management is fully
involved. This would mean more than a general "letter of endorsement"
of planning by the C.E O., some general urging that the organization "go
out and plan." What is needed is that the C.E.O. actually start the
process he should signal his own aspirations, intentions and performance requirements to the division heads as the first step of the annual

planning process. He should be as specific as he feels he can realistically be, but stress that his ideas are tentative at this stage. The C.E.O.'s inputs should serve as a vehicle for giving a useful and stimulating context to planning; it will consequently be natural and desirable that revisions, modifications and improvements are likely to result from the planning process itself.[2]

Corporate assumptions with regard to interest-, inflation-, wages-, and currency-levels should also be communicated at this stage. These too should be tentative, in that if a given business has a particular reason for not following the common assumptions as a result of unusual circumstances in its setting, then the management of this business should be encouraged to state this. Each business should be convinced that the general corporate assumptions are valid in their own setting; if not, it should be up to the division itself to raise the issue.

In our experience, it often happens that the C.E.O. does not come out with an adequate statement of involvement at the outset of the planning process. This, in our experience, has detrimental effects on the subsequent planning effort, for several reasons. First, the C.E.O. might not feel himself really committed to the planning process yet, in that he has not put his own thought "on the block." This implies that time will be wasted on unrealistic "planning exercises" until he commits himself. Secondly, the key line executives will hesitate to put efforts into the process because they feel that the process is "unreal" without the C.E.O.'s involvement. Many may hold back on their own positions until they get a better feel for where the C.E.O. stands and what direction he prefers. Thirdly, lack of realism and focus at the objectives-setting stage will at best imply that much more time will have to be spent before a meaningful decision-making focus can be instilled, at worst, it means

that corporate planning as a strategic decision-making process is "dead,"
given the lack of realism and the "political" ambivalence about what might
be a useful strategic direction of the firm. If the C.E.O. is unwilling
to commit himself to the planning system as a viable strategic decision-
making tool, the one to lose is above all himself. He is depriving himself
of a management tool which can significantly increase his discretionary
ability to manage the firm strategically, or stated differently, shift
the power balance of the firms more towards himself. (This shift toward
relatively more top-down emphasis might be a strong reason for resisting
planning by the line in many companies, their bottom-up influence might
be seen to be threatened.)

Let us illustrate further the importance of the C.E.O.'s involvement
in starting the process off by means of two examples. The first example
refers to a consumer products food company with annual sales of approximately half a billion dollars. An elaborate set of corporate assumptions
are being disseminated to the divisions by the corporate planning department at the outset of the first planning cycle. These fall into the
three categories, summarized in a condensed version below

a) General assumptions. no unforeseen major environmental event
that would dramatically change the company's environment should be
planned for.

b) Managerial assumptions no fundamental change in organizational
structure should be assumed. rapid changes in society and business
will call for a need to review current competitive situations and re-
evaluate future business plans; capital will continue to be in
short supply; consequently, return on investment concepts will be
emphasized.

c) Environmental trend assumptions   a general economic environment
analysis indicates an expected overall economic trend as well as
expected developments for monetary conditions, labor, consumer spending,
prices and raw materials supply patterns; a consumer attitudes
analysis indicates trend shifts in lifestyles, changes in consumer
attitudes and awareness, and expected implications of these consumer
attitudes and trends; finally a demographics analysis spells out the
population characteristics of the United States for the next five
years.

The above set of corporate assumptions is stated with more thoroughness
and spelled out in more detail than in many companies. Nevertheless, it
falls short of what seems to be a necessary starting requirement for
initiating the planning process for two related reasons. First, given
that the corporate assumptions have been prepared by the corporate planning
group, with the assistance of other corporate staff groups as well as some
outside environmental trend service organizations, but with no apparent
involvement of the senior management, the line was reluctant to accept
several of the key implications stemming from the corporate assumptions.
Thus, it is important to give the corporate assumptions "credibility" by
having them being stated as the C.E.O 's assumptions. At the minimum
they should go out under his signature. Preferably, he should also be
actively involved during the review of these assumptions so that he can
make the substantive impacts he might want. Needless to say, the staff
should of course undertake most of the burden of preparation, for reasons
both of availability of time as well as its possession of high specialized
needed competencies. Secondly, the corporate assumptions do not go far
enough, in that they do not directly signal the C.E.O.'s aspirations
and tentative objectives. The indirect inferences that the line might

draw about the C.E O.'s intentions may even be conflicting. For instance,
under the section of managerial assumptions it is stated, on the one hand,
that rapid environmental changes will call for a high planning responsiveness, i.e. a strong adaptive thrust. On the other hand, the shortage
of capital and the emphasis on strict return on investment measures is
also stated, i.e. a strongly integrative. Thus, it seems necessary that
the C.E.O. comes out with his aspirations about what general direction he
wants the firm to go, in addition to the statement of corporate background
assumptions Further, one should avoid the risk of stating so many corporate assumptions that they become entirely conflicting, and, thus, more
or less meaningless, unless a careful prioritizing is introduced among
the assumptions

The second example refers to the European-based diversified corporation discussed in the Appendix of Chapter Two. The major business involvements of this company fall within the pharmaceutical area. Corporate management has stated that the emphasis in the future should be
shifted relatively more towards internal growth, a shift away from the
relatively predominant mode of growth through acquisitions of the past
Given this it will be important to encourage a heavy involvement, by the
businesses in order to capitalize on their familiarity with and understanding of their businesses when identifying internal growth opportunities.
However, a seemingly almost total lack of top-down initial input into the
planning process on behalf of the C.E.O causes concern and anxiety among
line managers about the role of the planning system as a vehicle for
pursuing the internal growth strategy. Above all, this seems to cause
each of the businesses to develop their plans in much of a vacuum, and
with a lot of caution. The emerging plans generally seem to be uninspiring

and conservative. The C.E.O. has not been able to instill much of a sense
of direction and relevance about what are reasonable strategies from his
point of view By foregoing the opportunity to give the organization
clear signals about his ambitions and desires about where he hopes to
take the company as well as indicating his belief in planning by making
clear his readiness to participate at this logical point in time, the
C.E.O. leaves the planning process in a state of ambivalence and degradation.
The potential seriousness of this deficiency can be seen from examining
decisions related to the company's entry into new business areas, which
as we have pointed out in the past have been largely been facilitated by
means of acquisitions, and primarily within the divisions themselves.
Particularly the Home Products Division was still active however in continuing to attempt to acquire a relatively large number of companies over
a quite diverse area of activities. Such "diversification by subunits"
might be seen as potentially a serious indication of lack of corporate
top-down portfolio direction. The undesirable implications of this are
particularly apparent when it comes to the company's risk-taking. A particular division is likely to evaluate a given diversification proposal
from the point of view of the activity level of its own business, i.e.
more or less whether the acquisition makes sense risk-wise as if the division was an independent company. The company as a whole, however, is
in a position to take far larger selected risks, simply by benefiting from
being larger and being dependent on a wider number of sources of funds
flows than a single division. Consequently, it may seem right at the
corporate level to acquire one or a few relatively large companies, moves
that never would have been taken by a division on its own. Thus, "delegation" of the acquisition aspect of portfolio planning implies that
there will be a likelihood of the creation of a too fragmented and

conservative acquisition pattern, with too many small entities. One of the few advantages of being a relatively large company is thereby not being pursued. Thus, lack of a clear statement of the C E O.'s aspirations, including the nature of risk-taking that he might want to involve the company in, seems to have led to a breakdown of top-down corporate leadership of the firm's direction-setting in this case. A "mushrooming," overly conservative bottom-up diversification drive seems to be the result.

In summary, then, it is critical that the C.E.O. initiates the planning process. In our experience problems with effective planning systems can quite commonly be traced back to a lack of top management involvement at the outset. As we have seen, several dysfunctional effects from this are likely to occur, leading to significantly less useful planning in most cases.

11. Assessment of business opportunities and threats.

A second implementation problem relates to each division's business opportunity assessment, as part of their development of objectives and goals statements for "where they want to go" with their respective businesses, responding to the initiation of planning that has come from the C E.O. It is critical that each division management team, being the closest to a particular business environment, skillfully and imaginatively assess the major opportunities and threats that are facing their business. These managers should not only have the best insight into the opportunities their business environment can offer. They should also be in the best position to perceive how to take advantage of these opportunities in modifying the objectives and goals of their businesses It is of critical importance that a creative element of environmental awareness and "gutsy" business entrepreneurialism to pursue new, unconventional leads is captured in the corporate planning process at this step.

Unfortunately, for many companies such an open-minded, environmental opportunity orientation of the planning efforts at this stage may be next to non-existant. Instead, the normal is a tendency for division management to treat the environmental outlook and the assessment of business opportunities and threats as an exercise that can be taken quite lightly. A common feeling might be that in most likelihood the business next year will continue to be more or less the same as the business in the past. Such a mental extrapolation of the past into the future typically might fit a manager's comfort quite well, not only because it will typically be quite comfortable to continue pursuing what one more or less already has been doing, but even more so because it avoids threatening the vested interests that a manager typically might have in his present organization. Thus, there is a natural tendency among many managers to actually <u>wish</u> that there will be no major environmental changes affecting their business so that they can keep on doing business in the future the way they have done it before, and are comfortable and familiar with. Thus, managers resistance to facing needs for change might add to the problem of taking too lightly the task of assuring one's business opportunities. There will therefore easily be a temptation for the division manager to address the critical task of business opportunity and threat identification by merely doing a brief editing and updating of last year's statement.

This might of course by particularly difficult for senior management to detect, given that one would actually normally <u>expect</u> relatively little change from year to year for many of the businesses. The critical issue, however, is that such a conclusion, that small changes in one's business only will be necessary to incorporate new business opportunities and/or threats, has been made after a thorough assessment of the business environment.

It is thus important that the analysis focus on issues in the business' environment, not inward on the problems of "business-as-usual " The focus should be on the strategic effectiveness of the business, not on strategic efficiency; "are we in the right business," not "are we doing this business right." The approach developed in Chapter Three for risk/return assessment of businesses faced with potential positive or negative impacts from environmental factors might be used by a division manager as a basis for assessment of his opportunities. The issue for him is to assess the positive as well as negative factors as well as his own response potential. He might also follow a set of "leading questions" in order to detect pertinent environmental changes are there any differences in the attractiveness of the business?, in our own competitive strength? New opportunities should be discussed in terms of potential impact on the business' strategic position in a more narrow sense as well as in the sense of the broader issue of risk/return impacts on the corporate portfolio.

A major problem in many cases, thus, might be that an explicit or implicit extrapolative thinking on the part of the business managers might prevent a more meaningful assessment of the strategic opportunities and threats of the business The result is often conspicuous lack of new and innovative ideas in the plans. Having missed out on this creative input to the planning process the result is often that the planning steps subsequently to follow will be more or less meaningless too, i.e. the well-known "garbage in-garbage out" syndrome Many companies experienced this during the first wave to undertake long-range planning, during the mid to late sixties These planning efforts tended to be heavily numbers-oriented, which does not necessarily have to be bad, except, when the numbers have been developed primarily through extrapolation,

providing a more or less useless picture of the strategic opportunities
of the future. When we have such a highly numbers-oriented planning
emphasis the temptation seems to be particularly strong that extrapolation
replaces real and hard thinking. Needless to say, however, even without
a heavy numbers emphasis we might still have a "verbal extrapolation"
planning exercise, again just as useless.

The failure to have innovative and highly involved divisional futures-
oriented opportunity assessment, not allowing it to be constrained by
one's present business situation, represents a serious obstacle to realistic planning, particularly so for companies that base themselves primarily on an internally generated corporate growth thrust. Particularly
for a company in rapidly changing environments that might be a very
serious limitation to effective planning.

iii. Portfolio focus in corporate level's reviews.

A third implementation problem deals with the mode the C.E.O. and
his corporate office often tends to be following in reviewing planning
inputs generated further down in the organization and giving feedback to
the divisions. We shall discuss this issue in relation with the objectives-
setting stage because it typically might first surface as an implementation problem here. However, an appropriate mode of corporate review and
interaction with the divisions might tend to be a serious implementation
problem at any of the stages of the planning process. We shall discuss
two aspects of the issue of implementing a proper mode of corporate level
planning reviews, namely the need to follow a so-called portfolio review
approach as opposed to what might be called a sequential review approach,
and the need to install a degree of procedural discipline among the
parties in the review process. Let us first turn to the portfolio review
issue.

The corporate level's strategic task is to be responsible for the development of a corporate portfolio strategy, as we have discussed. This, however, implies that any review and evaluation of a particular planning input from a business should be carried out to assess the relevance of this piece of input within the context of the overall portfolio pattern of the company. Thus, each business plan should be reviewed in a way which stresses that its merit has to be judged conditional on the other business plans

Unfortunately, however, corporate reviews of divisional planning inputs often do not follow the portfolio mode that we have just described. Instead, corporate management often tends to review divisions one at a time, in a sequential fashion. This, of course, will not facilitate the development of a corporate portfolio strategy given that it will be more or less coincidental what the approved business inputs might add up to as a corporate portfolio pattern. To underscore this when a sequential corporate review mode is followed, it will probably matter for a particular business when it is being reviewed relative to the other. For instance, while the first businesses to be reviewed might receive relatively encouraging corporate responses for expansion policies implying commitment of significant funds, the later businesses reviewed might be penalized by a shortage of discretionary corporate funds, accompanied by a tightening up of resource allocation criteria and tougher corporate review. While this simplified example is perhaps exaggerated, it is nevertheless clear that a sequential corporate review makes it virtually impossible to apply a consistent risk/return criterion for approval of the divisional planning input proposals, given that the contingent nature of the portfolio interdependence between the business inputs will have been overlooked. It is also clear that the corporate review process in principle cannot be decomposed into reviews of smaller clusters of businesses, say within a group, for subsequent corporate review of the aggregate outputs from the groups. Here too, the overall comparability between the risks/returns of the businesses gets lost. When it comes to how to ameliorate in practice the problem of groups thus becoming "strategic filters" in the review process, this might be very hard within a large, diversified firm, leading the C.E.O. to conclude that he might have an impossible task dealing with the complete overall portfolio of businesses directly. We shall not discuss how to approach this problem here, however, but postpone this until Chapter Six.

Let us reiterate how a corporate review approach approximately has to be carried out in order to facilitate proper corporate portfolio strategizing: First, all of the divisions must provide corporate head-quarters with their business planning inputs. This will provide the corporate level with a complete set of data to carry out the next step, namely to review what seems to be the emerging pattern when seeing all the business inputs within a single context Only then, as a third step, should feedback be made to a particular business individually about potential modifications that it should carry out to provide for this business' fit within the portfolio.

Unfortunately, we have seen several examples of corporate plans being developed through a "step-wise" corporate review process and also by a simple notion of stepwise aggregation. A division manager might develop his plan by reviewing the SBUs reporting to his division, group plans might then be developed by aggregating and reviewing the plans of each group's divisions, and the corporate plan might come about by adding the group plans. Even in companies where corporate management recognize the need to be closer to "the grassroot," by having a closer understanding of the

nature of each business, going at great length in its efforts to give
attention to each business, a sequential pattern of review might still
prevail preventing an appropriate risk/return tradeoff between the business.

Let us now turn to the other aspect of the issue of implementing
proper corporate review practices. Needless to say a proper corporate
review procedure requires considerable discipline on the parts of the
various organizational units involved. For each of the divisions, there
will be a requirement that planning outputs are developed in such a way
that they are relatively easily comparable. They have to rest on a common
set of consistent premises, both in terms of data inputs, definitions and
analytical approaches. Further, each division must deliver its output
on time; if one division fails to come up with its plan then the entire
corporate review process will have to be delayed because of the impos-
sibility to establish an overall corporate portfolio context until all
business elements are available. The role of the planning calendar is
therefore critical - much more so, of course, for companies which recognize the nature of corporate portfolio reviews than for companies that
follow a corporate sequential review. Thus, added standardization of the
format of business planning as well as cutting down on the flexibility
of each business in having to conform to the deadlines of the planning
calendar should be seen as necessary conditions for portfolio planning.
This is a consideration often overlooked by executives who might be
criticizing such a relatively rigorous planning system, faultering it
for being too much of a "straight-jacket" on the creative drive of the
businesses.

For the corporate level there will also be an added need for discipline, however. Senior corporate management of a company might typically

be under virtually constant pressure from the operating divisions to give
its okay for various new projects. However, it will not be enough for
senior management to merely convince itself about the soundness of a
project, even though it might be evaluated as part of the strategic
programs that the division is in the process of carrying out in order to
implement its business objectives. Many projects, of course, are not
even tested in terms of strategic program fit, all that matters is that
the project's projected return on assets is satisfactory. It will be
necessary for corporate management to view the project in a portfolio context: does the company benefit more from investing in this business than
in other businesses? It is extremely difficult to carry out corporate
reviews of divisional proposals which will be strategically valid, given
that a project in fact will have to be evaluated along three dimensions:
its impact on the overall fit of the entire corporate portfolio strategy,
and, finally, the need for the project to satisfy a minimum financial
hurdle rate. It will as a practical matter become extremely difficult
for senior management to approve major projects during the year that are
not part of the corporate planning process. As we recall, the planning
system is intended precisely as a decision-making tool for resource allocation decisions such as these. Corporate management which approves
major projects outside the context of the planning cycle will thereby
jeopardize the future effectiveness of corporate planning. There might
be obvious dysfunctional motivational effects among division line managers if they develop the perception that it will not be all that difficult to get away with breaking the discipline of the orderly resource
allocation process by succeeding in securing funds on an ad hoc basis.
An even more serious and fundamental unfavorable effect for corporate
management is the potential for distorting the overall balance of the

corporate portfolio strategy   Thus, there is a heavy demand for discipline on the part of corporate management as part of managing the company in a strategic mode; the corporate planning process in fact ties corporate and divisional management together in a "contract."

We saw the corporate-divisional "discipline" problem being a major
obstacle to progress on strategic planning in a European-based corporation
which was engaged within several businesses within the building materials
and construction fields. This example is quite revealing in terms of
shedding light on the general nature of this problem and merits a brief
discussion. One of the smaller divisions of this company manufactured
ready-mixed concrete from a relatively large number of small plants which
had to be located near their end-use markets. This division was however
considerably larger than any competitor in the business   There were a
large number of small independent local producers. Many of these represented "tempting" takeover opportunities for the concrete division. The
division manager capitalized on exactly this when he was stressing the
unique ad hoc strategic opportunity to take over a competitor and prevent
anybody else from doing this when he approached corporate management for
funds to carry out an acquisition move. These acquisitions however were
entirely out of context from his agreed-upon strategy, which stated that
he should concentrate concentrically around the one largest market. After
several "extraordinary" resource allocations the other divisions too
started to bring up extraordinary requests. Only a strong reinforcement
of a portfolio-type approach restored the necessary strategic discipline.
Needless to say, a company must act on an opportunity when it arrives, and
typically cannot foresee or plan for such an exact happening   However,
the strategies should have been developed so that they are available
when the opportunity arrives, so that the decision can be taken within a
strategic context. An acquisition, for example, then becomes merely another

strategic program for how to achieve a particular strategy, not a random
shift (and shock) for the corporation. Thus while corporate management
as well as division managers might urge that strategic decisions be taken
when they arise, given that it will be undesirable or not feasible to
delay a critical decision until next year's planning cycle, this line
of reasoning tends to be a straw man argument in that the issue of having
to take critical decisions outside of the ordinary planning cycle fortu-
nately seldom happens.

If the planning system is functioning well, the "homework" for
evaluating an opportunity is largely done beforehand. The reason for
this is as follows   The corporate planning system is intended to provide
a gradually sharpened focus for the strategic context within which resource
allocations are to be taken. As we have seen, the objectives-setting
cycle culminates in a corporate-wide consistent set of objectives which
provide the context for the strategic programming activities. As long
as a strategic programming activity is consistent with the agreed-upon
objectives it is desirable and normal that decisions relating to the fulfillment of this activity go on through the year. Some programs will
be new ones, under preparation for more in-depth review and approval
during next year's planning cycle. For the latter type of programming
activity there is again established a sharpened contextual focus within
which alternative investment decisions can be taken, as long as they fall
within the program. Thus, as long as the broader strategic context for
a particular decision has been established through the strategic planning
process the follow-up execution will go on over time. It is critical,
however, that a proper sense of discipline and responsibility exists
among the participating parties in order to avoid the emergence of strategic program undertakings that are abuses of the strategic objectives

directions agreed upon

Ideally, what the planning system should provide is enough
curtailing of decision-making flexibility to be rigorous, but rarely
so much curtailing as to foster indecisiveness. Line management should
understand that it will be rare that an entirely new strategic alternative
suddenly emerges; in those instances the significant additional, analytical
workload to carry out a proper portfolio strategy reassessment should be
met. On the other hand, there might be a danger that the willingness and
ability to reach a decision gets lost in an abundance of analysis and
future revisions. The decision-making focus of strategic planning must
therefore always be kept in mind.

iv. <u>Functional departments' involvement in objectives-setting.</u>

A fourth implementation issue in connection with the objectives-
setting stage has to do with the nature of the formal involvement of the
managers at lower levels in the organization than the divisional managers
during the objectives setting stage of the planning process. It should
be pointed out that the nature of the planning process during the
objectives-setting stage is different from the nature of the process
during subsequent stages, in that <u>a general management point of view</u>
should be dominant: The issue is to decide on the general strategic
direction of the firm, which business activities should be expanded;
should growth of present business operations be curtailed in order to
acquire new businesses; should some of the present business activities
be divested in order to free up funds for reemployment in some of one's
other businesses or in acquisitions, so that one might achieve a better

corporate portfolio balance? Clearly, a predominantly general management point of view is needed in order to address these critical issues. We shall give three reasons for this.

First, it seems reasonable to assume that only corporate management will be in possession of a sufficiently broad set of corporate-wide information. Presumably also, corporate level managers are likely to be in a better position to exercise more of a "healthy emotional detachment" from a particular business than the division managers so that they might better see what relative business involvement balance will be the best for the company as a whole. The general managers of the divisions snould however be able to appreciate the general nature of evaluating a business problem with its broader portfolio context. By grasping the significance of this, should be able to contribute to the development of a portfolio-based set of corporate objectives in a "disciplined" manner, despite the obvious belief that each division manager should have in favor of his own business. The division manager's rationale should be that, even after having attempted to do his utmost to convince corporate management about the viability of his business as part of the corporation's portfolio, having been given ample opportunity to bring up his viewpoints and to be heard by corporate management, if it still turns out that other divisions can provide better business opportunities from a portfolio viewpoint, then the entire "corporate family" is better off this way. The long-term opportunities of a manager of a business that is being curtailed are probably better served this way too, in that the corporation will be able to create more new resources and long-term opportunities for all.

When it comes to the rest of the management within a division, such as functional managers, SBU managers or area managers, one should not expect a general management point of view to prevail. In fact, a very parochial commitment to one's special task is the key ingredient for managerial success at this level. Thus, the inputs from these managers is not central to the general direction-setting management decisions of the objectives-setting cycle. Consequently, the special task managers within the divisions should not be formally involved in the planning process at this stage. We have of course assumed that the general manager of the division is intimately familiar with his business, its opportunities and threats, its capabilities and limitations, its strengths and weaknesses To the extent that he needs to strengthen his understanding of the business he should of course be in intimate contact with his specialized line managers on issues that will help him formulate his general management judgments. As such the special tasks managers within the divisions are informally involved in the planning process during the objectives-setting cycle, being part of the management teams of the division general managers.

A second reason for the need to only have a limited involvement of the specialized managers within the divisions during the objectives-setting stage of the planning process relates to a latent and potentially serious dysfunctional motivational effect. By formally soliciting the function-, SBU-, and/or area-managers' viewpoints on objectives, goals and strategies but then having to disregard or modify these contributions in order to satisfy a general management viewpoint to fit within a portfolio strategy, there might be a high risk of loss of morale. The divisional general manager's role will of course also easily become difficult if he has to interact with corporate management backed up with explicit statements about policy suggestions from his own subordinates, he will, so to speak, find himself "between the bark and the wood". Emphasis on an ad hoc informal planning activity within the divisions should ameliorate many of these problems.

Finally, the time constraint issue should be kept in mind. A frequent objection to planning has been that it seems to require exceeding amounts of time. At the extreme, a typical manager might find himself spending his day preparing materials for the planning documents, attending planning meetings and reviewing planning reports, no time is left for running the business! Therefore, there should be a general requirement not to involve management in planning activities that are not essential. Particularly given the central and typically elaborate and time-consuming involvement of function-, business- and area-managers in the strategic programming stage of the corporate planning process, it is desirable to keep the involvement of these managers to a minimum during the objectives-setting stage.

In one company we examined the issue of the functional management's involvement seemed to become confused due to a strong desire among top management that it would be critical to involve management in the strategic planning activities several levels down in the organizational hierarchy in order to enhance strategic thinking and be able to have some real impact to achieve relevant strategic changes through planning. When calling for the organization's participation senior management seemed, however, to make little distinction between objectives-setting and strategic programming. While its desire to "tap the organization's ideas and creativity" seemed to have a lot of merit when it came to the strategic programming stage, which by design would be heavily bottom-up oriented through the critical role played by the functions in developing program alternatives, top management did not fully realize the typically more top-down general management nature of the preceding objectives-setting cycle. The task of setting objectives was thus just not satisfactorily achieved; the functional inputs did not add up to generic strategic statements of directions. In this instance, as well as in many other cases when it comes to the design of a planning system, it is beneficial to ask whether the way a particular aspect of planning is executed makes explicit logical sense, given the nature of the aspect of the planning task one attempts to achieve. An extreme bottom-up approach to a task which is essentially more top-down in its nature should thus not be expected to work.

v.   The iterative feedback loop

During our discussion of the conceptual model for corporate planning in Chapter Two we pointed out that our model places heavy reliance on its iterative properties, the assumption being that good plans are most likely to be developed as a result of an interplay - back and forth - among managers with different strategic outlooks and responsibilities. Such an interplay, however, might easily end up hampering the planning process, unless the nature of the interplay is spelled out in some detail. Thus, we need to establish a set of rules to guide the feedback process We shall discuss this implementation phenomenon at this point because it first appears during the objectives-setting stage; however, just as was the case for the corporate portfolio-type review requirement, this issue is of relevance during all of the stages of the planning process.

We recall that during the objectives-setting stage there were three distinctive steps of the planning process (See Exhibit 2-6), namely an initial statement of tentative objectives and expectations by the C.E.O., an assessment of the business opportunities by each of the divisions, and a corporate portfolio consolidation of these business objectives. The pattern of organization interaction is thus clear· a top-down initiation and a bottom-up response. However, there is an additional element of "closing the loop"; when the C.E.O. compares the consolidated output of the third step of the process with his initial expectation stated in the first step there might be a discrepancy, in fact, this would probably be the normal. We recall from Chapter Two that we have called such a discrepancy a planning gap. The way such a planning gap is established, analyzed in terms of options for closing it, and finally being closed before proceeding to the next cycle of the planning process is a critical implementation issue for the effectiveness of the planning process.

During the objectives-setting stage the planning gap will be defined by comparing the risk/return characteristics of the expected funds flow pattern that emerges from the portfolio strategy of where the company attempts to want to go (Step 3, Exhibit 2-6) with the initially stated expectations of the C E.O (Step 1). If there is a discrepancy, i.e., a

planning gap, then this will have to be closed in accordance with one or
more of the following four approaches·

- a lowering of the C E.O.'s initial expectations, i.e., a
  realization that the initial "push" just seemed to be too
  ambitious. A downward revision of his aspirations will then
  be needed in order to obtain a more realistic focus for the
  subsequent planning.

- a corporate demand on one or more of the divisions to develop
  more aggressive business plans. To some extent this option
  might be available because of the existence of "slack" in the
  business organizations - in fact, some of the more publicized
  benefits from planning have been with respect to how the C.E.O
  has used the planning system in pushing for more aggressive,
  achievement-oriented divisional performance.

- a corporate decision to shift the relative emphasis among the
  businesses. The C.E.O. would then attempt to reallocate
  discretionary resources away from some businesses and in the
  direction of other businesses, so that the commitment to
  businesses with higher future prospects get increased and less
  attractive business get de-emphasized. This change of emphasis
  in the balance among the divisions requires an _ability_ on the
  part of the C.E.O. to make strategic priorities and a _willingness_
  to reallocate resources accordingly This is the essence of
  corporate portfolio strategic management, the overriding the

purpose of strategic planning is to act as the tool in facilitating these decisions.

- a realization that the portfolio balance should be changed through acquisition and/or divestiture in order to achieve more rapidly the intended properties of the strategic portfolio. Above all, potential savings in _time_ is an important factor in achieving strategic changes through acquisitions/divestitures. Internal developments of new businesses of enough substance to have a meaningful impact on changing the corporate portfolio balance typically take longer time, and are often risky efforts.

It is important that a planning gap actually gets closed before the planning process is allowed to proceed to its next stage, and there are two reasons for this. First, the closing of the loop reinforces the decision-making nature of strategic planning. Specifically, top management will have to make some strategic choices. Conversely, by proceeding to the next stage of planning without resolving the issues of strategic choices that have been surfaced, as sticky and as complicated they might be, will weaken the decision-making realism of the planning process Management will be prone to relax their intellectual commitment and become less accountable to such process. It is significant to notice that it will require a top-down decision-making initiative to close a planning gap. The pressure is thus primarily on upper management to clear the way for the resolution of how to close a planning gap. A common implementation problem is often found exactly here, unfortunately,

in that upper management fails to demonstrate its willingness to commit
itself to specific strategic choice decisions

A second reason for the importance of closing a planning gap is due
to the desirability to provide a gradual sharpening of the focus of the
strategic direction as the planning process proceeds. Resolution of
strategic decisions with respect to how to fill a planning gap will
provide a necessary requirement for more targeted and relevant analysis
at the subsequent remaining steps of the planning process   If, for
instance, ambiguity still exists with respect to strategic choices that
have been left unresolved during the objectives-setting stage by not
closing the planning gap, then the subsequent strategic programming task
will have to be carried out within a much wider and less defined focus.
A likely result will be that the quality of the programming process might
suffer.

We recall from Exhibit 2-7 that the corporate level will be faced
with the challenge of closing of three distinctive planning gaps, namely
at the objectives-setting stage, the strategic programming stage and at
the budgeting stage. The specific focus of the strategic decisions to
be taken in closing each of these gaps will of course be difficult. The
general nature of these decisions will however be fundamentally the same,
in that they all affect the corporate portfolio strategy, and in that
each planning gap will have to close in accordance with one or a
combination of the four approaches just outlined. At the business level,
the division manager will be faced with closing only two planning gaps,
as we can see from Exhibit 2-7. The task of closing these planning gaps

will be fundamentally different from the closing of the corporate gaps,
in that the strategic decisions that need to be taken will affect a
particular business strategy There will basically be only two ways of
closing the planning gaps at the business strategic planning level, in
contrast to the four alternatives that apply to the corporate portfolio
level:

- one will relate to the extent to which "investments" will be
  made in market share for a particular SBU. Resources may be
  put into a product in order to "build" a particular business
  strength, or, to a lesser extent, to "hold" a particular
  business position. Resources might on the other hand be
  released from a product which is allowed to slip in market
  share - a "harvest" position. The transfer of funds among
  SBU's that have products at different stages of the product
  life cycle and in such a way that each of the products are
  managed along a deliberate evolutionary sequence of strategic
  positions, as indicated by the solid line in Exhibit 3-2, is
  critical to a "good" closing of the planning gap at the
  division level.

- the development of new products, in the "question mark"
  category, which can provide the basis for future growth and
  development of positions of future strength For this, funds
  need to be transferred from SBU's that are presently in the
  mature product stage to new product development, as indicated
  by the arrow in Exhibit 3-3.

For the planning gaps at the business planning level it is just as critical that they get closed before planning proceeds to the next cycle, for the same two reasons as already indicated, enforcement of strategic decision-making emphasis and a sharp as possible strategic focus.

We have now completed our discussion of five implementation issues that tend to occur during the execution of the objectives-setting planning stage, and shall proceed to a discussion of implementational issues at the next stage – strategic programming. However, as already noticed, several of the implementation issues discussed within the objectives-setting context also apply when it comes to other planning stages, notably the requirement for a portfolio mode of corporate review as well as the need for the closing of planning gaps apply at all of the three first stages.

4-3. Implementation pitfalls and problems during the strategic programming stage.

During the second stage of the strategic planning process, strategic programming, we shall discuss two fairly common implementation problems. These relate to how to enhance a predominantly cross-specialization nature of strategic programming for thereby to avoid functional compartmentalization, and the issue of aggregating strategic programs into "packages" that are consistent with the business strategy that the programs are intended to enhance   Let us discuss each of these issues in turn.

vi. Crossfunctional nature of strategic programming

The strategic programming activity is critical for a meaningful corporate planning system in that it is primarily during this stage that the foundation will have to be laid for implementing a particular set of decided upon objectives and goals. Specialized management functions within a division will be called on to provide specialized functional skills for execution of the strategic programs. In addition to the involvement of functional departments such as manufacturing, marketing or R & D, it is also critical that SBU managers participate intimately. Strong specialized competence within each of the organizational subunits involved is essential to good strategic programming; a high level of professionalism on the parts of each of the "components" that go into the programming process is paramount.[3]

A difficult implementation problem, however, often tends to arise when we are attempting to "blend" together the inputs of strong organizational functions into an overall cross-functional program. The nature of a strategic program is predominantly interfunctional, the specialized functions will have to cooperate in the execution of a particular program. Even the best functional inputs cannot ensure successful strategic programming if coordination between the various specialized activities is lacking. Specialized organizational subunits' attempts to take an overly independent stance may lead specialized professionalism to thrive, while creating barriers to the implementation of the strategic direction decided on.

There are several ways to counteract this tendency of organizational subunit compartmentalization, in order to enhance an appropriate implementation effort Above all, the resource allocation process implicit in the strategic planning framework which has been developed in this book implies that resources are being allocated to strategic programs, within the context of the objectives and goals. This is in contrast to the traditional allocation of resources to specific investment projects and to the organizational subunits' expenditure budgets. Thus, the various functions will have to develop program proposals together, be jointly subjected to the division head's general management review of strategic programs, and share the responsibility for subsequent execution of these programs. Thus, the nature of the programming task itself might reinforce the need for interfunctional cooperation.

An additional "precaution" that might be followed in order to strengthen the cross-functional flair is for the division manager to encourage the establishment of a "milestone summary" of each strategic program proposal that is being accepted. This is a way of summarizing what should be achieved at given times and who should be responsible. Such a summary helps pin-point the interdependence of the organizational subunits in a project's development. Above all it might create a stronger sense of shared responsibility among the functions; although at one stage of development one particular function might be most directly involved, another function will have to carry on when a particular point of progress has been reached.

A step related to this is to specify in considerable detail as part of a strategic program proposal the nature of the "interaction points" between the functions. For instance, a strategic program for developing a new pharmaceutical product from research into full commercialization might be "planned" in such a way that when a particular function has completed its task and is scheduled to pass the project on to the next function, a review of the program's progress would be made with the participation of all remaining functions which are expected to be involved in the program. Thus, what might seem to be a satisfactory completion of a particular function's input to a strategic program from a narrow point of view might turn out not to be satisfactory from the viewpoint of other functions. It is important that the functions will have a chance to jointly review the progress at a very early stage so that desirable modifications can be defined in a broad enough context to improve the chances of a final commercial success.

This brings us to yet another aspect of ensuring proper strategic focus of the programming activities. For each organizational subunit, in its involvement with the development of a strategic program, one might develop a checklist to ensure that the functional activity seems to be yielding strategic fit As we recall, such an approach was discussed in Section   of Chapter Two. It was suggested there that each function might approach this by developing an index with three classes of factors; an assessment of the technological possibility of carrying out the function - is this a difficult or easy problem given the state-of-the-art of this functional body of knowledge?; an assessment of the likelihood of the project leading towards a strategically attractive commercialization - does this research point towards applications that might fall within high-growth sales areas?; an assessment of the degree of fit of the commercialized output with one's own competitive strength and relation to one's other products - does the research point towards a commercialization that can be brought to yield a high market share, are our inhouse strengths

and skills adequate for this, does the product complement our other
products?

Typically, many division managers will feel that there might be a
need for development and analysis of separate functional "plans". Such
plans should however not fail to assess the extent to which the function
is tuned in with and contributes to the strategic programming activities
of the firm, to ameliorate apparent dysfunctional activities, and to
strengthen the strategic focus of each function. It seems the most
practical to develop such functional "plans", however, as a sequel to the
strategic programs, as a post facto "summary" of the roles that each given
function would be expected to play in the overall package of programs to
be pursued. Many companies, unfortunately, start out the strategic
programming process in reverse order, first developing functional plans,
then (maybe) attempting to reconcile these in terms of the strategic
program activities they imply Unfortunately, the strategic programs
that emerge from such a sequence of events easily end up being the results
of compromises between functional positions. The vitally important,
imaginatively developed strategic programs that are based on a more
unconstrained outlook of opportunities and/or threats will probably not
emerge.

vii. Consolidation of strategic programs.

Let us now move to another implementation problem that commonly
occurs during the strategic programming stage, namely the issue of
achieving appropriate choices among strategic program alternatives so
that they "add up" to the best program "packages" for progressing towards

the stated goals and objectives of a particular business.[4] There are two aspects of this that we shall discuss: how to avoid inconsistency between the anticipated impact from a strategic program package that has been chosen and the previously decided upon strategies and implicitly anticipated funds flow patterns for the business, and how to carry out the aggregation of the strategic programs - a so-called zero-based budgeting approach.

While the objectives-setting stage established a frame for "where to go", the purpose of the strategic programming stage is to operationalize "how to get there". It follows from this that the strategic program efforts should result in a directional thrust which is consistent with the objectives and goals previously agreed upon. A common implementation problem, however, seems to be inconsistency with respect to exactly this. At worst programming may result in a directional thrust which may be in sharp contrast to the intended strategic context. For instance, one particular division might have been arguing for an expansionary role for its business during the objectives-setting stage, resulting in the decision to let this division be designated as one of the major internal growth vehicles within the firm's business portfolio in the years to come. This strategic role of course has not been arrived at in a "vacuum", but as a pattern of interdependencies with the other businesses, where each has been designated a role as net contributor or net user of funds within the overall portfolio. If, during the subsequent strategic programming stage, it turns out that the division does not come up with a "package" of programs that provides the strategic direction assumed in the previous stage, then this will represent a potentially serious weakening of the

corporate portfolio objectives. The lack of proper implementation of
direction that emerges thus affects not only the business strategy of the
division itself but may also hold up the implementation of the corporate
portfolio strategy as well as potentially causing a need for modification
of other businesses' strategic programs, thereby frustrating the
implementation of direction here too.

There might be at least three different types of reasons why such
lack of consistency might emerge. One reason might be lack of emphasis
of the crucial interdependence between the two cycles. The organizational
units may simply never be challenged to come up with programs that are
consistent with the objectives in the directions of their strategic
impetus. An important implication of this is that the objectives-setting
cycle can be seen as being reduced to more of a brainstorming exercise
but with the realistic decision-making emphasis gone. Subsequent strategic
programs will be developed without benefiting from adequate strategic
context.

Another reason might be that a division lacks critical functional
professionalism and capabilities that will be needed to "deliver" an
adequate set of strategic programs. Typically there will be one or a few
functions that turn out to be the "bottleneck" In line with this there
might also be certain functions that are very strong but are not utilized
to their full potential. In a sense this represents an opportunity loss
in that the divisions' management might have potentially misjudged what
capabilities it might need to execute a particular set of strategic
programs as well as also potentially what capabilities it possesses. An

unrealistically large "gap" between needs and capabilities for specialized functional skills might cause serious implementation problems for the strategic programming efforts. Although to some extent the internal functional resources can be made available through ad hoc actions, it typically takes time to develop internal functional professional capabilities. Hence, a plan should be made to bring the functional capabilities up to the standards needed to fulfill the expected require- ments that the execution of the strategic programs will pose. To the extent that this does not seem reasonably feasible within a given period of time the strategic programs themselves become unworkable and must be modified. We are in fact here potentially faced with a dilemma in our planning approach We recall that a major premise for the conceptual framework that we have developed is the emphasis on searching for new environmental opportunities and/or threats as the driving force for dictating the firm's direction. We also stressed the sharp contrast between this approach and "extrapolation" based on one's present strengths and/or weaknesses However, the pursuance of new opportunities and/or threats cannot be carried out without taking into account the internal strengths and/or weaknesses as constraints Thus, a reconciliation will have to take place between what would seem to be a more open-ended determination of what opportunities and/or threats to follow, as determined in cycle one, with what would actually be feasible, given one's own internal strengths and/or weaknesses as surfacing during the strategic programming stage. This important modification activity is an essential part of the strategic program consolidation The challenge, of course, is to take maximum advantage of internal strengths and attempt to

ameliorate the effects from internal weaknesses as much as possible. In
this way the strategic programming process can solidify and boost the
intended strategic direction set during the objectives-setting stage,
not dampen the pursuance of creative and opportunistic direction-setting

This brings us to a related issue with respect to the problem of
setting directional congruence between strategic programs and objectives,
namely that of dealing with unrealistic (too optimistic or too pessimistic)
managerial judgments For instance. a set of objectives may be so far out
and ill conceived that executing a strategic thrust through concrete
programs might not be feasible In such instances. if the deviations and
unrealism are great enough it might be necessary to redo the entire
objectives-setting cycle, not only for the division in question, but
because of their portfolio interdependencies, all the business plans It
is of course equally undesirable, and quite common, that some divisions
"understretch" their business potential during the objectives-setting
cycle, so that there is little challenge to attain what might be seen as
a "safe" strategic programming tasks during the next stage

The potential problem of lack of consistence between the strategic
thrusts of the objectives-setting and the strategic programming cycles
might to a considerable extent be ameliorated through emphasizing an
important consequence of the decision-making nature of the planning process,
namely, that every manager will be expected to live with what he has
committed his organization unit and himself to. Realism, when it comes
to objectives-setting as well as strategic programming, is thus essential,
rather than unrealistic objectives followed by unimaginative strategic

programs   The key is to hit a reasonable balance between the consideration
of opportunities and threats, and strengths and weakness. Useful in this
respect will be the linking of managerial performance towards the fulfillment
of each planning cycle to the managerial incentive schemes, thus reinforcing
managerial credibility for delivering what has been promised.

The problem of incongruence between the planning cycles might partly
also stem from procedural shortcomings in the way that program alternatives
are being evaluated, chosen and aggregated into an overall business strategic
program package for a division. The so-called "zero-base approach" might be
useful here   A first step in zero-base budgeting, assuming that the
objectives and strategic tasks have been translated to each function
beforehand, is to identify alternative ways of fulfilling the tasks that
have been assigned to a particular function. The various alternatives for
achieving a particular task are then ranked, and the most cost/beneficial
alternative is chosen. After this all the tasks themselves are ranked,
again in terms of the cost-benefits from the task. A cut-off point is
established and all tasks above this will be passed up to the next level
of management   At this level the tasks from all this manager's subordinates
will be consolidated and ranked again, and so on.

Due to the interfunctional nature of most strategic program alternatives, it will be a general management task to rank these alternatives.
Thus, while alternative ways of executing each function's part of a
particular task should be explored by the function, a function would be
unable to pass a strategic judgment in isolation as to which specific tasks
should be done. This can only be done by considering the inputs from the

various functions when forming a total strategic program. Thus, ranking
of strategic programs must be done from the general management point of
view, i.e., by the division head, and not be left in the hands of each
function. It follows from this that the strategic direction determined
for a business during the objectives-setting stage is particularly useful
for the general manager in putting a necessary focus to strategic programming. Without this a straightforward zero-base budgeting aggregation/
ranking approach would not necessarily lead to an appropriate strategic
direction.

4-4. Implementation pitfalls and problems during the budgeting stage

Let us now turn to implementation pitfalls and problems that tend to appear
during the budgeting stage. There are at least three concerns that commonly
might be raised in this respect, namely difficulty in actually allocating the
necessary strategic resources to the decided-upon strategic programs because
of conflicts with traditional resource allocation mechanisms in the firm which
tend to put strong pressures on allocation to departments and/or investment
proposals, because of inadequate recognition of the need for building the
budget around key variables, of the dollar as well as non-dollar types; and
failure of providing a mechanism for personalizing elements of the budget by
the various relevant managers throughout the organizational hierarchy,
"management by objectives" being an integral approach for facilitating this.
We shall discuss each of these three issues in turn.

viii.   Resource allocation to strategic programs, not project or expenditure
         proposals.

As already discussed, the advent of a corporate planning approach
brings along an important implication in terms of a shift in the resource

5
allocation mode. Major strategic resource allocations will be decided on
during the strategic programming cycle as a reflection of how to achieve
the objectives and strategies of the first planning cycle. This thus calls
for a revised and scaled down role for traditional capital budgeting in the
resource allocation process. In companies with no corporate planning
procedures in place as a strategic decision-making tool the resource
allocation process will be heavily focused around the capital budgeting
process and the approval of expenditure budgets. Capital budgeting's
role in such a situation would be as the central vehicle for the allocation
of funds to investments in plants and machinery. The core unit to be
evaluated would be each capital request proposal - say, a project which
involves a new plant or a new machine. Traditional analytical tools from
the capital budgeting body of knowledge were brought to bear in order to
judge the desirability of the project. Prominent techniques include time-
adjusted hurdle rates of return on investment such as net-present-value or
internal-rate-of-return, as well as the simpler pay-back method. These
ratings may be further adjusted for the riskiness of the project. They
may also be classified in terms of size, i.e., whether they exceed the
limits of managerial discretion associated with the manager who is deciding
on the project. Finally, an investment which, for instance, is an essential
replacement of a part in a large continuous process machinery might be
treated differently than an investment which falls within an entirely new
area. The expenditure budget's role in a situation with no strategic
planning would be to provide certain limits for the levels of discretionary
expenditures of various kinds that each department might spend each year.

A vast number of more or less elaborate techniques exist for the development of expenditure budgets too   Typically, however, less analytical effort tend to go into the resource allocations of discretionary expenditures than what is the typical case for capital budgeting decisions. Without elaborating further it is clear that there exists a well established and widely accepted body of traditional methods for aiding in the resource allocation decisions within the firm.

With the advent of resource allocation's role as corporate management's major device for influencing and reshaping the strategic direction of the firm, we have argued that the roles of capital budgeting and the expense budget should be seen in a different light. However, even though a company may have adopted corporate planning and in principle is allocating resources to major strategic programs, it may be easier said than done to modify accordingly the traditional well established systems for allocating capital investments and discretionary expenditures   Thus, it is conceivable that a strategic program which has been approved through the planning process might be frustrated or even halted in the further implementation due to delays in the appropriation of particular projects which are vital parts of the strategic program but which do not yield the necessary hurdle rate when taken out of its strategic context for appropriation according to the classical procedures. Similarly, necessary allocations to some functions' capital expenditure budgets may be insufficient for the functions to carry out their intended strategic roles. Needless to say, serious disturbances in the implementation of strategic direction might result from the pheonomenon that elements of a strategic program, be it expense-elements

or capital investments, are being evaluated separately and according to
non-strategic criteria.

There might be several reasons for this, out of which we shall
discuss two here. The most nasty problem exists when friction between
a strategic resource allocation mode and a "classical" resource allocation
mode can be largely attributed to a "power struggle" between different
groups of management, often associated with changes in generations of
managers. Typically some executives, for instance, the board of directors
and/or the staff executive heading the office evaluating capital requests
(usually the Controller or V P. Finance) have retained considerable "power"
as a result of their heavy involvement in the capital budgeting process
Similarly the staff executive heading up the analysis of the expense
budgets (for instance, the Controller) would have considerable power over
the allocations of discretionary expenditures. These groups might
implicitly or explicitly resist redefinition of their roles in the resource
allocation process, particularly if they feel that a "new" group of managers
are increasing their influence at their own expense.

Another source of friction might simply be due to lack of appreciation of and attention to this as a problem. It is a common experience that
it is easier to add routines to the management system than it is to dismantle or modify administrative routines. This is a reflection of the
common lack of attention for managing the evolutionary direction of the
management system so that its various elements may continue to be consistent
although noticeable changes or additions may have been made to parts of the
system over time. (We shall discuss an approach towards managing the

evolution of systems in Chapter Six.) One difficult issue in managing
the management system is to reconcile how to run the "old" and the "new"
resource allocation systems "in parallel" until the new system has been
"debugged" and is functioning with a reasonable reliability. A second
issue is to determine exactly what the modified role of the "old" resource
allocation system should be. Both issues merit some further discussion.

It is clearly a complicated and far-reaching decision to attempt to
implement a corporate planning system. Such a system cannot be expected
to operationally function overnight. Not only will there be a large
number of formats, routines and communication channels that will have to
be developed. A heavy burden might also fall on the operating managers
in learning and internalizing how to actually work within such a system.
It is not likely that every aspect of the system can be operationalized
at once nor that all managers involved know how to use the system
immediately. Thus, a period of learning and fine-tuning will be normal.
There will typically also be considerable learning associated with the
gradually increased explicit recognition of the strategic position of the
company and its parts; to go through the planning exercise will probably
heighten the strategic understanding and allow for this being stated in
more explicit operational terms. There will of course always be this
learning effect in terms of improved strategic understanding, a major
reason for planning, but this effect will probably be most dramatic during
the first years of planning. Given these considerations it seems necessary
to maintain the traditional resource allocation systems in its original
form for some time in parallel with the strategic planning system. Efforts

should however be made during the execution of capital budgeting to
reconcile the emerging resource allocation decisions with the strategic
programming efforts   If for instance a capital budgeting project is being
proposed which is not part of a strategic program at all, then this should
be resolved on an ad hoc basis. Similarly, if the necessary capital for
an investment which is an integral element of a strategic program is
turned down through the capital budgeting process, then this should also
be resolved on an ad hoc basis. An analogous argument can be made with
regard to the allocation of discretionary expenditures. The critical
issues is to force reconciliation between the "old" and the "new" resource
allocation procedures, so that the importance of corporate planning is
underscored early. Even though planning might still be in its infancy
every attempt should be made to stress that it is going to have effects
on how strategic resources are being used within the company.

The modified roles of the capital budgeting system and the discretionary expenditure budget should be seen as vehicles for "fine-tuning" of
the major resource allocation thrusts decided upon in principle during
the strategic programming stage. Subsequent to this the resolution of
many smaller resource allocation issues typically will remain. Another
important role would be as a "safety-mechanism" to detect unrealistic
assumptions behind strategic program decisions. Modifications and
reassessment of a strategic program might be appropriate if it turns out
through the subsequent more detailed capital budgeting process that, for
instance, the assumed general level for the cost estimate does not hold.
Needless to say, with the modified roles of the capital budgeting and the

discretionary expenditure budget, senior management's time involvement
with these tasks should diminish substantially, and instead shift towards
the strategic programming decision-making process as this becomes the
major resource allocation vehicle, replacing the traditional procedures.

ix. Choice of key variables in budget.

Let us now turn to a second implementation issue during the budgeting
stage, namely the one of choosing appropriate and relevant variables for
developing budgets, so-called key variables. Such a set of variables might
easily be quite different from the traditional all-dollar set of variables
commonly found in budgets.[6]

An operating budget will typically be broken down for each department.
Such a department is labeled a responsibility center; a functional department might either be cost-, revenue- or profit-centers, an SBU and/or area
organizational unit might typically be a revenue-, profit-, or investment-
center. It will be advantageous for control purposes to structure the
budget according to this breakdown. Typically dollar variables will
predominate in such budgets, now and then supplemented by non-dollar
variables which measure the physical activity levels that provide the
basis for the budget. It will however also be useful to reconcile the
departmental budgets into program budgets, reflecting the nature of the
strategic program pattern which the operating budgets are supposed to
represent, see Exhibit 2-5. This will enable management to identify the
function of each department's activity intended for each of the strategic
programs. All departmental operating budget items will of course not be
reconciliable as part of strategic programs, since a significant proportion

of the funds typically will be nondiscretionary For instance, to maintain
a given level of activity without attempting to develop a particular
strategic impact, virtually no strategic program funds might be appropriated,
thus when reconciled with the operating departmental budgets, it will be
only a small fraction of these. It is therefore important to be able to
break down the budgetary data according to such definitions that reconciliation with strategic programs becomes possible.

Another set of non-dollar variables also becomes important, however.
This is related to developing "milestones" for the progress towards
particular strategic programs, and for determining whether the progress
is satisfactory given the level of resources spent. Not only will this
call for the development of a set of operational milestone variables, such
as, for instance, measurement of deadlines, attainment of certain product
or process qualities, development of a distribution network, and so on.
Also it will be necessary to measure not only the rate of use of funds as
a strategic resource, but probably even more critically the "utilization"
of one's critical managers on strategic programs. In our experience this
critical issue is often overlooked and strategic programs are being delayed
as well as more expensive to carry out as a result. In line with this
there should finally be a measure of whether funds for each category of
strategic resources are being spent on a particular strategic project as
assumed, and not, say, on "overspending" to bail out another project or
on short-term performance boosting. Thus, physical measures are needed
to ensure that the timing of the spending on each project is in line and
that there is neither over-spending nor under-spending

Let us finally discuss how the operating budget also might be utilized for serving as a shorter-term indicator of one's progress towards objectives and goals. Let us as an example consider a particular business division For the division management it would be necessary to consider and interpret financial data in the light of what is happening with the strategic position of the business. For instance, a particular set of operating budget figures might be reasonable enough when the business attractiveness level for this business is assumed to stay the same However, if the business attractiveness can be assumed to increase significantly, say, as the result of a general increased trend of growth in sales of the products of this business, then the operating budget figures might be interpreted in a less favorable light Or, alternatively, if the general growth rate is expected to slow down, then the operating budget might be seen as quite favorable, given these adverse circumstances Thus, it is necessary to interpret budgetary performance figures according to changes in the levels of business attractiveness. Hence, a relevant measure of business attractiveness should be part of the budget One such measure might be the rate of growth of the business; if one assumes a certain growth rate, then the operating budget should be expected to take on certain values.

Similarly, the competitive strength of the business itself should be specified in order to state a meaningful set of expected budget performance levels. For instance, the market share of one's own business might be increasing in an effort to improve one's own competitive strength. This might be expected to be reflected in a reasonably moderate budgeting operating result. If one's market share is allowed to fall, on the other hand, then the operating budget should be interpreted in this light, with an expected relatively strong near-term budgeted performance. Figures for changes in one's own business' competitive strength should therefore be part of the budget in order to "peg" the budget to a particular level of competitive strength position. Other non-dollar measures of competitive strength level than market share might of course be relevant, such as for instance productivity measures (again relative to particular competitors, however).

Finally the budget of a business should be judged relative to changes in the relationships with other organizational units, so that it can be determined whether the level of consolidation attractiveness that the business is enjoying is the same or changing. If, for instance, overhead burden significantly changes due to large changes in the activity levels of other business units, then this should be reflected in the budget

Some businesses include adjustments for inflation and currency changes in their budgets. From a strategic management point of veiw there are two aspects of this. First, there is the issue of comparability over time When such comparability is needed for the development of strategic plans then the adjustments should be made, however, this is normally not a major issue when it comes to corporate planning. However, when inflation and/or currency changes have strategic effects then these should be included. For instance, devaluation of an export-oriented company's home currency might significantly improve the competitive position of the company We shall discuss the issue of modifying the planning system to encompass a multinational situational setting in Chapter Six.

In summary, the implementation problem seems to be that the operating budget often is built up exclusively around traditional internally-oriented variables, excluding non-dollar variables for activity level measurements, and that non-dollar variables for relating spending to the progress of strategic programs and for "normalizing" the operating budget for changes in business attractiveness position, own competitive strength and consolidation attractiveness changes are missing. The budget's role is "the tip of the iceberg" in terms of what can be done to implement the strategic programs during the coming year to proceed towards achieving one's objectives and goals. As such the budget's role is primarily to facilitate integration, coordination of the organizational activities with a clear internal focus However, the variables chosen must have the broader relevance to ensure that the budget becomes the culmination of the narrowing down of strategic options, i.e., is consistent with the broader contextual limits given through the objectives and strategic programs.

x. Accountability for budgets.

Let us now change our discussion to a third implementation issue associated with the budgeting stage, which might be analyzed together with the integration of the so-called "Management By Objectives" approach (MBO) in the corporate planning process. One important aspect of the budgeting process is that each manager should be in a position to identify clearly the tasks that will fall to him as a consequence of carrying out the budget. A related requirement is that each manager internalize and associate himself with the relevant part of the budget, next year's operation should make sense to him to the extent that he is indeed

motivated to pursue towards its fulfillment. There are several ways to
reinforce this. The major factor is of course the participation of
managers in the corporate planning process itself, which has involved
several levels of management in the development of a consistent set of
corporate objectives as well as strategic programs, i e , has provided
a basis throughout the organization for understanding the broader strategic
implications of the budget through their participation of the developments
in the previous stages. The budgeting stage with its culmination of the
narrowing down should therefore result in a clear task- and rationale-
identification for each manager with his part of a coordinated corporate-
wise action plan. A desirable effect of the process, therefore, is the
likely development of broad-based managerial commitment to a particular
strategic direction, through inviting the managers to participate in the
process in a manner which will make common sense to them.

To reinforce this sense of commitment even further it might be useful
to tie this added sense of direction in with a management by objectives
scheme. A first step in this direction is to have meetings between each
manager and his superior to review what the budget implies in terms of an
action program for him during the coming year. Each manager relevant to
the implementation of the budget in the organizational hierarchy should go
through this. This might provide a basis for evaluation of each manager's
short-term job performance after the year is over in a mode which underscores the longer range strategic significance of near-term performance.
Management incentives might be tied to such an evaluation - we shall
discuss this a little later.

One implementation problem with respect to the above is that the budgeting process may not emphasize enough the action-oriented task implications for each manager   It is not only necessary that the budget has been developed with enough detail to facilitate this, but also that near-term action-responsibility on the part of a manager can be reconciled with longer-term program responsibility   Failure to develop this degree of specificity in the budgets is often an indication that the entire corporate planning process is not functioning as expected, and to ameliorate this attention should be focused on cycles one and two of the process with respect to whether the outputs of these cycles are specific enough to be useful as well as to whether preliminary patterns of manage-ment accountability have been established. To address the above question is a critical check of whether the corporate planning process has been functioning so far, i.e., that the stages of the process which are concerned with identification and narrowing down of strategic opportunities are operational.

A smaller and much easier implementation problem to handle stems from the fact that the management by objectives approach often tends to be detached from the strategic planning effort. This might actually result in dysfunction unless modified to be consistent with the rest of the strategic management process. An example of a problem of this kind might stem from the fact that management by objectives might already have been introduced well before planning, to create more of an action-oriented task-emphasis to the traditional budgeting. As such, management by objectives would have a highly bottom-up dominated nature, with lower-level managers playing major roles of what they see as relevant aspects of their job, and with heavy emphasis on behavioral/job evaluation aspects. Of course, it could not be expected that the management by objectives process would bring out an adequate general management strategic context for such task-identification. With the advent of a corporate planning approach what is needed is the modification of the management by objectives approach so that it can be executed within the necessary strategic context and thereby become a useful reenforcement of the strategic management process.

We have by now discussed a total of ten implementation issues that relate to the three first stages of the strategic planning process. It should be noticed that all these issues are concerned with aspects of how to establish strategic direction for the company and/or its parts. Thus they deal with how a company might prepare itself to improve the pattern of strategic resource allocation <u>before</u> it actually will have to act. We shall now change focus and discuss four additional implementation issues, fundamentally different in nature from the former in that they deal with aspects of cycles four and five of the planning process, i e , post facto concerns

-5. <u>Implementation pitfalls and problems during the monitoring stage</u>.

We shall discuss two implementation problems that seem to be common when it comes to an effective monitoring of progress towards the fulfillment of the strategies decided upon during the previous three cycles of the corporate planning process These issues relate to taking a "mechanistic" approach towards monitoring actual results relative to plans, without proper reflection on the specific nature of the phenomenon being monitored, its predictability,

the strategic response potential at hand, and the relative importance of the
phenomenon in a risk/return sense. A second implementation concern is that
the monitoring tends to emphasize short-term progress, with little or no
regard for the monitoring of progress towards long-term objectives. We shall
discuss each of these issues in turn.[7]

    xi.   Tailormade monitoring to the phenomenon at hand.

        We recall from our discussion of the concept of risk/return as part
of the corporate portfolio analysis in Chapter Three that it is meaningful
to consider the degree to which we are able to predict a particular
phenomenon as well as the extent to which we are able to respond in a
discretionary fashion to the phenomenon. We isolated four environmental
factor archetypes, from this, according to differences along the above
two dimensions, each factor having a different degree of risk associated
with it. However, the diminished risk associated with a strategy which is
heavily dominated by an environmental factor that can be reasonably well
predicted and which also can be responded to will not automatically be
enjoyed; we have to carry out an adequate monitoring in order to be able
to predict the factor and we also have to prepare the form of ameliorating
response we might want to take. Thus, the approach that is taken to
monitor performance is critical in containing strategic risks to the
levels we assumed when we developed and approved the strategy. Given the
different environmental archetypes we shall benefit from employing a
situational monitoring/control systems approach, contingent on the degree
of predictability and the degree of discretionary response potential. It
shall thus be a major requirement to the successful implementation of the

monitoring stage that a general overly standardized monitoring approach
is avoided.

For the monitoring of a phenomenon which has a relatively high
degree of predictability potential and also a relatively high degree
of discretionary response potential, an approach that we shall label
steering control is the one most appropriate. This implies that
forecasting of environmental phenomenon will be done with enough
frequency and detail to predict changes, if any, with a reasonable
degree of accuracy. This in turn allows for a relatively immediate
response as soon as the predicted deviation emerges, and permits carrying
out the corrective action before the strategic program actually has been
completed; this reduces the potential for adverse effects by making
corrections in time or increasing the potential for favorable effects
by taking action in time to go after a particular opportunity. Because
the nature of the corrective action typically will be rather incremental
it is analogous to a self-correcting positive feedback phenomenon; it is
being steered towards the target through the monitoring process.

Our capability to carry out this highly advantageous before-the-fact
steering control depends above all on the potential for reasonably
accurate forecasting. However, in many situations forecasting an
environmental phenomenon will be virtually impossible, even though we
might have been able to respond if we had some reliable forecasting
information. In such a situation we shall propose a contingency control
approach This implies that for each of several alternative outcomes of
such an unpredictable environmental phenomenon a particular managerial

response is developed. The monitoring function then consists of observing when a change actually takes place, and as rapidly as possible executing the appropriate predetermined response pattern. A strategy which relies on this type of environmental phenomenon is more risky than one that relies on a more predictable phenomenon, however, a contingency control monitoring approach which lays out prepared response patterns beforehand can at least significantly reduce the risk.

We may also be in a position where there is little we can do to respond to a development of a particular environmental phenomenon, even though we might be able to predict the development of an environmental factor there is little we can do in terms of corrective actions <u>after</u> we have committed ourselves to the particular strategy. We shall apply an <u>anticipative go-no go</u> control approach in monitoring this class of environmental phenomena. This implies that we might be able to scale the strategic program activity up or down, or abandon the program altogether, however, we might be able to reduce the consequences of an adverse development (or increase the potential for benefiting from a positive development) if we take advantage of the "early warning" that the relatively high degree of predictability can give us. Thus, this monitoring approach implies that ample attention should be put on forecasting and that the necessary reactive managerial consequences for the strategic program in question should be faced up to at once.

The final situational setting implies that the key environmental phenomenon influencing a strategy can neither be well predicted nor easily responded to In such an instance we might adopt a <u>post-facto</u> <u>go-no go control</u> approach Given that there is little we can do through

monitoring in terms of taking corrective actions to contain the risk
associated with a strategy, there is not the same compelling reason for
allocating time and money to the monitoring function in this case. We
might therefore conclude that monitoring should be kept to a minimum or
abandoned - if not for the following two secondary benefits. First, to
register through monitoring that an environmental event has taken place
which is different from that assumed in the plans will allow for
reassessment of the corporation's portfolio strategy in case the effects
are serious enough. Secondly, through careful monitoring we might be
able to learn, and improve our judgment so that we can make sounder
strategic choices next time around.

A related benefit from the fact that we have been able to designate
different modes of monitoring for phenomena with different risks is that
we also may make use of this as a vehicle for setting guidelines for
when to pass on information and decision-responsibility upwards in the
organization versus when to carry out corrective actions at the decentralized level. A strategy which might be monitored primarily through
a properly developed steering control approach can be left in the hands
of subordinate management in terms of discretionary responsibility for
execution to a much larger extent than a more risky strategy. Thus, the
bottom-up flow of monitoring signals in cycle four should also be tailored
to the nature of the monitoring task.

The contingency approach towards monitoring just discussed seems
unfortunately to be far from the state-of-the-art of implementation of
the monitoring function. Instead, much of the monitoring tends to be
standardized according to principles that do not substantially allow for

differentiation between the monitoring tasks at hand, and neither for a
tailoring of centralized versus decentralized response to monitoring data.
This emphasis reflects a tradition of making use of the budgets as
simplified tools of measuring by the end of a given period whether an
organizational subunit has actually achieved its budget or not. This
"stick and carrot" approach clearly puts too little emphasis on developing
innovative strategy-based monitoring tailormade to various subunits of
the organization An effective monitoring approach represents an essential
element in the implementation of strategies, providing an opportunity to
modify strategic programs in time, and thereby reemphasizing an element
of responsiveness and alertness to critical factors outside the firm in
order to reduce and contain risk. It is a serious implementation problem
that the monitoring function tends to be so deficient as an element in our
strategic decision-making context, particularly in that opportunistic
responsiveness gets quashed and unnecessarily high risk-taking will be
the result.

xii. Near-term monitoring only

Let us now turn to a second and highly related implementation issue
which has particular relevance to the monitoring stage, namely the need
to monitor not only short-term performance but also longer-term performance.
We recall that the budget should represent the "tip of the iceberg" in
terms of next year's action plan towards the fulfillment of agreed upon
longer-term objectives, goals and strategic programs However, as we
also discussed, budgets are not complete mappings of strategic programs
or objectives, none the least because they only represent near-term aspects

of the longer-term strategic direction Thus, monitoring of budget
fulfillment does not necessarily imply that we are progressing as
intended towards the fulfillment of strategies, hence, it is necessary
to monitor separately progress towards the fulfillment of particular
objectives and strategic programs When it comes to strategic programs,
"milestones" should be established for the progress review and reevalua-
tion of each, as already discussed Separate monitoring should be done
for the longer-term progress of each of these programs. Similarly, when
it comes to business objectives the progress along a transition path
towards achieving a particular new long-term position for one's own
competitive strength, say, by increasing market share, should be monitored.
Changes in business attractiveness and consolidation attractiveness should
also be monitored. We have already discussed the choice of appropriate
variables - monetary as well as nonmonetary - for facilitating the
monitoring of long-term performance in addition to short-term performance.
We have also discussed the need to monitor key environmental factors,
particularly in connection with the monitoring of progress towards the
fulfillment of business as well as corporate objectives. The implementation issue of providing for both longer-term and shorter-term monitoring
is related to these issues already discussed and shall not be elaborated
further here.

One final aspect of the implementation of monitoring long-term
progress relates to the attention that senior management puts on the
interpretation of these monitoring signals relative to the attention being
paid to the interpretation of short-term results. There is a tendency
among some senior managers to pay inordinate attention to short-term

performance-deviation problems, going from one "firefighting" situation to another. For lack of time (or mental energy) relatively little or no attention will be paid to monitoring signals that indicate more fundamental weaknesses with the general strategic path. Also, pressures toward showing consistent short-term performance, a feature which tends to be highly appreciated by the stock market, might diminish senior management's relative attention to long-term corrective actions. We are of course not claiming here that short-term performance should not be attended to. Rather, our position is that monitoring of both long-term and short-term results should be attempted. The issue of how much relative emphasis should be put on short-term versus long-term performance fulfillment attention is however a question that will depend on a company's particular situation, and we shall discuss this further in the next chapter on tailormaking of the corporate planning system's design

4-6. Implementation pitfalls and problems during the management incentivating stage.

Let us now discuss two implementation problems that relate to the fifth and final stage of the corporate planning process, the determination of management incentives. The first implementation issue here is that the granting of management incentives should reflect the nature of the strategic tasks at hand. If a particular strategic success is due largely to environmental effects outside the control of a manager then he should not receive additional compensation for this, if, on the other hand the success was largely attributable to the manager's strategic insight, then this should be reflected in the way he is compensated The second implementation issue in connection with the final cycle is to pay attention not only to incentives that honor short-term performance excellence but to strike a balance between these and those that honor long-term performance excellence. Let us discuss each of these two issues in turn.

xiii. Strategic focus on managerial incentives.

The nature of the strategic task at hand should be reflected in the incentive system, so that managers can be motivated in a way which facilitates congruence between the strategies to be pursued by the organizational unit and the manager's personal goals. Let us illustrate this issue by considering how to motivate the manager of an SBU as an example. The nature of the strategic task facing the manager might for instance vary significantly with the type of life cycle that the SBU's business is in. For instance, the major determinants to success for an SBU which is in its early growth stage are probably adaptive entrepreneurial moves to develop an effective niche in the marketplace, breadth and type of span of products, channels of distribution, pricing and financing policies, and so on. To a large extent the success on this is likely to depend on the manager in charge of the SBU. He might be incentivated towards this by receiving a relatively large share of his compensation as a variable function of his organization's performance. The emphasis on the key role of this manager as an individual may further be under-scored by giving the major part of the incentive to him as an individual and not the broader group of managers in the SBU. If on the other hand we have an SBU which is positioned within a business which is considerably more mature, the keys to strategic success will probably be different than

in our growth-business SBU example. Now the success is more likely to
hinge on outperforming one's competitors in terms of cost efficiency, a
smooth production and distribution process, lean policies for purchasing
and inventories, maintenance of stable levels of product quality, and so
on. In this case the team of managers as an overall team rather than
individualistic performance is likely to be critical. Thus, incentives
should be focused more on the performance of the management team as a
group. However, a relatively larger number of factors outside control
of the management team will probably also dictate the performance in this
case than in our earlier example, above all the SBU's built-up position
of business strength over past years. Thus, a larger fraction of the
executives' compensation should probably be considered as fixed, the
incentives should probably only apply to a relatively small porportion
of the overall compensation. In line with this, a strategic emphasis on
managerial incentives might involve a tailormaking towards the given
situation; individual versus group incentives as well as relatively high
emphasis on fixed compensation versus on compensation variable with
performance.

However, we see that incentives should relfect the nature of the
strategic task of a particular business, depending on the life-cycle stage
that the business is in   There will typically be an additional consideration that might further modify the nature of the strategic task, namely
the extent to which the management of a business is in a position to
predict and respond to the development of key environmental factors. If
a manager has little or no opportunity to predict significant developments
in the environment that might dramatically influence his strategic

performance, then his incentives should reflect this· a relatively
smaller share of the incentives should be variable, so that effects from
unpredictable fluctuations can be eliminated. Similarly, if there is
little the manager can do in terms of discretionary reaction to environmental factors then too the variable fraction of the incentives should
be relatively smaller, it would be meaningless to develop incentives that
are not the function of discretionary managerial action. Thus, incentive
systems should be applied only in situations where opportunities exist for
forecasting events external to the business and/or for discretionary
managerial responses.

Unfortunately, in practice there seems to be relatively little
reflection regarding the nature of the strategic tasks in the design and
implementation of managerial incentive schemes The incentive systems
often seem to be designed as a general set of rules that apply across the
company, thus disregarding to modify the scheme so as to reflect wnether
strategic success will be heavily dependent on variable factors outside
the control of the managers or not. Whether a manager has a relatively
large or limited potential for influencing his strategy does not seem to
be reflected in most incentive schemes. Worse than this, in several
instances there is no apparent tie between the incentive scneme and the
strategy-fulfillment performance of managers at all, rather, highly
informally set incentives, often with a strong element of nepotism, tend
to be common This lack of emphasis on the reinforcement of strategic
direction-setting when developing management incentives may not only be
an important barrier to the implementation of strategic planning as such
Worse, it is even conceivable that the implicit thrust of managerial

motivation actually might be counterstrategic, thus providing even more
serious momentum against the implementation of planned strategic direction.

xiv. <u>Balance between incentives for long-term and short-term performance</u>

This brings us to another implementation problem, namely that
incentive schemes do not tend to reach a reasonable balance between
motivating towards short-term versus long-term performance. Unfortunately,
in most cases the emphasis seems to be heavily skewed towards appreciation
of short-term performance in the incentives schemes. For instance, year-
end profit performance, particularly when it exceeds the budget, tends to
count heavily. This is likely to introduce a snort-term performance
maximizing bias into a company, with possibilities of dangerous non-
strategic suboptimizations that might erode the potential for long-term
success. One of the objections to including long-term performance
fulfillment criteria in management's incentive schemes is that these
schemes must be based on reasonably "objective" measures and that it
generally is too subjective to assess a manager's contribution towards
long-term performance. However, with the advent of the set of variables
and measures that have been devised during the previous four cycles of
the strategic planning scheme, there is a much better basis for carrying
out assessments of longer-term performance; hence, this concern should no
longer be seen as a major objection.

Another factor which traditionally has detracted from emphasizing
long-term performance as a criterion in the incentive schemes is based on
the observation that the frequency of job rotations among managers is so
high that it will be virtually impossible to hold a manager accountable
for longer-term performance. This is a valid objection, indeed a

fundamental potential obstacle to the implementation of a strategic mode of managing the firm. One approach to reducing this problem would be to cut down on the frequency of managerial job rotations Excessive job rotations may in many companies indicate a lack of thorough planning of key management resources, and may also be seen as a symptom of under-estimation of this obstacle's role as a barrier to the implementation of strategic planning. The epitome of this may be a rapid assignment of a succession of managers to try to turn around a troubled business, instead of attempting to come to grips directly with the basic strategic problems facing this business. In any case, rapid job rotation seems to have become a part of the management style of some companies, probably with more negative than positive benefits (A conscious attempt to reduce the frequency of job rotation of course does not mean that one should have to go to the other extreme.)

Some companies systematically reassess managers' key strategic decisions even after the responsibility for a manager's business domain has been transferred to his successor. Such a "dossier" of a manager's back history of substantive input on strategic decisions and plans might be a useful tool in ameliorating some of the dysfunctional effects of job rotation by reserving a sense of long-term accountability for strategy fulfillment. The "administration" of such a file would of course have to be done carefully, both in terms of who should have access to it and the right of each manager concerned to include his point of view in the file. Probably the most useful purpose of such a file system is to have on record the backgrounds for the business successes, credit is very easily given to the manager who happened to be at the helm at the time when a business experienced a successful break, and not to the managers who laid the foundation through long-term strategic insights.

Lack of proper balance between longer-term and shorter-term criteria for performance as the basis for managerial incentive schemes provides an important implementation barrier to strategic planning, above all because of the decline of an important opportunity to bolster planned strategic direction that this represents   While this implementation problem, as well as the other one discussed in the context of the final cycle of the planning system may be seen as relatively indirect barriers to the implementation of corporate planning, they are still important. Proper integration of management incentives with the rest of the planning system can provide a significant reinforcement of the indended strategic thrust.

4-7. Summary

This chapter has laid out the initial issues in our discussion of how to implement corporate planning systems   Rather than embarking at a contingency-based discussion at this point we found it useful to discuss fourteen different general types of implementation pitfalls and problems that tend to be common when adopting the three-by-five conceptual approach to corporate planning. The issues raised here should serve as a first "checklist" for the implementation of corporate planning, without at least being aware of, or, even better, having attempted to resolve these issues it is more or less futile to expect planning to be effective. Having tackled the problems outlined in this chapter does not, however, guarantee success in the corporate planning function, additional tailormaking of the system to the particular situational setting at hand will have to be done - the topic for the next chapter.

Let us briefly review the thirteen areas of immediate concern when implementing a planning system. During the objectives-setting stage there were five issues that seemed particularly common the active and open involvement of the chief executive and senior management during the first step of the planning process; the penetrating assessment of business opportunities by each of the divisions, through open-ended assessment of key environmental factors rather than through a mode of extrapolation, the mode of review of planning inputs by the corporate management, emphasizing a portfolio approach whereby each business is assessed in relation to the others; the limited and informal involvement by the functional departments during the objectives-setting cycle - this aspect of planning is rather a general management key concern, and, the need to make decisions to narrow down options in order to close planning gaps.

It should be noticed that two of the issues discussed in connection with the implementation problems of the objectives-setting cylce have general applicability in all five cycles of the planning process. Thus, we should always be concerned with stressing the need for a corporate level portfolio review of bottom-up planning inputs as well as the issue of closing the planning gaps during the various stages of the planning process by executing the necessary decisions. For practical reasons, we have found it useful to discuss these implementation issues when they first occurred, namely during the objectives-setting stage.

During the strategic programming stage we discussed two common implementation concerns, namely that the development of strategic program alternatives is typically cross-functional, and that when aggregating and choosing between strategic program alternatives there should be consistency

with the objectives set during the previous stage. During the budgeting
stage we raised three areas of implementation concern   that strategic
resources should be allocated to the strategic programs and not to the
proposals of the capital budgeting process nor to the departments' discretionary expenditure budgets, that the budget should be seen as an action
plan reflecting next year's intended progress towards the fulfillment of
strategic programs, objectives and goals, and hence should be built up
around key variables, and that the budget should assign clear responsibility
for execution to the relevant managers, consistent with the underlying
objectives, goals and strategic programs. During the monitoring stage
there were two issues of particular concern   that the monitoring task
should be strategic in outlook, i e., have a focus on the forecasting of
a given environmental phenomenon as well as the strategic response potential,
also, the monitoring task should reach a balance between a long-term primary
external focus and a shorter-term primary internal focus   Finally, during
the management incentive setting stage we raised the issue that the specific
nature of the strategic task should be reflected in the management incentive
system's execution, and that the incentives should reach a balance between
emphasizing shorter-term and longer-term performance fulfillment.

Having by now completed our task of identifying and discussing a set
of general planning implementation and pitfall issues, which seem to be
more or less relevant to all corporate planning settings, our next step
shall be to discuss how to approach the tailormaking of a planning system
so that it might possess an appropriate set of capabilities to meet the
particular needs for planning that a given company might face. We shall
dsicuss this in Chapter Five

Chapter Four - Footnotes

1. This chapter follows a structure which in most instances is similar
   to that reported in Lorange, Peter, "Implementation of Strategic
   Planning Systems", in Hax, Arnoldo C. (editor), Advances in Operations
   Management, North-Holland Publishing, Amsterdam, 1978. For other
   discussions of pitfalls and problems, see Warren, E. Kirby, Long-Range
   Planning: The Executive Viewpoint, Prentice-Hall, Englewood Cliffs,
   1966, Gilbert, Xavier and Peter Lorange, "Five Pillars for Your
   Planning", European Business, Fall, 1974, Eliasson, Gunnar, Business
   Economic Planning, John Wiley & Sons (also, Swedish Industrial Publi-
   cations), New York, 1976, Koontz, H., "Making Strategic Planning Work," Busines.
   Horizons, April, 1976, and Steiner, George A., Strategic Managerial
   Planning, Planning Research Institute, Oxford, 1977.

2. See Koontz, H., "Making Strategic Planning Work", Business Horizons,
   April, 1976, Quinn, James Brian, "Strategic Goals: Process and
   Politics", Sloan Management Review, Fall, 1977.

3. See Ansoff, H. Igor and John M. Stewart, "Strategies for a Technology-
   Based Business," Harvard Business Review, Nov.-Dec. 1967, and Vancil,
   Richard F., "Better Management of Corporate Development," Harvard
   Business Review, Sep.-Oct., 1972.

4. See Carter, E. E., "The Behavioral Theory of the Firm and Top-Level
   Corporate Decisions", Administrative Science Quarterly, Vol. 16, 1971,
   Phyrr, Peter A., Zero-Base Budgeting: A Practical Management Tool for

Evaluating Expenses, John Wiley & Sons, New York, 1973, Stonich, Paul J.,
Zero-Base Planning and Budgeting, Dow Jones-Irwing, Homewood, 1977, and
Anand, Sudeep, Resource Allocation at the Corporate Level of the Firm:
A Methodological and Empirical Investigation of the Dimensions Used by
Managers for Evaluation of Investments, Unpublished Ph.D. Thesis,
M.I.T., Cambridge, 1977.

5. See Berg, Norman A., The Allocation of Strategic Funds in a Large
    Diversified Company, Unpublished Doctoral Dissertation, Harvard Business
    School, Boston, 1963, Ackerman, R. W., Organization and the Investment
    Process: A Comparative Study, Unpublished D.B.A. Thesis, Harvard
    University, Boston, 1968, Bower, Joseph L., Managing the Resource
    Allocation Process: A Study of Corporate Planning and Investment,
    Division of Research, Harvard Business School, Boston, 1970, Carter,
    E. Eugene, Portfolio Aspects of Corporate Capital Budgeting, D. C.
    Heath Publishing, Lexington, 1974, and Anand, Sudeep, Resource Alloca-
    tion at the Corporate Level of the Firm: A Methodological and Empirical
    Investigation of the Dimensions Used by Managers for Evaluation of
    Investments, Unpublished Ph.D. Thesis, M.I.T., Cambridge, 1977.

6. See Schiff, M. and A. Y. Lewin, "Where Traditional Budgeting Fails",
    in Schiff, M. and A. Y. Lewin, (editors), Behavior Aspects of
    Accounting, Prentice-Hall, Englewood Cliffs, 1974, and Carter, E. E.,
    "Designing the Capital Budgeting Process". in Nystrom, Paul C. and
    William H. Starbuck, (editors), Prescriptive Models of Organizations
    North-Holland Publishing Co., Amsterdam, 1977.

7. See Footnote 6. Also, see Newman, W H., <u>Constructive Control</u>, Prentice-Hall, Englewood Cliffs, 1975, Lorange, Peter, "Strategic Control: A Framework for Effective Response to Environmental Change" Sloan School Working Paper, Cambridge, 1977, and Bales, C. F , "Strategic Control: The President's Paradox", <u>Business Horizons</u>. August, 1977.

CHAPTER FIVE

Tailormaking the Corporate Planning System's Design

5-1. Introduction

We have developed a conceptual scheme for corporate planning (Chapter Two)
but seen that the successful implementation of such a conceptual scheme
for planning will not only depend on the avoidance of a number of "pitfalls" of implementation (Chapter Four) but also and equally important,
that we are able to tailormake the planning system's capabilities to reflect the needs of the situational setting of the firm. The strategic
position of the firm (Chapter Three) was the most important source of
determination for planning needs. In this chapter we shall attempt to
develop an approach towards tailormaking the design of a firm's planning
system in order to meet the needs requirements at hand [1] We shall do this
by identifying a set of variables relating to the design of a planning
system. These variables will be under our discretionary control and can
be "manipulated" in such a way that the corporate planning system will
achieve desired capabilities for matching the planning needs. It is clear
that this will be an important step of sharpened focus beyond the more
general implementation issues discussed in the previous chapter. However,
we saw that these issues would seem to have relevance for all corporate
planning systems, and therefore represented a necessary step of clarification of the conceptual scheme.

We shall start our discussion of situational design of the planning
system by approaching how to tailormake those aspects of the planning system that apply to the SBUs in particular. We shall see how the planning
system might facilitate the setting of an appropriate strategic direction
of a SBU, in terms of this being a reflection of its needs for adaptation
and integration. The planning systems design issues that will help us

facilitating this shall consist of three classes of checklist factors to
facilitate the desired strategic thrust. The first dimension of the SBU
planning system will deal with the choice of specific strategic direction,
should it be an attempt to enter, build, hold, harvest or exit a business?
The second dimension deals with what would be a "natural" type of strategic
programming effort to reinforce the SBU's desired strategic direction,
should the strategic programming emphasis be on initial market development
for entry, on market penetration, on market maintenance, on vertical integration, on development of foreign business, on rationalization, on
efficiency improvements or, on unit abandonment and exit? The third dimension deals with the reinforcement of the strategic direction of a
SBU, as established through the choices related to the previous two dimensions, in term of selecting a particular competitive mode for strategic
niche "purification." Some of the factors here, such as emphasis on
quality or image, will tend to reinforce the adaptive thrust. Other factors might primarily strengthen the integrative side, such as choice of
policies for price, service and delivery reliance.

When it comes to the design of the part of the planning system which
is intended to facilitate the development of SBU strategies in a narrow
sense, our approach shall thus be one of suggesting a static, "checklist"
design, focussing on setting strategic direction, choosing an appropriate
strategic program thrust and reinforcing this with particular competitive
mode policy choices. Seen in isolation, such a static planning system
design would not appear to be all that useful, in that it might seem too
mechanistic and uninspiring However, we shall suggest that this component of the planning system should be used primarily for providing improved SBU strategic focus. Thus, it shall be intended primarily to

strengthen the planning inputs from the businesses into the interactive and iterative corporate planning process that was outlined in Chapter Two. The tailormaking of the design of this overall process shall be discussed in the latter part of this chapter.

It will primarily be the corporate level portfolio planning needs that will dictate the design of the overall planning process. We shall discuss a set of five tailormaking systems design devices which at least to some degree might be controlled or "manipulated" in a discretionary sense by the systems designer in order to achieve they desired adaptation and integration capabilities of the overall planning process. These factors will be the choice of relative emphasis on "front-end" versus "concluding end" of the strategy opportunity identification and narrowing down stages, the nature of the linkage among each of the five cycles in the planning process, "tight" versus "loose," the relative amount of executives' penetrating involvement and time spent on each of the five cycles of the planning process, the relative emphasis in the control system on monitoring "front-end" versus "near-term" phenomena, and, finally, the relative emphasis in the managerial incentives system on assessing "front-end" versus "near-term" performance fulfillment. As a way of summarizing our approach to tailormade design of the planning system we shall finally illustrate by means of an extensive example how this "battery" of planning systems design factors can be changed when needed, in order to reinforce a strategic shift, either for the company as a whole or in some of its parts.

5-2. Designing a Planning Systems Module to Meet a SBU's Planning Needs.

We recall from our discussion of a SBU's planning needs in Chapter Three that the absolute and relative need for adaptation and integration will be a function of the location of a SBU's strategic position within

the business attractiveness/competitive strength matrix. Thus, a so-
called "question-mark" position would imply a high need for adaptation but
a relatively low need for integration; a "star" position implies a high
need for both adaptation as well as integration, a "cash-cow" position implies a relatively higher need for integration than for adaptation, and
a "dog" position implies a relatively low need for both adaptation and integration. We also recall that to evolve a SBU from a "question-mark" to
a "star" position will require an inordinate emphasis on both adaptation
as well as on integration, but that the integration dimension is the one
that will have to be strengthened relatively the most. When evolving from
a "star" to a "cash-cow" we recall that the adaptive needs actually will
diminish somewhat relative to integration The challenge for a SBU's planning system is to facilitate the choice of a strategic direction that
actually provides the adaptive/integrative thrust to meet these identified
needs. [2]

     The planning system for a SBU shall facilitate the execution of stra-
tegic direction. As already indicated we shall propose three sets of
"checklist factors" which should facilitate the proper focus on the execution effort These checklists relate to the choice of basic strategic
direction, the choice of strategic program thrust and the choice of competitive mode reinforcing policies. The contingency-based design approach
of planning systems for SBUs implies that the actual span of each of these
choices will indeed be relatively narrow, given that there will be a few
"natural strategies" that most properly will provide the desired adaptive
and integrative thrust for a particular SBU. Thus, the major purpose of
the design of the SBU's planning system is to ensure that the relevant
"checklist factors" are being chosen which allow such a "natural strategy"
execution to be followed, consistent with the SBU's needs. The system

should be a tool for the SBU manager for his own planning of his strategic
direction. Let us in turn discuss the three classes of check-list systems design choice factors for a SBU's strategic planning systems module.

When it comes to the first set of factors, namely to check what should
be the basic direction of "where to go," or, in other words, to check what
should be the basic direction coming out of the SBU's objectives there
seem to be five broad directional alternatives:

i) To <u>enter</u> into a business, typically creating a new SBU within the
"question-mark" area.

ii) To <u>build</u> a strategic position. This will typically imply the
development of competitive strength, say by increasing one's
market share.

iii) To <u>hold</u> one's strategic position. This implies the embarking on
a strategy that attempts to maintain one's competitive strength
posture without major shifts in, say, market share.

iv) To <u>harvest</u>, which will imply that one's strategic position will
gradually be allowed to be weakened, there will probably be more
resources extracted from a SBU than what is reinvested to maintain its competitive strength.

v) To <u>exit</u>. This implies withdrawing from the business by divesting
of the SBU or closing down its activities.

We recall from Chapter Two that the objectives-setting stage of the
strategy-formulation process is particularly important for influencing
the adaptive thrust of a strategic direction. Considering the above directional alternatives in this light we might say that the "entry" and
"build" direction choices typically will be imply a rather highly adaptive
thrust. A "hold" direction will probably imply a less intensive adaptation
thrust. This is likely to be even more so for a "harvest" setting, where

to "exit" no active adaptation thrust is implied.

Let us now move to the second class of checklist factors for the execution of a proper strategic direction for a SBU, namely what might be
the type of strategic program that most appropriately should be chosen
for "how to get there." We shall identify eight major classes of strategic
program directions, all signifying alternative ways of "how to get there,"
but each being the "natural choice" in a different SBU direction need
situation

     i)   Initial entry into a business by means of initial new market and
          new product development.

    ii)   Market penetration. This implies the execution of strategic
          programs, either for penetrating new markets with ones existing
          products, for penetrating one's existing markets with new prod-
          ucts, or for penetrating new markets with new products.

   iii)   Market maintenance. A strategic programming effort of this type
          implies that the present markets and products are being maintained

    iv)   Vertical integration. Such strategic programs will attempt to
          facilitate either backward integration or/and forward integration.

     v)   Expanding into foreign businesses Strategic programs to facil-
          itate this might include moves to export one's same products, at-
          tempts to arrange for licensing abroad, development of overseas
          facilities to carry out, say, some of the SBU's manufacturing-,
          distribution-, and/or marketing-activities, or development of
          more or less "complete spin-off SBUs" abroad.

    vi)   Rationalization. Strategic programs of this kind might include
          making moves to trim excess capacity, attempting to carry out
          market rationalizations, distribution rationalizations, product

line rationalizations and/or production process rationalization.

vii) <u>Increased efficiency</u>. Such a strategic programming thrust would
      include attempts to gain increased technological efficiency,
      elaboration of methods for further pursuance of functional ef-
      ficiency improvements, as well as traditional cost cutting ef-
      forts.

viii) <u>Terminal exit</u> would imply strategic programs for gradual aban-
      donment and/or divestiture.

We recall from our discussion of Chapter Two that the strategic programming activities typically tend to imply a relatively much higher emphasis on integration than on integration taking place "later" in the
planning process. If we consider the eight types of strategic programs
that just have been identified above, however, we can see that these do
not all seem to be equally integration-oriented. For instance, a programming thrust that emphasizes initial market development, market penetration or market maintenance seems much less oriented towards integration
or expansion of foreign businesses. Strategic programming activities
which are based on rationalization or improved efficiency will typically
be even more extensively integration-dominated. Thus, if we exclude for
now the terminal exit strategic program thrust we see that the integrative
dominance of the strategic programming activities seems to increase as we
go from the first type of programming to the seventh.

Before introducing the third list of check-list factors, policies for
fine-tuning of the SBU's competitive niche, let us see how the combined
use of the two checklists already discussed provide the management of a
SBU with quite accurate guidelines for developing a "natural strategy"
to correspond to its identified needs for planning. In Exhibit 5-1 we
have plotted the alternatives along the five basic strategic direction

horizontal axis according to its adaptation-orientation. Along the vertical axis we have ranked the seven first strategic program alternatives
according to their integrative orientation. We have indicated with check-
marks what appear to be relevant "natural strategy" combinatio- of these
objectives and strategic program thrusts. For instance,

	Direction of Objective	Entry	Build	Hold	Harvest	Exit
Low In-tegra-tion	Initial Entry	v				
	Market Penetration					
	Market Maintanance		v	v		
	Vertical Integration		v	v		
High inte-gra-tion	Foreign Business Expans.			v	v	
	Rationalization			v	v	
Low inte-gration)	Efficiency Improvem.				v	v
	Terminal Exit.					v

Exhibit 5-1. Checklist of "Natural Strategies" in Terms of Basic Strategic
Direction and Type of Strategic Program. V Represents Feasible Objective/
Program Strategy Combination. ____ Represents Borderline for Strategy Com-
bination Alternatives for different Strategic Positions: I = "Questionmark"
(High A/Low I Need); II = "Star" (High A/High I Need); III = "Cash Cow"
(Low A/High I Need) · IV = "Dog" (Low A/Low I need). ____ Represent Evolution
A from "Questionmark" to "Star;" B from "Star" to "Cash Cow."

if the basic direction of the objective is "entry," then one type of
strategic program will fit logically with this, namely "initial entry."
If we take any of the other strategic program thrusts, such as for instance
"vertical integration" or "rationalization," none of these will blend
with the "entry" objective into a "natural strategy." If we take the
"build" basic objective, on the other hand, we see that there are three
alternative strategic program types that fit with this, namely "market
penetration," "market maintenance" and/or "vertical integration." One
or a combination of these strategic programs will form another "natural
strategy" when connected with the "build" objective. Similarly, from
Exhibit 5-1 we can see in an analogous manner what the other "natural
strategy" alternatives might be.

From the vertical and horizontal axes of Exhibit 5-1 we can determine
the nature of the adaptation and integration capabilities of the various
"natural strategies." For instance, a "natural strategy" of "build by
means of market penetration" will imply a relatively high adaptive but
low integrative thrust. A "harvest by means of efficiency improvement"
strategy, on the other hand, will imply a low adaptive but high integrative
emphasis. Given that we therefore can classify all the "natural strategies" in terms of adaptation/integration capabilities it follows that
specific sets of these strategies will provide the most adequate response
to different SBU planning needs. Specifically for a SBU which is in a
"question-mark" strategic position and thus is facing relatively high
adaptive needs but relatively low integrative needs, we have indicated
that two alternative "natural strategies" might be relevant. These are
located inside the area marked I and are either "entry by means of initial market development" or "build by means of market penetration." Let
us similarly also consider what would be the "natural strategies" that

would fulfill the needs of a SBU in a "star" position. These have been encircled within the area marked II on Exhibit 5-1. We see that there are four potential strategies that would have the appropriate capabilities in this instance, namely to "build by means of market position mainte-nance," "build by means of vertical integration," "hold by means of mar-ket position maintenance" or "hold by means of vertical integration." In a similar fashion we can see from Exhibit 5-1 what will be the "natu-ral strategies" for SBUs in the "cash cow" or "dog" positions.

We can also see from Exhibit 5-1 what will be the "natural strat-egies" of primary relevance to consider for a management which intends to evolve its SBU from a "question-mark" to a "star" position. This is indicated by arrow A on Exhibit 5-1. Clearly the basic direction of the strategies to follow in this case would be to "build." In line with this the arrow falls within the "build" column in its entirety. We see, how-ever, that there are three "natural strategies" that are applicable in this case, namely to "build by means of market penetration," "build by means of market maintenance, and/or "build by means of vertical integra-tion." In a similar fashion we can see what would be the relevant strat-egies for a SBU which is to be evolved from "star" to "cash cow," see arrow B on Exhibit 5-1.

From the discussion of the preceeding paragraphs we see that the "checklist" approach to the design of a planning system module for the SBU level leads to the development of a tool which helps the SBU mana-gers to develop strategies relevant focus so as to respond to the needs for planning identified. We shall now introduce the third class of "checklist" factors which shall be intended as helping devices to sharpen the strategic capabilities even further. As indicated, the third class of factors relate to how to reinforce an appropriate competitive niche for a SBU.

We shall indicate four different competitive mode factors for reinforcing a competitive niche.

1) _Image_. A product's image might be developed to reinforce the
strategic direction, and probably with particular effect in
the "build" and to some extent in the "hold" strategic direction
cases.

11) _Quality_. The quality of the product that the SBU is offering
might be developed to reinforce a strategy. This is probably
particularly relevant for reinforcing a "build" or a "hold"
strategic momentum.

111) _Service_. This factor, which also includes reliance of delivery,
might be particularly useful to employ for a SBU which is following a "hold" general strategic direction, and is attempting
to further strengthen its competitive niche.

1v) _Price_. While the price of a product has to be competitive for
the SBU to stay in business at all, it will probably be for
SBUs which follow a general "hold" or "harvest" direction that
price might be a useful tool to be actively used to strengthen
one's competitive niche position.

We have attempted to order these factors in terms of how they might
reinforce an adaptive or an integrative thrust. The first factor, "image,"
for instance, seems particularly appropriate for strengthening a highly
adaptive strategic thrust, such as those applying to a SBU in an "entry"
position. On the other extreme the "price" factor seems to be particularly
appropriate to ripe competitive benefits for SBUs that are following a
highly integrative strategic direction, such as "harvest." The "quality"
and "service" factors would seem to have strengthening effects above all

on general strategic thrusts that fall in-between the two examples cited,
such as applying in particular to "build" and "hold" strategic directions
respectively. Thus, we see that the competitive niche reinforcement
factors 1) - iv) seem to apply along the upper-left to bottom-right continuum indicated as the evolutionary stages of a SBU in Exhibit 5-1.
Consequently, this third set of checklist factors contributes to an even
further sharpening of the strategic capabilities in response to a SBU's
particular planning needs.

Before concluding our discussion of how to tailormake the set of
check-list factors to different situational settings in order to come up
with useful planning system components at the SBU level, let us briefly
touch on the particular problems concerning the analysis of the planning
needs and capabilities associated with the exit decisions. We have seen
that while it has been relatively easy to come up with a concept for how
to match the planning systems capabilities with the particular needs for
planning when we are dealing with SBUs which find themselves in various
ongoing operations settings, it is difficult to extend this analysis to
an exit decision setting, given that this implies the discontinuance of
this operation. In such cases the intended mode of exit will determine
the needs for planning and the corresponding planning system support.
If, for instance, management's decision is to phase out a "dog" SBU slowly
as its net funds generating capabilities dwindle, then the future business potential of the SBU will indeed be so low that it will not be well
justified to spend extensive management resources on revitalized adaptation
and/or integration directions. As such, we might state that the relevant,
opportunity-weighted needs for planning would be low, both with respect
to adaptation and integration. The planning system should reflect this
If, on the other hand, management is attempting to divest of the SBU,

then different planning needs will be created. There might be a need to
"dress up" the SBU itself, calling for the pursuance of various adaptive
and/or integrative planning moves at the SBU level. In addition, the
need to search for divestiture candidates will typically create added
adaptation planning needs at the corporate level. We shall not pursue
the issue of modifying further the approach proposed in this book for
matching needs and capabilities when it comes to SBU exit situations,
given the highly atypical anture of these situations.

We have now concluded the first part of our analysis of how to approach the task of tailormaking the design of a planning system so as
to reflect a particular situational setting's needs. Specifically we
have seen how at the business level a SBU with a particular set of planning needs might be equipped with a planning system which facilitates
the development of a focussed business strategy, relevant to the setting
of the SBU at hand. The design of the SBU-related planning system took
place by choosing guideline factors for facilitating the establishment of
the relevant basic direction as reflected by proper choice of objectives,
by choosing factors to guide the development of an appropriate strategic
programming thrust, as well as by choosing factors for developing an appropriate competitive mode to strengthen the SBU's competitive niche.
Thus, the planning system for the SBU level consists of three sets of
strategy formulation guideline parameters, for each of which we have
chosen a relatively narrow set of parameter values to reflect a given
situational setting.

It should be clear, however, that while this approach has the potential of providing a useful guidance to the development of more focussed
plans at the SBU level, the approach might easily lead to the development
of too mechanistic and static SBU plans if being used as the only planning

system tool. When integrated as part of a larger, overall corporate-wide strategic planning system, however, the SBU-level approach gains the potential of becoming highly useful. We recall from Chapter Two that our conceptual framework is heavily based on interaction, iterations and information-exchange. It is as a vehicle to sharpen this group decision-making process that the SBU planning approach becomes useful.

Let us therefore now turn to a discussion of how the overall corporate planning system itself might be tailormade so as to better reflect a particular corporate setting. The task at hand, then, will be to develop guidelines for how to tailormake the conceptual framework for corporate planning that we developed in Chapter Two to the particular needs for planning that a company faced, as seen from the corporate level. Thus, the corporate planning system's design should reflect the corporate portfolio needs for planning, as determined in Chapter Three

We shall discuss five situational design issues that relate to the corporate planning system, namely the extent to which there is a "top-down versus a bottom-up" general emphasis in the communication and interaction process, the extent to which the focus is concentrated on the earlier part versus the later parts of the planning process, the nature of the "linkages" between the various cycles of the planning process in terms of which linkages should be "tight" and which ones should be "loose;" the choice of which issues to emphasize heavily and which to treat more lightly in the performance monitoring; and, finally, the choice of management incentives to honor strategic relative to near-term performance fulfillment.

5-3. "Top-down versus bottom-up" Planning Emphasis.

Before starting disucssing any of the corporate planning systems
design tailormaking issues it is useful to recall the nature of the
situational design task that we are faced with. We recall from our discussion of the needs for planning at the corporate level in Chapter Three
that three basic types of need "imbalances" might be created as a result
of shorter-term financial as well as longer-term structural pressures on
the corporate management. One situation would indicate a high need for
facing integrative types of issues. This might dictate a corporate planning system design approach which modifies the conceptual scheme in such
ways that its integrative capabilities will be strengthened. To do this
added emphasis should probably be given to the elaboration of the strategic programming and budgeting cycles, as well as to the tie-ins between
these two cycles and the monitoring and incentives-scheme cycles. A
second corporate planning need situation, we recall, might indicate that
the pressures would primarily be of an adaptive nature   In such a case
the design of the objectives-setting cycle of the corporate planning system should be elaborated, together with the aspects of the monitoring
and incentives-scheme cycles that relate to this. The third major type
of corporate level planning need indicates that there might be both adaptive as well as integrative pressures. This would call for a strengthening
of the planning system's capabilities all across, i.e. when it comes to
both adaptation as well as integration capabilities. It should be stressed
that the task of tailormaking the design of the corporate planning system
is one of starting out with the conceptual scheme that has been outlined
in Chapter Two, i.e. viewing this as a "base case." The particular need
pressures which apply to the corporate level should then dictate how to
modify the basic scheme so that relevant planning capabilities might be

put in place to contribute towards the lessening of the pressures that
apply to the corporate level over the longer run. Each of the five
classes of design factors that shall be discussed in the next sections
are thus primarily intended for tailormaking the overall capabilities of
the corporate planning system in accordance with what we just have discussed. The five tailormaking design considerations to be discussed
are.

- the degree of "top-down" versus "bottom-up" emphasis in the planning process
- the degree of concentration on the "front end" versus the "later
  stages" of the planning process.
- the nature of linkage of each of the stages of the planning process to the monitoring and management incentive cycles.
- the emphasis of the performance monitoring process on objectives
  fulfillment versus on fulfillment of more near-term performance.
- the emphasis of the management incentives process on rewarding
  objectives fulfillment versus rewarding more near-term performance
  fulfillment.

Let us first discuss the planning system design issue which relates
to the nature of the "top-down"/"bottom-up" balance which should be attempted for various situational settings. "Top-down" and "bottom-up" are
expressions which are examples of the unfortunate tendency towards jargon
which so often tends to creep up within the field of planning; a digression
for a clarification of their meaning is consequently in order. "Top-down"
is used as a label for the initiative and direction that top management
gives to the planning process. This will of course typically be particularly associated with portfolio planning, a top-down emphasis might be
seen as almost a prerequisite in order to achieve a deliberate shift in

strategic direction through influencing the resource allocation pattern.
Such top-down emphasis will thus be manifested through the resource allocation decisions by the deliberate transfer of funds from one business
to another, as well as deliberate curtailing of some business involvements
through divestiture and/or expansion into other areas through acquisition.
The key to achieving such strategic shifts is a strong corporate level
integrative focus on the funds flow patterns within the company, so that
it will be quite explicit which will be the sources of strategic resources
and which will be the users. Through an integrative focus the corporate
management diminishes the likelihood of "surprises" and unexpected changes
in these planned shifts of its strategic resources, thereby avoiding that
the intended shift in portfolio strategy will be frustrated.

Another aspect of the top-down/bottom-up balance emphasis, however,
relates to the relative impact that senior management might have on planning within the divisions through its guidance or involvement in the
setting of assumptions and premises for divisional plans as well as
through reviews, discussions and approval of these plans. Let us see,
for instance, what effect a highly "bottom-up" orientation might have
with respect to the planning activities of the businesses, particularly
in terms of planning for the ongoing success of each of the businesses.
Such a heavy bottom up emphasis will put a strong pressure on the management of each of the businesses to show initiative in coming up with internal growth opportunities of its business and in attempting to tackle
potential threats facing its business as well. Thus, a bottom-up orientation will also be necessary to achieve effective adaptation of the business level to pursue internal growth. In this way it will be possible
for the corporate level to receive more relevant inputs about the potentials of each business. It seems that a bottom-up emphasis is likely to

yield strong business level adaptation planning dominance. On the other hand, a heavy top-down emphasis is likely to yield strong integration planning dominance at the business level, in that the businesses will have received much more specific inputs from the top with respect to where they are expected to go, and how to utilize their internal strengths.

We thus see that a relatively heavy bottom-up emphasis might tend to strengthen the organization's capabilities for internal growth through adaptive moves of its own businesses. A relatively heavy top-down emphasis, on the other hand, will have as an effect the strengthening of the integrative planning capabilities with respect to the firm's ongoing businesses. The significance of this will be that strategic resources more easily might be freed up for redeployment by the corporate level, either by means of significant shifts in emphasis among the company's internal businesses, or by means of acquisitions. This implies that the corporate level must have an adaptive planning capability to orchestrate these portfolio strategy shifts. It is important, however, to recognize that this is a different planning capability from the planning capability which will be created through the "top-down"/bottom-up" design choice. The latter is addressing the planning capabilities necessary to pursue in a desired direction with the ongoing operations. In addition a separate corporate level capability is needed when one wants to change the basic balance of the mix of the ongoing operations. Typically one might pursue to develop such a strong portfolio change adaptive capability in combination with a strong "top-down" corporate integration capability with respect to the ongoing businesses.

It may well be that neither an extreme "top-down" nor an extreme "bottom-up" approach will be appropriate in most real-life situations. A reasonable balance between the two is often more in line with what is

needed, allowing for some internally generated growth through business
level growth, as well as for facilitating some corporate level portfolio
adaptation.

5-4. Front end versus back end.

Another systems design issue which is highly related to the top-down/
bottom-up design consideration just discussed, is the degree of emphasis
on the "front" end of the planning process versus the "back" end, i.e.,
the relative amount of management time and intellectual effort "invested"
in planning activities that relate to the first planning cycle, versus
the second cycle versus the third. A relatively heavy emphasis on the
front end of the planning process will imply a relative strengthening of
the adaptive planning capabilities, with added emphasis on an assessment
of and attempt to improve the objectives and goals of the organization
and added emphasis on reexamining the basic relevance of strategic programs.
A relatively heavy emphasis on the "back" end of the process, on the other
hand, implies that the integration capabilities of the system will be
relatively strengthened because of the closer emphasis on strategic program efficiency through budget emphasis.

The choice of front end emphasis relative to back end emphasis or
vice versa will have to take place at the corporate management level as
well as at the division management level. The key is how much real intellectual effort and commitment is being put into the development of
plans proposals and plan reviews and discussions by the various management groups. One achieves neither proper adaptation nor proper integration just by committing a lot of time unless the "quality" of the time
spent is high.

It should be noted that the balance between front end versus back
end management emphasis does not need to be identical when it comes to

each of the organizational sub-units within the firm. Some SBUs or divisions, for instance, may be primarily into the "cash-cow" strategic mode, with heavy need for integration. The management of these units should spend their efforts more heavily on the back end of the process. For an SBU which is heavily into a growth mode, on the other hand, such as a "star" or a "question-mark," its management should spend relatively more efforts on the front end process issues. The corporate management may have to spend relatively more efforts interacting with the internal growth business units while spending relatively less front end efforts on the mature businesses by merely stating relatively clear top-down guidelines for these. Later in the process, however, relatively more top management efforts might be spent with the detailed strategic programs and budgets of the mature businesses. The growth businesses, on the other hand, would need relatively less corporate attention at this point, given that the objectives already chosen will more or less dictate what types of programs and budgets that need to follow.

A relatively simple, but straightforward device to influence the adaptation/integration capabilities, as we have seen, is to manipulate the effort-spending pattern that managers follow when it comes to their involvement in planning. With relatively more efforts being spent on the front-end planning activities than the back-end activities, the more relative emphasis will be given to adaptation, and vice versa One design aspect of the formal planning system which therefore is important is the lay-out of the so-called planning calendar. This spells out the deadlines for the various inputs, presentations and reviews that have to take place, according to some time sequence. A critical constraint on the lay-out design of the planning calendar must be that it sequences the various planning activities in a way which will have to be consistent with the

conceptual planning framework that we have outlined. Beyond this, however, there is typically ample flexibility to design the planning calendar
so as to give relatively clear suggestion as to the general time limits
that various line executives should   spend on the different aspects of
planning. Thus, the planning calendar is a simple and important device for
influencing the time-spending pattern. Too often, unfortuantely, the
design of the planning calendar is done without keeping sufficiently in
mind that we here have a useful source for influencing the planning capabilities. At worst, a carelessly designed planning calendar can actually
influence the planning capabilities in unintended directions.

    There will of course be conisderable flexibility in determining the
actual time-spending pattern within the relatively broad limits set by
the planning calendar. However, given the needs to have the entire set
of the businesses' planning inputs available at the corporate level in
order to make portfolio considerations, and facilitate the "closing" of
each particular planning cycle, it is also important that the planning
calendar is being strictly adhered to. Failure of one SBU to deliver
its planning input on time will delay the progress of the entire corporate planning effort.

    As in the front-end versus back-end design issue discussed in the
previous section, senior management will have a considerable impact on
this final determination of planning time-spending. If the C.E.O through
his own example shows his determination to influence the planning effort
in the way needed, then the rest of the organization will "pick up the
signal." Unfortunately, however, planning takes time and it might be
tempting for the C.E O. not to spend the time needed, particularly on
more far-reaching adaptation planning issues; the rest of the organization will be quick to cut down on its own time-spending too. Thus, what
might at first have looked like fairly insignificant concessions to

short-term pressures by the C.E.O. in terms of "postponing" planning,
might in the end have serious adverse effects for planning as a strategic
decision-making tool. The planning calendar is therefore an important
tool for the C.E.O in signaling to the rest of the organization how he
expects them to spend their involvement in planning.

5-5. Linkages between the five cycles of the planning system.

Another useful planning systems tailormaking devise is the nature
of the linkage between the five stage elements of the planning system.[4]
To consider what we mean by the "linkage" concept we may recall that
there will be a set of outputs from each of the three planning cycles
relating to the identification and narrowing down of strategic options.
One cycle's output will thus constrain the execution of the planning
function that has to be undertaken by the next stage in the planning
process. If the output from one planning stage heavily constrains the
span of the next cycle's planning activities, then we shall say that
there is "tight" linkage between the cycles. If, on the other hand, the
output of a prior planning cycle to a considerably lesser extent constrains the planning activities of the next planning cycle, then we are
dealing with a "looser" linkage. A tight linkage implies a rapid narrowing down of strategic options, a loose linkage implies a slow narrowing down Exhibit 5-2 indicates the difference between a rapid narrowing down of the alternative strategic options, i.e , a tight linkage
between the cycles (dotted line), versus a slow narrowing down of the
strategic alternatives, i.e., a loose linkage between the cycles (solid
line)

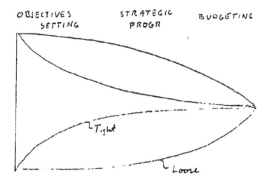

ObJECTIVES   STRATEGIC   BUDGETING
SETTING   PROGR

Tight

Loose

Exhibit 5-2. Loose vs. Tight Linkage; Slow vs Rapid Narrowing
Down of Strategic Options.[5]

We might also consider extending the linkage concept to address
how the monitoring and managerial incentives cycles relate to the three
strategic direction-setting cycles. When it comes to looking at the
monitoring cycle's relationship with the previous three cycles we shall
want to apply the term as follows. If progress towards fulfillment of
the output of a given cycle is monitored in much detail and with quite
accurate measurements being attempted, then we have tight linkage, if,
on the other hand, the monitoring efforts are done in less detail and
one is attempting to measure progress in a broader manner, then we have
loose linkage. In an analogous way we shall apply the linkage term with
respect to the incentives system: If managerial incentives and compensation are closely tied to the fulfillment of the output of a particular cycle then we have tight linkage, if, on the other hand, the compensation is more informally and loosely tied to the performance fulfillment of a given cycle, then we have loose linkage

We shall distinguish among three types of linkage. The most obvious
one, substance linkage, relates to the relationship between the substantive

output of one planning cycle which then will be the basis for the resolution of the substantive planning issues in the next planning cycle. For instance, at the corporate level it may be decided that the discretionary funds flow resources of a certain magnitude might be channelled into a new business area, primarily through internal developments within a new direction. These issues have been identified and resolved in principle during the objectives-setting cycle. Thus, important limitations will thereby have been set for what the substantive context of the subsequent strategic programs will be like.

Another type of linkage shall be labelled <u>organizational linkage</u>. This refers to the extent to which the same managers are centrally involved in the execution of or with the responsibility for planning all the way through the five planning cycles (tight linkage), versus that different managers may be having basic responsibility for the different cycles of the planning process (loose linkage). We might, for instance, have the corporate and divisional planning departments heavily involved in the execution of the objectives-setting and strategic programming cycles while the controller's department might be centrally involved with the execution of the budgeting and monitoring cycles. Further, a human resources department might be responsible for administering the management incentives cycle Thus, in this case we have a situation where three different corporate management staff groups are involved in various aspects of the planning process - what we would consider a loose organizational linkage. If, for the moment, on the other hand, we are assuming that the three groups are reporting to a common senior vice president for administration, then we would have a tighter organizational linkage If, at the extreme, one manager is directly in charge of the staff activities relating to all five cycles, then we have a tight organizational linkage.

The third type of linkage might be labeled <u>timing linkage</u>, relating
to whether or not the activities on the planning calendar follow each other
in such a rapid sequence that there are few or no vacant periods between
the activities to complete the various cycles (tight linkage), or that
there is considerable unused time between two cycles that thus is not
being spent on planning activities (loose linkage). We have already discussed the role of the planning calendar, whether we have tight or loose
timing linkage between two cycles can be seen from this.

Exhibit 5-3 shows the various linkage possibilities among the five
elements of the planning system. As we seen we have a total of eight different linkage types. First, we have two linkage types which are directly
associated with the interrelationship between the three elements that
represent the "narrowing down" procedure of the planning process. These
are labelled types 1 and 2 on Exhibit 5-3. Then we have three linkage
types associated with the interrelationship between the monitoring cycle
and each of the three cycles that perform of the narrowing down part of
planning, marked as Types 3, 4 and 5 on the exhibit. Finally, we have
three linkages types between the management compensation cycle and the
three narrowing down cycles, indicated as Types 6, 7 and 8 on Exhibit
5-3.

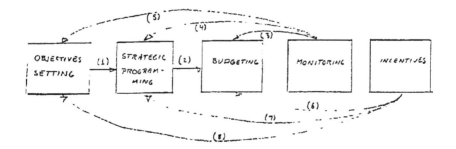

Exhibit 5-3. Linkages in the Planning Process.

Linkage Type 1   Between the objectives-setting and strategic
                  programming cycles.
Linkage Type 2   Between strategic programming and budgeting
Linkage Type 3   Between performance measurement and budgeting
Linkage Type 4   Between performance measurement and strategic
                  programming.
Linkage Type 5   Between performance measurement and objective
                  setting
Linkage Type 6   Between the management incentive scheme and
                  budgeting.
Linkage Type 7   Between the management incentive scheme and
                  strategic programming
Linkage Type 8·   Between the management incentive scheme and
                  objectives setting.

Let us now consider how the linkage concept can be utilized as a design tool to influence the adaptation and integration capabilities of planning. Let us first assume that we intend to strengthen the adaptation capabilities. Hence, we want to emphasize the "front end" objectives-setting related aspects of the overall planning effort This means that we would attempt to make linkages Types 1, 5 and 8 tight In a tight linkage of Type 1, the objectives and goals would be fairly explicitly developed, so that they provide a relatively narrow set of constraints for the strategic programming activity, i e., the objectives and goals would be followed up by the development of a set of strategic programs that correspond to the intended adaptive direction. Assuming, of course, that the objectives and goals cycle has produced an appropriate adaptive strategy, then the tight linkage of Type 1 will facilitate the follow-through with the implementation of this. Linkage Type 5 ensures that progress towards objectives and goals is being closely monitored. A tight linkage implies that we will have a careful and relatively detailed monitoring of progress towards the strategic direction towards which we intend to adapt the firm. Linkage Type 8, which connects the objectives and goals cycle with the managerial incentives cycle, should also be tight in order to emphasize the importance of encouraging managerial performance towards the longer term strategic direction necessary to achieve adaptation.

Turning now to a situation where we want to strengthen the integration capabilities of the planning system, tight linkage should be attempted for Types 2, 3 and 6 for the following reasons. Linkage Type 2 ensures that the strategic programming and budgeting fit together as one efficient activity so that the budgets merely represent more detailed developments of the strategic programs, thereby strengthening the integrative thrust. Linkage Type 3 facilitates a close monitoring of the budget fulfillment performance, again essential for efficient integration so that corrective action can be taken in time. Linkage Type 6 ties executive compensation to managerial performance's fulfillment towards budgets, underscoring the importance of integration. We have not discussed linkage Types 4 and 7 because these seem to possess a middle ground position in between adaptation and integration in terms of their emphasis. However, while they might have no extreme effect in reinforcing either adaptation or integration, they may still have important effects in strengthening a particular adaptive or integrative capability trust. For instance, by monitoring and motivating progress of the strategic programs directly as part of an attempt to strengthen integration tight linkages of Types 4 and 7 should facilitate this. An examination of the specific nature of the strategic programs, whether they are primarily adaptation-oriented or integration-oriented, would, however, be necessary in each such case.

Let us now consider the interplay between the linkage types that primarily facilitate adaptation and those that primarily facilitate integration. To some extent we might be able to strengthen adaptation further by loosening up somewhat on the linkage types associated with integration, Types 2, 3 and 6, in addition to the tightening of the adaptive linkage Types 1, 5 and 8. Conversely, if strengthened integration was the intention, then we might have implemented exactly opposite linkage tightening and loosening procedures. It is necessary in this context to remind ourselves that both adaptation and integration capabilities are needed in any planning system; what we want to do when redesigning a system is to change the relative emphasis on the one versus the other aspect of planning, but within limits. We must therefore be particularly careful not to dichotomize between adaptation and integration by overemphasizing one aspect of planning to such an extreme that the necessary absolute minimum capability level of the other dimension is being violated.

5-6. The Monitoring System

As already implied in the previous section, the monitoring system typically might play a significant role in affecting the adaptation/ integration balance of the planning capabilities of a planning system, depending on how the monitoring stage is linked to the other cycles of

the planning system. As such, we do not need to discuss this further
There are, however, additional aspects of the monitoring cycle's interplay with the rest of the system that need to be pursued. A major concern is the almost generic tendency of the monitoring cycle to often reinforce stronger integration than actually intended and thereby often to
weaken the adaptation emphasis indirectly. This is probably due in part
to the nature of the traditional role of the control system as a key tool
for managing companies that do not have a planning system. The emphasis
in such cases tends to be more focussed on more near-term, often somewhat
crisis-laden issues, rather than on systematically pursuing a long-term
strategic direction. Thus, even though a firm's senior management may
have participated wholeheartedly all the way through the implementation
of a planning process, there is always the danger that when an adverse
quarterly performance report hits the desk of the C E.O., he may overreact.
His old working habits call for his involvement in the details of sorting
out a problem, including putting heavy immediate pressure on the subordinate managers in question to ameliorate the problem, but often with
little or no regard for the underlying strategies previously decided upon.
This is, however, exactly the kind of situation in which the "homework"
done during the planning process should pay off to avoid hastily perceived
and executed reactions, which might be likely to violate the strategic
thrust agreed upon for the business. The involvement of senior management in near-term fire-fighting to a considerable extent may easily have
a somewhat overpowering effect on the subordinate managers who should be
primarily accountable for the strategic success. Erosion of discipline
in connection with reacting to monitoring outputs might thus represent a
serious problem.

The nature of superior management's involvement in interpreting and

reacting to monitoring feedback is a function of the degree and nature
of autonomy that subordinate organizational units may be enjoying. What
constitutes an appropriate level of delegation is a complex issue which
we shall only be able to touch upon in part, and briefly, in the next
paragraphs. Our general position is that the pattern of delegation, i.e.,
the degree of decentralization is an issue that should not be decided on
as an overall general policy, but should reflect the strategic issues of
the given corporation at hand. We can illustrate one aspect of this by
extending on our analysis for assessing the riskiness of a business strategy when strategic risk is seen as a function of the nature of the strategy's exposure towards the environment. We recall that we might be able
to position each environmental factor critical for the success of a particular strategy in terms of the potential degree of predictability of
this factor as well as in terms of the organization's own options for
making a discretionary response to such a particular development in the
environment. We argued that the riskiness of a strategy was high if its
links to the environment were more heavily dominated by factors that might
neither be easily predictable nor offer much response flexibility. Conversely, the strategy was dominated by more easily predictable factors
that also offer much response flexibility, the risk would be lower. Assuming for now that the environmental factors which we have identified to
be of potentially major significance in terms of their impact on a strategy generally fall within the no predictability and no response potential
category, we might presume that management would be less inclined to delegate extensive autonomy to respond, given the high risk of such a strategy. When on the other hand the riskiness is less, say when key environmental factors generally fall within the high predictability and high
response potential category, we would expect that senior management would

be more willing to delegate responsibility for evaluation of and response
to monitoring feedback. In Exhibit 5-4 we have indicated how the pattern
of delegation, autonomy in monitoring and responding, might be seen as a
function of the riskiness of a strategy. Let us stress again, however,
that environmental risk posture typically will be only one of several
factors determining patterns of delegation. Let us therefore raise two
related additional issues with respect to this.

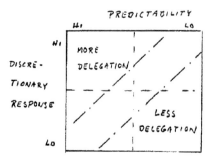

Exhibit 5-4. Influence on the Pattern of Delegation in the Monitoring and Control System Stemming from Environmental Risk Exposure.

    First, while one factor to influence the general degree of SBU au-
tonomy with respect to monitoring and discretionary authority to carry
out corrective action will be the overall pattern of environmental exposure, there might be one or a few environmental factors in a particular situation that cause a risk exposure substantially different from
the general pattern. Consequently, there might be a need for a different
mode of top management monitoring and control involvement when it comes
to such exceptional factors than what would be the general norm. For
instance, a SBU which is facing generally low risk might, however, also
be exposed to one critical environmental factor that implies high risk

exposure. Therefore, while the management of this SBU might enjoy a high degree of monitoring autonomy in general, the monitoring of this exceptional environmental factor might involve a higher degree of senior management involvement.

Secondly, in general one might expect that the _frequency_ of decisions tends to be higher and the magnitude of each single decision tends to be less when it comes to corrective response to phenomenae that fall within the lower risk segment of Exhibit 5-4. The normal mode of corrective action here will typically be relatively small incremental steps, often in sharp contrast to more fundamental changes that may have to be taken as one move towards the "bottom-right" side of the exhibit. Thus, while such major decisions might be reserved for senior management, the more incremental decisions can more easily be delegated. Again, we see the need for a tailor made monitoring and control approach.

Let us conclude this section with a caveat. It should be obvious from the discussion of the planning approach advocated here, that a strategic mode, as opposed to an ad hoc mode, of interpreting performance evidence from the monitoring cycle, does not imply that management would have to be insensitive to significant changes and fail to make decisions. It will in fact be an indication that the corporate planning system is not effective as a strategic decision-making tool if the planning exercise contributes to indecisiveness. All that is required is to make use of the "homework" already done through the planning process when interpreting monitoring feedback for making a corrective strategic decision. Environmental altertness is essential. Needless to say, the planning process will not give us the "right" answer about what the future will look like, and it will not reduce the uncertainty in our business environment. What meaningful monitoring of progress towards plans fulfillment can do is to improve a firm's ability to cope with this uncertainty, so that the risks in business policy decision-making can be contained at an acceptable level.

5-7. The Management Incentive System.

As was apparent from Section 5 of this chapter, the management incentive cycle also offers unique opportunity to influence the adaptation and/or integration capabilities of the planning system. Specifically, when we put relatively more emphasis on motivating managerial performance which contributes towards the fulfillment of objectives and goals as well as strategic programs, as opposed to more near-term budget-fulfilling behavior, then we strengthen the adaptive capabilities of the system. In order to create more goal congruence between long-term performance fulfillment and managers' individual goals, thus, there will have to be tight linkages between the objectives-setting cycle and both the monitoring and the management incentives cycles (Linkage Types 5 and 8 in Exhibit 5-3). Implicit from this follows that the monitoring cycle also must be linked to the three first cycles in an analogous way. In case we want to strengthen the integration capability, an analogous argument can be made for this, by strengthening linkage types 3 and 6.

As we have discussed the major leverage points for facilitating adaptation typically lay within the "front end" of the planning process, particularly during the objectives-setting stage. We recall that the number of executives participating during this stage typically is relatively low, basically the C.E.O and the division heads only. As progress is being made in identifying the strategic options and in narrowing these down, however, a gradual shift tends to take place towards involving more and more executives. Thus, by the time organizational consensus has been reached for next year's budget a large number of executives will have been inverted. They must have delineated for them their roles in the fulfillment of the near-term, primarily integrative, tasks by this point. The implication of this for the tailormaking of incentives schemes would be that incentives for the individual executives might be relatively more applicable when it comes to inducing adaptive behavior, while group or team incentives, on the other hand, may be relatively better suited for inducing integrative behavior. Thus, we would find relatively more individual incentives tied in with the fulfillment of objectives, and relatively more group incentives when it comes to near-term performance fulfillment.

It has been postulated that when it comes to the management of SBUs in different strategic positions distinctively separate executive styles might be appropriate. For instance, a SBU in a start-up position would benefit from more of an entrepreneurial type manager, while a SBU in the cash cow position might better be managed by a manager who has a strong aptitude towards cost efficiency and performance detail. The implication of this for the design of incentive scheme would be that manager of the former types of SBUs, with their relatively high adaptive challenges, would receive predominantly individual incentives while the managers of the latter type of SBUs would receive relatively more group incentives, given their integrative tasks.

There is however another incentives tailormaking dimension in addition to the individual versus group incentive tradeoff. This stems from the fact that the actual degree of success in the fulfillment of adaptive targets typically tends to be lower than when it comes to the success rate for the fulfillment of integrative targets. The reasons for this might be several, longer term versus shorter term time horizon, less versus more highly structured managerial tasks, the inherent degree of risk

involved, and so on. Thus, if a manager is given a certain function of
his salary as fixed, i.e. independent on his success in target fulfillment,
and another fraction of his salary as a potential bonus, dependent on
his success in achieving the targets, then it follows that the degree of
variability of the compensation of the managers who face more integrative
tasks will be less than for the managers who face more adaptive tasks.
The implication is that bonuses can have a relatively higher effect when
it comes to motivating adaptive behavior. Thus, the function of variable
to fixed compensation might be higher for SBU managers who are managing
question-marks versus for cash-cow SBU managers.

The number of factors playing a role in inducing different types of
managerial behavior is large. It is beyond the scope of this book to
discuss the many incentive schemes that have been proposed. In summary,
however, we shall stress the need to see the decisions on choice of management incentives as part of the overall strategic management system
design task. Too often are incentives being developed in a less than
adequately focussed strategic decision-making context, the result invariably being that the incentives become at odds with the strategic
decision-making thrust of the firm.

5-8. Tailormaking the Planning System to Reinforce Shifts in Strategic Direction: An Example.

Let us consider a company with annual sales of approximately $500
million. The company is active in businesses domestically and internationally within foods products, children's toys and industrial chemicals.
Diversification internationally and into toys and chemicals have been
relatively recent strategic moves, primarily through acquisitions The
company has recently reorganized from what was predominantly a functional

to a divisional structure. Presently there are four groups, more than twenty divisions, and close to seventy SBUs. The recent reorganization called for a relatively higher emphasis on integration during the years just after the reorganization, so that transitional inefficiencies associated with the institutionalization of the new management tasks might more rapidly be sorted out.

The C.E O has adopted a philosophy of high performance aspirations, including, as noted, with heavy emphasis on growth through acquisitions. The diversity of the company is therefore rapidly increasing. One consequence is that senior management can less and less comfortably know all the businesses with some reasonable degree of detail. Senior management thus increasingly realizes that it will have to rely on the more specialized business knowledge of the various division managements. The portfolio/business "division of labor" with respect to the strategic planning tasks of the firm in achieving its strategy of growth has thus only recently been proliferated.

In terms of the planning needs facing the company at this point in time the continued acquisition drive might call for strengthening of the adaptive planning capabilities at corporate in order to identify, analyze and consummate acquisitions. Also, however, a strengthening of the integrative planning capabilities when it comes to the ongoing operations of the company seems in order, so that dysfunctional efficiency problems due to the recent reorganization might be overcome. This would apply to the existing operations at the divisional/business level, but would also be reflected in the corporate management's mode of interaction with the divisions We thus seem to have a different adaptation/integration balance need for the planning at the corporate level and at the divisional level, in the former it seems appropriate with relatively more emphasis on adaptation, while in the latter, relatively more emphasis on integration should probably the case. Of course, if at some later stage the emphasis on internal growth through the existing businesses is to be stressed, then the adaptation capabilities at the division/business level need to be strengthened relatively more at that time.

The key implication in terms of designing the linkages of the planning system, however, is that the needs for linkage might be _different_ at various organizational levels - relative tight linkages of Types 1, 5 and 8 (see Exhibit 5-3) at _corporate_ level, relatively tight linkages of Types 2, 3 and 6 at divisional levels. Also, we see that changes in linkage patterns might be appropriate at a particular level at a given point in time when the adaptive/integrative balance of a subset of organizational subunits might change. In instances of this kind linkage changes across the entire organization would be inappropriate - a potential loosening of linkage Types 2, 3 and 6 and tightening of linkage Types 1, 5 and 8 would be appropriate for thoses divisions at the business level where more internal growth gradually would be pursued.

The increased diversity of the company provides the company's senior management with the opportunity to develop a corporate "portfolio" strategy that emphasizes the balance between net funds generating business divisions and funds "consuming" growth divisions, as we have seen. This added diversity calls for increased realism with respect to adaptation needs and capabilities among the high growth divisions, so that the corporate level can be fully aware of each business' growth potentials. Also, there is a need for increased integration needs and capability realism, particularly among the net funds generating divisions, to facilitate the gauging of the discretionary funds flow generation. This is necessary to estimate reinvestment capacity for going into other business segments, how dramatic a corporate portfolio strategy change that can be pursued. Thus, added diversity typically calls for increased adaptation emphasis at the corporate level so that appropriate rebalancing of the portfolio can be carried out. Given their different roles in the portfolio strategy, the nature of the linkage might be different among different divisions, as we have seen with relatively tight linkage of the Types 1, 5 and 8 among the growth divisions and relatively tight linkage of the Types 2, 3 and 6 among the net funds generating divisions. This again underscores the need to tailormake planning among divisions within a company - too inflexible formalized planning rules applied to all divisions for the company as a whole may be dysfunctional Thus, we see an added dimension to the richness of the linkage problem in that the nature of linkage probably should be expected to differ depending on the life-cycle/ competitive strength posture of the division. In general, we see that the maturity of the system, the nature of the company's growth strategy and the characteristics of its portfolio pattern of diversity are factors that typically will be of relevance in dictating the needs for tailormaking of the linkage aspects of the planning system.

As we have seen to be the normal, the emphasis on pursuing a corporate or business strategy is likely to change over time in most real-life settings, so that the relative need for adaptation versus integration changes due to strategic shifts. It will therefore be a normal procedure that the relative emphasis on the different linkage types should change. This "management" of the shifts in linkage emphasis is probably one of the most important "plan for planning" tasks. We shall pursue this further in Chapter Six. At this point, however, let us give another example which describes how such shifts actually might come about.

A 1.5 billion dollar sales company was pursuing two major groups of
businesses, one rapidly growing and high technology-based and one more
mature and within the consumer products area It went through an evolutionary pattern for planning, which in many ways gives a quite typical
illustration of the linkage type problems associated with changing the
relative balance between adaptation to more long-term environmental opportunities and/or threats and integration in order to cope with the
often somewhat more near-term internal issues of utilizing own strengths
and diminishing effects from own weaknesses.

_   The company got started within an emerging high technology business
area some three decades ago and grew rapidly based on the entrepreneurial
insight of its founder and C.E.O The company's performance was outstanding, as measured by means of its growth in sales as well as in return
on stockholders' equity (ROE) over the first two decades. However, from
year to year the performance was often quite erratic, a phenomenon which
the C.E.O. felt was a natural reflecting of his strong desire to continue
to take innovative risks, some of which would result in success, some in
failure. Through a major acquisition about a decade ago, the company
took over a well established stable consumer products company, the strategic rationale being to provide for a stabilizing effect on the corporation's cash-flow pattern. The high-technology business end of the company soon after experienced a series of serious set-backs - even with the
stable cash-flows from the other end of the company, the overall corporate
performance became so poor that both stockholder pressure as well as
pressure from the firm's bankers eventually caused a dramatic shift towards
near-term actions, so as to get costs under control and to "clean up"
obvious inefficiencies. This manifested itself within the high-technology
business by the adoption of a rigid budgeting system, cost-cutting across

the activity areas, particularly within personnel, and a dramatic reduction
of discretionary expenditures Within the consumer business end, an even
more conservative, heavily contingency-oriented plan than before, was
adopted The result of this reorientation towards more integration was a
stabilization of the performance of the company's performance, as indicated
by a more stable ROE.

The level of the more stabilized ROE trend was, however, far below the
performance levels of what comparable competing corporation seemed to be
able to come up with. Thus, in order to attempt to improve on long-term
performance prospects beyond the gains from stabilization achieved through
the integration-dominated efforts, increased emphasis was being put on allocation of resources, discretionary development expenditures and channeling
of capital to new profit lines judged to have higher longer term strategic
potentials Soon it was further felt that the more or less even approach
towards cost cutting across the company also needed to be adjusted, so
that costs were not cut as hard in instances where this would clearly
frustrate the attempts at new strategy development. This was, in fact, an
approach very close to zero-base budgeting In order for the senior management of the high-technology group to better see where to allocate discretionary resources and where to cut free resources, they more and more
felt a need for concern with longer-term priority-setting. In fact, what
was taking place was a relative increase in the adaptation emphasis. Thus,
the "pendulum" was swinging back again for the high-technology part of the
company, away from a one-sided integration emphasis and towards a more
balanced adaptation/integration planning thrust For the mature consumer
products part of the company, however, the predominantly integrative emphasis largely remained.

The major lesson from this example is that it took the top management of the company a long time and a lot of frustration and agony to realize that shifts in the company's direction might more fruitfully be pursued in a less grand-scale and sweeping way. It was neither necessary nor beneficial to encourage cross-company changes of such a magnitude. Belatedly, the senior management came to the conclusion that tailormaking of the planning system was necessary within the company itself. Not only should the linkage design be more "front-end" oriented for the part of the planning system that applied to the high-technology part of the company versus more "back-end" oriented for the consumer products part. Also, the other tailormaking design features should be applied differently. Thus, in handling the task of management of the evolution of a planning system, one must typically recognize the need to allow different parts of the organization to receive the types of planning support that <u>they</u> need, while of course also keeping an overall corporate focus in mind.

As a way of summarizing the major systems design options available for influencing the capabilities of the corporate planning system let us consider Exhibit 5-5. We recall from Chapter Three that the overall corporate planning needs generally were focussed on bringing the corporate planning system back to an equilibrium position in terms of its adaptation and integration capabilities, by redesigning the corporate planning system so as to either improving on its adaptive or the integrative capabilities, or both. We have identified a total of five systems design variables, combinations of which might be employed to facilitate such tailormade design. The choice of values for these design variables will thus depend on the direction towards which we wish to change the planning system, as indicated in the exhibit.

Corporate Planning Systems Tailormaking Design Factors	Ameliorate High Integration Pressure	Ameliorate High Adaptation Pressure
"Top-down versus Bottom-up"	Top-down	Bottom-up
"Front end versus Back end"	Back end	Front end
Linkages	To Back end	To Front end
Performance Monitoring	Of Budgets Fulfillment	Of Objectives Fulfillme[r]
Management Incentives	Tied to Budgets	Tied to Objectives

Exhibit 5-5. The Corporate Planning System's Tailormaking Design Options.

5-9. Summary.

In this chapter we have attempted to discuss approaches towards tailormaking the strategic planning system so that the capabilities of the planning system can be developed in such ways that they meet the particular needs for planning that different companies have, in accordance with the adaptive and integrative planning needs patterns identified in Chapter Three. We approached this task at different organizational levels.

For the business planning level we saw how the adaptive versus integrative tasks would call for different sets of "strategic guidelines" for the development of the desired strategic thrusts. We identified several aspects of such guidelines.

We then examined several corporate systems design factors that the planner to a greater or lesser degree might control, in order to achieve the needed adaptation/integration focus of the planning system. These tailormaking factors were: relative emphasis on "top-down" versus "bottom-up" inputs in the planning process; relative emphasis on "front end" versus "concluding end" of the strategy opportunity identification and narrowing down stages; the nature of the linkage among each of the five cycles is the planning process - "tight" versus "loose;" the pattern of executive involvement and time-spending patterns; the focus of the control systems for monitoring the "front end" versus "near term" parts of the planning process, and, finally, the relative importance on "front end" versus "near term" in the management incentives formula.

We finally gave examples of how the tailormaking emphasis might differ in relation to different organizational sub-units within the same company. We also saw an example of how changes in tailormaking emphasis might reinforce successful shifts in firms' strategic directions.

Appendix. Business Planning Capabilities of a Highly Diversified Company

In this appendix we shall describe how one company has approached the task of tailormaking its planning system at the business level to the strategic needs of various types of its businesses. The company is highly diversified, with more than 150 SBUs, but all the businesses fall into what one might characterize as the high technology field. None of the businesses fall within the consumer products area. The company has placed heavy reliance on planning as a key tool for managing a highly diversified, high growth company. Performance results in general have been very good. The present planning system has been in effect since 1971, and is considered highly useful among most of its SBU managers.

In order to develop and communicate a SBU strategy the company has identified three classes of choices that need to be resolved:

- What type of strategy to follow, choice of how to compete in terms of market share target and corresponding investment policy

- What strategic direction to attempt to follow; choice of what types of products and markets to emphasize.

- What competitive posture to pursue relative to one's major competitors, choice of pricing and quality policies.

In terms of choice of type of strategy, i.e. goals for market share as well as corresponding investment policy the company has identified five alternative modes:

a) Build - expand market share

b) Hold - maintain market share over the longer run.

c) Harvest - maintain market share in the near term, but do not invest for long term position in the market.

d) Withdraw.

e) <u>Explore</u> - (This strategy type is limited to 6 months before having
to be reclassified into one of the other types).

In terms of choices of <u>direction</u> of strategy, i e. what types of
products or services as well as what market segments to emphasize the
company has identified five different options of strategic direction.

a) <u>Base</u> - this implies that the strategic direction should be maintained as present, i.e. no change in what products and markets
to be pursued.

b) <u>Market segmentation</u> - this implies that the markets to be pursued will be segmented so that only a limited subset of particularly attractive markets will be pursued.

c) <u>Market development</u> - this implies that a broader set of markets
will be pursued, i.e. the opposite of market segmentation.

d) <u>Output differentiation</u> - this implies that a more specialized
set of products or services will be developed.

e) <u>Output development</u> - this implies that the SBU will attempt to
develop a more complete line of products or services, i.e. the
opposite of output differentiation.

The third aspect of determining a SBU's strategy is to decide on a
<u>posture</u> for what kind of competitive position to be taken relative
to the SBU's major direct competitor, when it comes to one's pricing policy
as well as one's policy with regards to the quality of one's product or
service. A SBU's own pricing policy posture is defined in a straightforward manner. whether one's own relative price is higher, averaging or
lower than the major competitor's. The product or service quality posture
is defined as an industry-specific composite measure, on the other hand.
A keen understanding of what quality value the customers are looking for
is essential in coming up with a meaningful measure of relative performance.

The leader is defined to have an average relative pricing posture as well as an average relative performance posture. A total of seven posture modes are then identified:

  a) <u>Leader</u> - The company's own SBU is the major force in the business

  b) <u>"Me too"</u> - The SBU is adopting a similar pricing and quality posture to the leader

  c) <u>"Prestige"</u> - The SBU is adopting a higher pricing policy posture than the leader, while the product quality policy posture remains more or less similar to the leader's.

  d) <u>"Performance"</u> - The SBU is pursuing a set of competitive policies which call for both taking a relatively higher price as well as providing a relatively higher quality than the major competitor.

  e) <u>"Value"</u> - The SBU offers an output with a relatively higher quality than the major competitor, while charging a price which is more or less on the same level as the competitor

  f) <u>"Price"</u> - This competitive posture implies that one's SBU is charging a relatively lower price than the major competitor, while maintaining more or less the same output quality policy as the leader.

  g) <u>"Economy"</u> - In this case the SBU adopts a competitive posture which implies both relatively lower price as well as relatively lower quality than the major competitor.

The experience of the company is that the two most profitable and thereby most advantageous postures are either a <u>leader</u> or a <u>performance competitor</u> All the other posture positions seem to require much more special efforts in order to return a reasonable profits For instance, a "me too" or a "Value" posture often imply a competitive "jungle," and the company never maintains a presence of SBUs in these postures unless one's own market share is number two or number three at a minimum If not the cost disadvantages relative to the leader usually tend to become too large A "prestige" competitive posture is typically profitable but but tends to be unstable, in that it might be difficult to be able to pass on the price to the customer for too long by "living on past good-will." An "economy" position might often also be quite exposed in the sense that one typically will be vulnerable to the leader's cost/effec-tiveness. It is quite remarkable that the "performance" posture has been found to be as profitable as the "leader" posture, in the sense that the former posture typically corresponds to a "questionmark" strategic position while the latter typically corresponds to a "star" or a "cash cow." This illustrates that carefully conceived products, positioned in emerging market niches, indeed may become highly profitable at an early stage. The opportunities for this may be particularly high in the high technology fields.

It is useful to evaluate the strategic characteristics of the port-folio of SBUs, in terms of how the frequencies of these break down for each of the strategic elements. Tables 5-1 to 5-3 illustrate this:

Table 5-1. Types of Strategies, Relative Frequencies.

Type	Relative Frequency
"Build"	42%
"Hold"	47%
"Harvest"	7%
"Withdraw"	2%
"Explore"	2%
	100%

Table 5-2. Relative Contribution to Sales and Profitability by Different
Market Share Categories.

Market Share Category	Sales Contribution	Profits Contribution
0-20%	35%	26%
20-40%	23%	24%
40-60%	30%	33%
60-80%	6%	9%
80-100%	6%	8%
	100%	100%

Table 5-3. Types of Postures, Relative Frequencies.

Type	Relative Frequency
"Leader"	51%
"Performance"	17%
"Prestige"	0%
"Value"	18%
"Me too"	10%
"Price"	4%
"Economy"	0%
	100%

Chapter Five - Footnotes

1. The contingency approach or situational design approach to the design
    of management systems underlines this chapter. Among the more
    influential articles and books that have relevance within the context
    of corporate planning are Chandler, Alfred D., Jr., Strategy and
    Structure, M I.T. Press, Cambridge, 1963, Thompson, James D , Organ-
    izations in Action, McGraw-Hill, New York, 1967, Newman, William H ,
    "Strategy and Management Structure", Journal of Business Policy,
    Winter, 1971-72, Lorsch, Jay W. and Allen, Stephen A 1II, Managing
    Diversity and Interdependence An Organizational Study of Multi-
    divisional Firms, Division of Research, Harvard Business School,
    Boston, 1973, Newstrom, John W , William E. Reif and Robert M. Monczka,
    A Contingency Approach to Management Readings, McGraw-Hill, New York,
    1975, and Lorange, Peter and Richard F. Vancil, Strategic Planning
    Systems, Prentice-Hall, Englewood Cliffs, 1977, Part Two.

2. The following articles or books address important aspects of how to
    develop situationally tailormade product-market strategies Marquis,
    Donald G., "The Anatomy of Successful Innovations", Innovation,
    November, 1969, Hofer, Charles W., "Some Preliminary Research on
    Patterns of Strategic Behavior", Academy of Management Proceedings,
    August, 1973, Arthur D. Little, Inc., "A System for Managing Diversity"
    Cambridge, 1974, Schendel, Dan E., Richard Patton and James Riggs,
    "Corporate Turnaround Strategies", Working Paper, Purdue University,
    West Lafayette, 1974, Wasson, C R., Dynamic Competitive Strategy and

Products Life Cycles, Challenge Books, St. Charles, 1974, and Hofer, Charles W., "Towards a Contingency Theory of Business Strategy", Academy of Management Journal, 1975.

3. See Lorange, Peter and Richard F. Vancil, "How to Design a Strategic Planning System", Harvard Business Review, Sept.-Oct., 1976.

4. See Shank, John K., Edward G. Niblock, and William T. Sandalls, Jr., "Balance Creativity and Practicality in Formal Planning", Harvard Business Review, Jan.-Feb., 1973, and Hobbs, J. M. and D. F. Heany, "Coupling Strategy to Operating Plans", Harvard Business Review, May-June, 1977.

5. See Lorange, Peter and Richard F. Vancil, "How to Design a Strategic Planning System", Harvard Business Review, Sept.-Oct., 1976, Exhibit 2.

6. See Ansoff, H. Igor, "Managing Surprise and Discontinuity - Strategic Response to Weak Signals", Working Paper No. 75-21, EISAM, Brussels, 1975, Newman, William H., Constructive Control, Prentice-Hall, Englewood Cliffs, 1975, Ansari, S. I., "An Integrated Approach to Control System Design", Accounting, Organizations and Society, 1977, Metcalfe, Les and Will McQuillan, "Managing Turbulence", in Nystrom, Paul C. and William H. Starbuck, (editors), Prescriptive Models of Organizations, North-Holland Publishing Co., Amsterdam, 1977, Ouchi, William G., "The Relationship Between Organizational Structure and Organizational Control", Administrative Science Quarterly, March, 1977, Vancil, Richard F., Decentralization: Managerial Ambiguity by Design,

Financial Executives Research Foundation, New York, 1978, and Ball,
Ben C. and Peter Lorange, "Managing Your Strategic Responsiveness to
the Environment", Sloan School of Management Working Paper, Cambridge,
1978.

7. See Clifford, Donald K , Jr , "Managing the Product Life Cycle", in
Mann, Roland (editor), The Art of Top Management   A McKinsey Anthology,
McGraw-Hill, New York, 1971.

CHAPTER SIX

Managing the Evolution of the Corporate Planning System

6-1. Introduction

In the previous chapter we discussed the needs for, and approaches
to, tailormaking a corporate planning system to the particular needs of
a given corporation, so that the capabilities of the planning system might
be developed in a useful direction. The particular planning needs will,
however, seldom be constant, but rather keep changing. Partly, this will
be due to changes in the firm's environment, thereby creating new strategic pressures on the corporation. Also, however, revised planning
needs might stem from changes in the strategic position within the firm
itself

In this chapter we shall first discuss how one might approach this
issue in general of how to modify the planning system so that it may stay
"current" over a longer period of time. Our approach shall be that the
task of "managing" the evolution of the planning system should be based
on an anticipation of the nature of upcoming planning needs, not a reactive process. We shall take an overall management systems point of
view on the challenge to carry out such an evolution, in that we would
want it to be consistency among the various elements of the management
system; thus, the five systems elements proposed in our conceptual scheme
need to be managed as a whole.

Having established a general framework for how to manage the evolution of the strategic planning system we are in a much better position
to approach a number of specific evolutionary issues that also need to be
tackled. Specifically, we shall be focussing on seven issues relating to
implementing this "managing of the planning system approach." These will
be how to cope with "overloading" of the planning system the issue of

how to minimize potential dysfunctionalities with the hierarchical structure of the firm, so that an added "group" level does not become a "filter"
in the strategic process, how to assess whether a particular SBU pattern
still remains reasonable or whether further delineation of organizational
boundaries between SBU's should be undertaken, the issue of how to modify
the planning system so that it might be workable within a so-called matrix
organization structure, how to cope with differences in executives' personal attitudes towards risk in planning in order to facilitate a relatively consistent pattern of risk-taking over time, the issue of how to
attempt to maintain vitality as a central ingredient of planning as the
process becomes older, and, finally, how to incorporate considerations
for particular strategic problems of planning within the multinational
corporate scene, not only as a company grows abroad,   but also as
the multinational scene becomes more complex.

6-2. The Task of Managing the Corporate Planning System over Time.

Exhibit 6-1 gives our view of the dynamic nature of the task of managing the evolution of the corporate planning system. · Let us first give
a brief general description of the nature of this management task, by
explaining the overall rationale of the process implied by the exhibit.
Subsequently we shall elaborate as needed on several aspects of the
process [1] Starting with the top box of the diagram of Exhibit 6-1, we

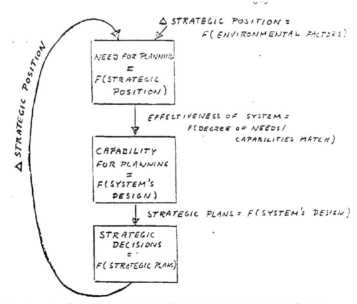

Δ STRATEGIC POSITION = F(ENVIRONMENTAL FACTORS)

NEED FOR PLANNING = F(STRATEGIC POSITION)

EFFECTIVENESS OF SYSTEM = F(DEGREE OF NEEDS/ CAPABILITIES MATCH)

CAPABILITY FOR PLANNING = F(SYSTEM's DESIGN)

STRATEGIC PLANS = F(SYSTEM's DESIGN)

STRATEGIC DECISIONS = F(STRATEGIC PLANS)

Δ STRATEGIC POSITION

Exhibit 6-1:   The Dynamic (Closed Loop) Task of Managing the Planning System.

merely state that the particular needs for planning is a function of a
specific organization's strategic position. This is in accordance with
what we discussed in Chapter Three. The planning system, then should be
designed in such a way that the capabilities built into the system as
much as possible will meet the particular needs identified. This is
exemplified by the middle box of Exhibit 6-1. The actual approach for
how to tailormake the planning system's design was outline in Chapter
Five. Strategic plans will be shaped through the planning system, leading
in turn to strategic decisions which will be functions of the strategic
plans. We have illustrated these outcomes of strategic planning as a
decision-making in the bottom box of Exhibit 6-1.

At a first glance we might conclude that our task of designing a
useful corporate planning system will have been successfully concluded at
this point, particularly if the capabilities of the system seem to reflect

the company's needs On second thought we will, however, probably realize
that the emerging strategic decisions in turn will inflict changes on the
previous strategic situational position of the firm, and thereby cause
changes in its planning needs. Environmental factors are also likely
to inflict changes on the firm's strategic position We have indicated
this on Exhibit 6-1 by means of the two arrows which respectively identify
internally and externally generated changes in the firm's strategic position. Thus, the company's planning needs will be expected to change
over time, partly because of environmental factors outside the control
of the firm, but partly also as a result of the firm's own discretionary
decisions. Revisions will consequently have to be incorporated in the
design of the planning system, in order to provide for the modified capabilities that now will be called for by the new needs. Recognizing that
we have a "closed-loop" system at hand, a more or less continuous updating
of the planning system will therefore normally be required in order for
the system to maintain its effectiveness. If not, the planning system
will contribute to its own obsolescence by "destructing" itself.

As indicated on Exhibit 6-1 we can in fact develop a concept of planning's effectiveness as a function of the degree of match between the
planning needs and the system's capabilities to meet these needs. Discussion of the preceeding paragraph should make us realize that effective
planning is a "fragile" phenomenon and might easily deteriorate unless
one almost continuously works at it.

Having now completed the discussion of the basic dynamic issues applying to the evolution of planning systems let us attempt to get a
better perception of how this evolutionary process might work in actual
life. We shall start on this by giving some examples of strategic decisions and see how they might affect the company's strategic position.

Considering a SBU, for instance, these might be strategic decisions that
relate to changing its strategic direction such as to invest to "build"
a stronger competitive strength position, alternatively to "harvest" by
allowing the competitive strength position to become weakened. For a
division we might have decisions that relate to developing new SBU's
as well as phasing out older ones. For the corporate level we might have
strategic decisions that affect a relative shift in emphasis on certain
businesses at the expense of others, in that particular businesses will
be allocated a relatively larger share of discretionary resources than
others. Other examples of portfolio level strategic decisions are acquisitions and/or divestitures. In all these instances we see that the
internal situational setting of the firm will change as a result: emphasis on new product lines -- deemphasis on others; expansion into new geographic areas, investments in new plants, entry into new businesses --
divestiture from others, and so on. Clearly, the planning needs of the
firm will change as a consequence of this. Therefore, unless the planning system is modified to reflect the evolving planning needs, the system will less and less reflect the needs dictated by the situational
setting. As already stated, the planning system will contribute to its
own destruction.

The other major element to influence the situational setting will
of course be changes in the firm's relevant environment. Some companies
are such dominating factors in their business settings that they can significantly affect their environments themselves through their own actions
Typically, however, such companies are relatively few. Most companies will
not be in a position to significantly impact on the major factors of their
environments, at least not for an extended period of time. Thus, most
firms' environments will change largely due to factors outside the control of the firm.

It is important to make a distinction between changes in the planning needs that stem from internally generated decisions versus those that
stem from external, environmental pressures. These latter factors are
particularly significant, not only because they too might impact the need
for planning, but because they are largely outside the control of the
firm's management and cannot easily be well anticipated in most cases.
This is in contrast to the effects from the firm's strategic decisions
on its own internal situational setting, which at least in theory should
lend themselves to be anticipated reasonably well, thereby facilitating
modification of the planning system in time The environmental factors
are often much harder to anticipate, and it should be a major task in
the effort to manage the planning system's evolution to pay attention to
this, so that the reactive element of the mode of evolution of the planning system might be kept to a minimum.

When analyzing the "history" of many real-life planning systems in
the light of the dynamic evolutionary model for a planning system's design
that has just been developed, we feel that many commonly found planning
"growth-pain" problems can be better understood. First, it makes us
realize that the planning system is in a sense close to a "temporary"
management system, in that it will only have applicability in a particular
form of design configuration for a relatively short period of time. Thus,
it will be important that the system relatively early should be brought
enough "up to speed" to function in such a way that it might contribute
usefully to at least certain aspects of strategic decision-making. Many
corporations, unfortunately, take such a long-term approach to the "in-
stallation" of a planning system that it might well be partly obsolete by

the time it will be supposed to be in operation. There is in fact some danger in allowing the consideration for learning during a planning start-up situation to be played up too much because of this Although there is a legitimate need for learning, little time should be wasted in emphasizing decision-making considerations as soon as possible. It might be deducted from this that a "modular" approach to planning might be useful, allowing planning to "come up to speed" within certain areas of planning at a time. In these instances there is, however, the danger that the overall consistency among the various elements of the planning system might get lost We shall discuss this in the next section.

A second evolutionary planning issue relates to finding a proper degree of rigidity and formality of the planning system. In general, a highly formalized system will be less desirable in the case of temporary systems than in the case of more permanent systems. Unfortunately, many companies tend to formalize aspects of the planning system more than necessary for the purposes at hand. As one indication of this we find some companies go through great efforts in having their planning manual printed, with fancy artwork and all. Although admittedly not necesarily a major stumbling block for proper evolution of planning, this might nevertheless easily lend a notion of permanence to the planning system that might be unfortunate Formalization and institutionalization might easily lead to the development of plans "for the sake of planning." In fact the planning approach to strategic decision-making discussed in this book would typically not be characterized by overly formalized systems routines, such as highly extrapolative, numbers-oriented "plans a la long term budgets" found in some companies

Thirdly, as for all temporary management systems, the corporate planning system needs to be associated with and managed by a specific group

of managers, who should be easily identifiable. The "manager" who is
the "prime customer" of this temporary system will be the C.E.O. above
all. As such he is also the one ultimately responsible for seeing to it
the planning system is being managed. He will of course have to draw on
a lot of staff assistance in having this task carried out. However, he
should not delegate the management of the system to a staff planner to
the extent that he loses the touch of familiarity with the system which
is necessary for him to have in order for him to judge whether the system
is fundamentally effective. Such familiarity is a requirement for building
confidence in the planning system. Also, it will open the possibility for
the C.E.O. to control the way he wants the planning system to evolve in
order for it to help reinforcing the strategic changes he is pursuing.

Let us stress as a preliminary conclusion then that it should be
clear that there typically will be a strong need for managing the evolution of a planning system, due to the fact that the situational setting,
and thereby the planning needs, will be almost constantly changing. It
is consequently useful to conisder a planning system as being analogous
to a temporary management system, stressing flexibility over formality,
requiring a relatively immediate pay-off in terms of results from the
system, and requiring the C.E.O 's involvement in the system's design in
his capacity as its key user. Beyond establishing the need for managing
the corporate planning system in general, as we have done in this section,
there will however be several critical issues that relate to how to carry
out specific aspects of this task. The rest of this chapter will in
fact be devoted to pursuing this. One critical issue in this respect is
to provide for a continued sense of consistency among the various elements
of a planning system as the system evolves over time   This topic shall

be discussed in the next section.

6-3. A Strategic Management System Point of View   Consistency

The key issue when discussing how to achieve an overall strategic management point of view for the design and implementation of the corporate planning system is the need to remind ourselves, in accordance with our conceptual scheme for planning discussed in Chapter Two, that there are _five_ cycles or sub-systems in our strategic management system, namely the objectives-setting system, the strategic programming system, the budgeting system, the monitoring system and the management incentives system. For each of these subsystems there will be the same need to tailormake it to the situational setting at hand. Needless to say, the _same_ general situational setting applies to all of these subsystems as the tailormaking base. This, therefore imposes a requirement for consistency among the subsystems in terms of their design and capabilities.[2] Exhibit 6-2 illustrates the need for a tailormade design of each of the elements of the strategic system so as to also underscore that the elements will have to be consistent with each other. The effectiveness of the strategic system, then, is a function of the matching of each system element's design to the particular needs of the situational setting. Assuming that an appropriate matching of needs and capabilities has taken place, this "automatically" implies that internal consistency in design is ensured among the elements of the strategic system.

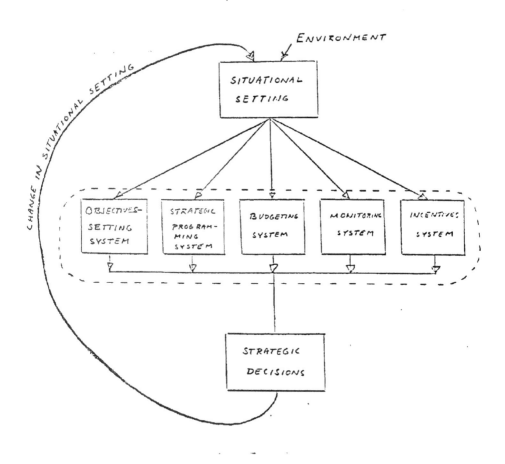

Exhibit 6-2: Tailormaking of each Element of Strategic System to Situational Setting, and with Consistency among Elements.

Unfortunately, there seem to be major problems in real life when it comes to achieving overall internal consistency within the strategic system Typically, management's attention will be on (re) designing and/or modifying one of the subsystems in particular at a given time, leaving the other systems as they are. For instance, the objectives-setting or strategic programming systems may receive major attention, becoming strengthened to reflect the given setting as of today The budgeting system, however, may not receive the same critical scrutinizing to assess whether modifications are needed here too. This sytem may have remained essentially the same over quite some time, having been tailormade to a situational setting long since changed. In such a case the budgeting system will not provide capabilities in accordance with the emerging needs and in line with what would be necessary to follow through with the benefits from the strengthening of the prior cycles. Hence, we might have a potentially serious element of inconsistency. For exactly analogous reasons to those above we might also have a management control system nad/or a management incentive system which does not reflect the present situational setting.

A typical reason for the situation with serious inconsistencies between the various systems elements might stem from the fact that the subsystems did not get installed at the same time, as already alluded The "age distribution" between the subsystems might even be so wide that the systems might reflect entirely different prevailing management settings. Another potentially prominent source of inconsistency might stem from the not uncommon fact that different management groups traditionaly may have been responsible for the management of the different subsystems, thereby not necessarily perceiving the same needs from the situational setting For instance, a corporate planning group might be responsible for the objectives-setting and strategic programming, a corporate controller's department may have major responsibility for the budgeting and monitoring stages, and a human development function might be primarily involved in the managerial incentives stage. These executives will approach the assessment of what will be the needs for system support based on their own frame of reference. Thus, unless coordinated, management responsibility segmentation, and potentially also an element of parochialism, might be likely to hamper the attempt to achieve overall consistency. Finally, it might be that management of a corporation is simply not sufficiently aware of the issue of potential subsystems inconsistency, possibly above all because they are not used to seeing the five various elements as part of one overall strategic system

What might be the consequences of lack of consistency among the elements within the strategic system? We have seen in our discussion of how an integrated overall strategic management system is supposed to work, that each element of this system is dependent on the others. Thus, the benefits as a strategic decision-making tool will not accrue unless there is a "tight logical linkage" among all the elemtns. There will be several specific consequences when such lack of overall consistency is the case, and we shall discuss each of these.

First, let us consider the consistency requirements among the objectives-setting, strategic programming and budgeting stages. If, for instance, the strategic programming activity is not done within the context of the focus set by the objectives-setting stage the effect will probably be that a much larger number of strategic program alternatives will have to be prepared and analyzed in order to come up with enough viable choices to be able to select a reasonably "good" package of strategic programs No prior focus will have been provided to limit the

areas of search for strategic programs, the most likely consequence being
that a lot of additional efforts will have to be spent on the strategic
programming aspects. This is of course normally not desirable at all,
given the heavy workload involved in preparing and analyzing a typical
strategic program A weakening of the quality of the strategic programs
to be followed is likely to result, given that management attention almost
inevitably will nave to be more thinly spread on a larger set of less
focussed strategic programs. Thus, inconsistency between the stages is
likely to lead to both a heavier workload and an "inflated quality" of
the managerial inputs into the process. Similarly, with inconsistencies
between the strategic programming and the budgeting stages there will be
an analogous set of problems, in tnat the strategic options will not have
been substantially narrowed down beforehand. We recall that the lack of
narrowing down problem was also discussed in Chapter Two, and illustrated
in Exhibit 2-4.

It should be noted that tne necessary narrowing down prior to the
budgeting process might be hampered even if we have a reasonable consistency between the stages of the process, namely as we have touched upon
several times, because of management's lack of willingness to execute the
necessary decision-making discipline during the earlier stages. Unless
management is willing to resolve which strategic choice to make among
several potential directions to go, i e., committing to a particular set
of objectives, it will be next to impossible to carry out a more focused
strategic programming Similarly, unless decisions are made concerning
which of the many potential programs to follow tne budgeting process will
be out of focus.

Returning to anotner related issue that was already touched upon
during our discussion relating to Exhibit 2-4 of Chapter Two, we see

that the distribution of the time spent on planning through the year also is critical, in terms of regulating the workload for reaching the "best possible" strategic direction. With gradual narrowing down of strategic options we see that the workload can be spread out reasonably well over the year. However, without the prior narrowing down management will be faced with the same broad set of strategic optins during the much shorter budgeting period This probably means an extraordinary peak workload for the management team, again likely to result in reduced quality of the strategic decision-making efforts Given that such a workload problem typically will create a natural and probably necessary tendency towards more ad hoc elimination of certain options. Thus, there will be a real danger that the "truncated" narrowing down that takes place will be out of line with what would seem to be optimal had the full range of relevant options been considered. A less than ideal final action program package might be the result

We have argued that lack of consistency between the first three stages of the strategic process might lead to serious distortions in the strategic decision-making due to dysfunctional effects on the narrowing down process. Beyond the arguments in this respect discussed in the previous paragraphs a more fundamental underlying problem will be that the adaptation/integration balance in the strategic decision-making process might get distorted. This, however, can more easily be discussed in connection with inconsistencies relating to the interrelationships with the remaining two factors, the monitoring and the management incentives components. We shall pursue this in the next paragraphs.

Considering problems that might arise due to inconsistencies between the monitoring function and the other stages, a basic requirement will be that the monitoring system must be structured in such a way that it actually

is able to monitor progress towards the fulfillment of the outputs for
each of the three previous cycles. When the monitoring system is out of
focus, the serious consequence might be that neither adaptive nor
integrative corrective actions will be taken. Beyond this fairly obvious
requirement that the monitoring system must adequately reflect the
variables it is supposed to monitor, there often exists a more subtle
source of inconsistency, due to the fact that the balance in the monitoring
efforts in terms of the relative emphasis on the monitoring of objectives
versus monitoring of strategic programs versus monitoring of budgets might
not fully reflect the intended adaptation/integration balance for the first
three cycles. Specifically, most monitoring systems tend to put almost
exclusive emphasis on the near-term budget-fulfillment monitoring. Some
also put emphasis on monitoring progress towards the fulfillment of longer
term strategic programs, while relatively few monitoring attempts tend to
be focused on the long-term objectives-setting fulfillment. Thus, there
might easily develop a bias towards the near-term and towards integration.
At least two factors tend to reinforce this bias. First, the fulfillment
of the budget might receive so much attention that management might become
too much geared towards integration problems. Secondly, the lack of
monitoring of the predominantly environmental issues associated with the
relevance of one's longer-term objectives might cause a further lessening
of the sensitivity towards adaptation-related issues.

Turning now to the management incentives phase, this system is maybe
the element which is most often substantially inconsistent with the other
parts of the strategic management system. For instance, a management
incentive system might consist of monetary elements, such as executive

bonus and stock option plans   Most often, however, these are <u>not</u>
specifically tied to each executive's performance in contributing towards
the fulfillment of the output targets of each of the three cycles.   In
cases where explicit rules exist for the distribution of bonuses and
options, these typically tend to heavily reinforce short-term budget-
fulfillment performance.   For non-monetary incentives too, there often
seems to be a lack of explicit tie-in with strategic performance.   For
instance, the promotion and reassignment of key executives is often not
systematically tied to explicit performance assessments.

The problem of the incentives system often not being explicitly
coordinated with the other elements of the strategic system may frequently
be reinforced due to the common practice of assigning the task of
administering the management incentives system to staff executives who
are not directly involved in the planning and control functions.   Even
more critically, these executives may typically not be very familiar with
the major strategic decision-making shifts that line management may be
attempting   Thus, by segmenting staff tasks without being explicitly
concerned about the system consistency issue, a company might not only
be denying itself the benefit from this source of reinforcement of the
strategic direction   Even worse, however, this might create pressures
that might specifically counteract the implementation of the strategic
plans.

It should be pointed out that to bring the incentives system in
line with the other elements of the strategic system will depend critically
on the availability of relevant information about strategic performance
fulfillment   Thus, the intention to emphasize both long-term and short-term

strategic behavior with the management incentives presupposes that the monitoring system has been developed sufficiently to allow for a useful assessment of managers' longer-term performance. Without this being realistic the basis for credibility would be gone

Given the importance of consistency among the elements of the strategic system, let us discuss a few approaches that management might take in facilitating that this might take place. A first step might be to carry out what might be labeled a consistency audit at certain regular intervals, say, every third or fourth year. The task here simply should be to determine whether each of the elements of the strategic system broadly seems to reflect basically the same common situational setting This consistency audit approach is useful because it explicitly creates an opportunity to focus on this overall consistency issue in large, complex organizations where the lack of an overall common viewpoint seems to be the normal.

A second approach for ameliorating inconsistency is to recognize the management task consequence of the overall integrated strategic approach, namely that it will be one task to manage the design and evolution of this system. Consequently, there should be one manager who has the overall responsibility for this task; this leadership will facilitate cooperation between, say, a corporate planner's department, a controller's department and a human resources department Given the critical importance of the strategic system as a vehicle for achieving strategic direction in a large, complex organization, it is necessary that the executive responsible for the overall system is sufficiently close to senior management to be able to internalize a realistic sense of direction as to the strategic direction

that the company will go   Thus, it will not suffice with a "remote" staff
executive in this position, such a person would not have the strategic
insight to be able to line up the strategic system behind the desired
strategic thrust

Thirdly, and probably equally important, by recognizing the complexity
of the task of managing the strategic system so that it stays relevant and
remains internally consistent, a company should develop a "plan for planning"
This should consist of an explicitly spelled out conceptual framework for
the system, identifying its components, how these are intended to function,
and their interrelationships   One example of a useful conceptual scheme is
the one proposed in Chapter Two of this book and summarized in Exhibit 2-6
Having put down, communicated and internalized such a conceptual framework
for planning, this should serve as a "benchmark" for any development and
improvement of aspects of the system, ensuring that improvements and
modifications will contribute in a common direction. Elsewise it might
easily be that energy gets wasted in developing aspects of a planning system
that eventually will not fit into a common scheme   Thus, an integral part
of the plan for planning will be to specify when to change what in the
planning system, and how as well as why such changes might be deemed
desirable. Without such an explicit plan for planning it is very common
that the planning system is subjected to shifts in direction, modifications
and additions that do not consolidate into a common strategic decision-
making thrust. Little by little the system might become so diffuse,
illogical and complicated that its effectiveness as a management tool is
diminished. A common feeling among the users in such situations is that
the strategic planning system has been "overloaded", an issue we shall
discuss in more detail in the next section

6-4. Overloading of the Strategic System

A common problem in the design, implementation and evolution of a corporate planning system is that there might be a tendency for such system to "mushroom", i.e., gradually become so complex, time-consuming and difficult to use that we might talk about a work-overload phenomenon on the part of the systems users. In such instances it will be exceedingly hard and time-consuming for the various line managers to prepare the necessary inputs to the various aspects of the planning documents, to participate in planning meetings, to report progress on strategic programs that they manage, and so on That this additional heavy work load and pressure may lead to a feeling of frustration is quite natural, especially when the not too uncommon perception develops among line managers that they seem to be preparing plans that are more useful to their superiors than to themselves. Further, they feel that the planning activities take time and energy away from the day-to-day business activities Given the typically quite formidable workload for a line manager, it should therefore be an essential requirement that the planning system be both conceptually sound as well as carefully implemented, so that there should be no wasteful activities Whatever requests on line managers' time, in the forms of additional meetings, new data inputs reports, extra follow-up studies, etc , that are not absolutely essential for the fulfillment of the strategic planning task should thus be eliminated.

Unfortunately, there seems to be a tendency for all management systems to keep growing as a function of time. In the previous section we discussed an aspect of this, namely that the system might thereby become less internally consistent and less logically focused over the years. Another real problem, however, is that while management tends to add new routines to the planning system, usually in response to a particular pressure (e.g., energy shortage leading to a need for the planning of energy sourcing, conversion and conservation, that soaring labor wages, social costs, and legislative labor restrictions will trigger off a corporate response in the form of a manpower plan; and so on). While such ad hoc additions might be necessary and legitimate given the circumstances, there is, however, not a similar tendency to delete those parts of the system that might have become less relevant; hence, tne system tends to grow

We snall offer three suggestions for dealing with this problem of keeping the line's time commitment within reasonable limits. The first will be to adopt a "zero-base" audit approach to the planning system. At certain time intervals, typically not too frequently, an internal audit might attempt to raise the question of _why_ each particular element of the planning system is justified, in terms of the benefits it yields relative to the "costs" of expending management time on executing this aspect of the system Essentially, the planning system will be examined as if it were redesigned from scratch It would be natural to perform this type of audit in conjunction with the consistency audit discussed in the previous section

A second approach would be to rely on ad hoc one-shot studies of various kinds to a larger extent in the planning process. For instance, a special purpose task force might be created to come up with strategies for how to approach each of the particular issues, such as energy or labor, referred to before. In line with this, it should more commonly be explicitly stated that certain of tne planning procedures that are being introduced are intended to have a very specific and definite lifetime only

There is another ad hoc aspect of planning which involves senior
management primarily, and has proven to be very useful in several companies.
Through this, senior management will get involved in an in-depth strategic
audit review of a few of the operating units each year, outside of the
recurrent reviews and interactions that are part of the annual strategic
planning cycle This might give senior management an opportunity to learn
more intimately about the subtleties of the particular business, and giving
the managers of the particular business an opportunity to better understand
senior management's point of view as well. In-depth strategic interchanges
of this kind might strengthen senior management's insight and feel for the
business, this being essential for giving the recurring annual planning
process corporate reviews a sense of realism rather than aloofness Also
it might open up a more free-flowing communication within the organizational
hierarchy. Incidents such as a corporate management visit to an operating
unit, for example, in connection with an in-depth strategic review, might
have dramatic effects on creating a sense of shared commitment to the
company's strategic direction.

This more in-depth business understanding on behalf of senior
management seems essential not only for efficient planning, in that it will
pave the way for a more focused, quicker, corporate-divisional pattern of
interaction for narrowing down strategic options, but more importantly, it
may provide an impetus for _better_ strategic decisions itself. As already
stated, the corporate-divisional planning review process might too often
deteriorate into an overly formalistic, intellectually unchallenging
exercise, overly financially dominated. Instead of pursuing planning with
such an unreal touch, a sound senior management business understanding and

judgment will better enable the corporate and the business strategic levels to work together to improve the strategic decisions The recognition of the need for appropriately chosen and insightful top management contribution to the business plans is essential; no top-down contribution should create a feeling of animosity at the business level, "artificial" or "shallow" top-down contribution might more than most factors lead to the deterioration of the effectiveness of the planning process

A final suggestion for keeping the overloading pressure of planning under control relates to the relationship between the corporate planning staff and the line It is not entirely uncommon to see corporate planning staffs that cannot resist the temptation to project themselves as "whiz-kids" relative to the line, or even developing an image of slight disrespect for the line. The danger of them becoming a little too close to planning might easily lead them to underestimate the time implications for the line of various suggestions they may come up with for planning systems "improvements" An effective corporate planning staff, on the other hand, will typically put much emphasis on working closely with the line to establish a line-staff consensus about the need to add to or to modify the planning system It might be advisable, for instance, to try out the format of any systems additions or modifications on a pilot subset of the divisions. It should be a definite requirement that a particular planning procedure has been thoroughly 'debugged" By actively involving the line in the implementation of modifications in the planning process, the likelihood of the line's acceptance of the modifications will be increased Equally important, the quality of the changes themselves will probably improve.

Despite the arguments in the preceding paragraphs to keep the time involvement required by both top management and the line within reasonable proportions, it should be strongly emphasized that good plans do not materialize without hard work. The considerable time and commitment needed in order to make planning work is a real requirement. Given that it is so time-consuming it follows that planning will probably not survive unless it provides sufficient useful input to the strategic decision-making process. It is through demonstrating a positive contribution that the planning tool can convince management (senior management in particular) that this is a worthwhile way of spending time and energy

Despite the requirement for extensive taxing of management's time and involvement, it turns out that strategic planning when properly functioning, actually might lead to savings in time spent by management on other management tasks within the firm For instance senior management's time spent on budget deviation analysis and short-term firefighting might actually be freed up somewhat. As a result of the planning efforts, a much more solid basis for the strategic direction of the firm now will exist Thus, a larger degree of delegation can typically take place when it comes to making decisions with regard to corrective actions for the implementation of strategies and programs. We recall from our discussion in Chapter Five, however, that extreme care must be exercised so that delegation is not carried out in such a way that senior management might miss critical signals when significant changes are taking place, thereby hampering senior management's involvement in executing a change in strategy. Despite this, having made "the investment" of involving a larger group of management in internalizing the strategic direction through planning should provide senior management with a real opportunity to free up time on ad hoc firefighting

Another potential area for senior management time-saving can be found
when it comes to involvement in the review and approval of capital budgeting
proposals and expenditure proposals. With prior planning and thereby an
established strategic direction as stated in a set of objectives and goals
as well as a focused set of strategic programs, the nature of the investment
proposal and expenditure review and approval process should get significantly
changed Given that investments and expenditures of course are parts of
particular strategic programs, the major review and approval effort from a
resource allocation viewpoint should take place at the stage when scrutinizing
the strategic programs Any investment of expenditure proposal should
therefore be evaluated in this context, i.e , as ways for fine-tuning the
particular strategic programs and for checking their continued validity.
Capital budgeting and expenditure budgeting should consequently not be seen
as a primary decision-making tool for strategic resource allocations as
such. Given the considerable senior management time involvement that the
traditional capital budgeting and expenditure review and approval procedures
typically require, planning might provide an opportunity to free up
considerable time Even more important than the actual time saved, however,
is probably senior management's increased sense of feeling that it can
exercise a more direct influence on the firm's direction through the
resource allocation process, as opposed to post-facto "rubber-stamping" of
investments and expenditure proposals.

Let us finally discuss an approach for keeping a potentially very
time-consuming aspect of planning within more reasonable proportions.
This relates to suggesting a more efficient way of carrying out the analysis
and evaluation of new product leads as well as potential acquisition leads.

It seems clear that a firm should strive to receive a substantially larger
number of such leads than what ends up being actually decided to positively
go ahead with. Such an "intentional overflowing" of alternatives will
probably be a significant factor for increasing "the batting average" of
the acquisitions and/or new product leads that turn out to be successful.
In terms of reducing potential "overloading" of the planning system, then,
it seems beneficial to develop a sequential approach for screening of new
product or acquisition proposals, with each proposal having to pass
increasingly more elaborate analyses. A minimum of time might thereby be
expended on proposals that are quite likely to be less attractive. Instead,
efforts might be concentrated on analyzing the more serious contenders.

Previously, we have discussed approaches for evaluating R&D projects
as part of a business strategy as well as for developing a business
attractiveness and planning need index for developing their fits as part of
a corporate portfolio. As we recall, these approaches were based on
developing overall measures of attractiveness based on a composite number
of relevant underlying factors. A similar type of approach might be
developed as the basis for a screening procedure for acquisitions. When
developing such an index-based sequential screening procedure it is important
to attempt to find the "right" level of discrimination. If the pre-screening
is too heavy then one runs the risk of turning down proposals that in
retrospect proved very advantageous. If, on the other hand, the pre-
screening is too light, then the problem of overloading in the planning
system will still remain.

There are two additional sets of issues that should be taken into
consideration when instituting pre-screening procedures for the handling of

new product and/or acquisition proposals in planning First, it should be kept in mind that the specialized know-how relevant for the evaluation of a new product and/or acquisition typically will have to be collected from a relatively wide number of executives within the firm, staff specialists, various functional representatives, line managers providing a business strategy perspective and senior management providing a portfolio strategy viewpoint. It is therefore essential that a formalized and standard information/interaction flow gets established among the relevant executives, so that it becomes clear who should evaluate what particular aspects of a new product and/or acquisition proposal as well as when this should be done. Such unambiguous assignment of tasks provides accountability in the time saving that this is likely to lead to on the analysis -- another critical factor for another reason too in that in many instances the ability to make a quick decision will be paramount in order not to lose an opportunity

In concluding our discussion on the problems of "overloading" the planning system stemming from the exceedingly significant calls for time and efforts that planning might require the potential dysfunctional effects on strategic decision-making might indeed be serious However, it will of course be other factors in addition to "overloading" that might lead to a diminishing of the decision-making focus. With the large number of executives that typically will be involved in aspects of strategic analysis, the pressure to decide might easily become diffused Planning might easily be synonymous with the situation where it will be nobody's responsibility to pull the snythesis together and make a decision' In the next section we shall discuss how the decision-making focus of planning might become blurred due to elements of inappropriateness in the ways the organizational subunits interact through the planning process What we shall identify as

"strategic filters" shall hamper in the development and implementation
of strategic direction.

.5   Strategic Filters

In turning to the task of discussing what we might call "strategic
filters" as another aspect of managing the evolution of the planning system,
let us first elaborate on what we mean with this phenomenon A strategic
filter is a feature of the organizational structure, formal or informal,
that will potentially jeopardize the development and implementation of
appropriate strategic direction, either when it comes to a corporate
portfolio strategy, divisional business strategies and (inter-) functional
strategic programs As we shall see in this section, the organization's
structure is of major importance as a facilitator of, or, alternatively,
as a barrier to the achievement of a strategic direction to be pursued.
It will of course normally be outside the scope of the corporate planning
system to be responsible for overseeing an organization's structure Thus,
it will normally not be an available planning systems design factor to
suggest organizational changes in order to improve the climate for strategic
management. However, the corporate planners should be aware of potential
dysfunctions associated with the organizational structure so that the
planning system itself may be modified to ameliorate such effects on the
strategic focus As we shall see, it is often possible to modify the
planning system as an alternative to undertaking large, expensive and
disruptive organizational changes to improve a company's strategic focus.
We feel that this opens up for a potentially very important benefit from
our approach to managing the evolution of the planning system By allowing
an updated planning system to remain a reasonably current strategic tool

for coping with the firm's challenges and threats at given points in time, the organization will already have a tool in place to respond to these emerging challenges without having to reorganize the firm's structure. To respond by means of reorganization is of course very expensive, given disruptions in communication- and learning-patterns. If the use of an evolving planning system can cut down somewhat on the need for and frequency of major reorganizations, the benefits from this might in fact put the costs of planning into a new perspective.[3]

It seems reasonable, therefore, that corporate planning should adopt the premise that one major purpose of planning is to keep reorganizations to a minimum. Thus, extreme care should be taken by the corporate planning executives to resist the temptation to suggest sweeping reorganizations as a "way out" whenever the planning system is not functioning as they wish Tendencies in this direction are however not entirely uncommon. This might indicate not only that the corporate planning executives might be unrealistic in terms of what should be the range of variables under their direction, but, more importantly, that the corporate planners have failed to realize that a major benefit from planning will be to keep major reorganizations at a reasonable level.

Let us now turn to a discussion of three specific types of strategic filters. These tend to be surprisingly common, and we shall discuss approaches both for identifying and for modifying the planning system to be able to cope with these.

The first type of strategic filter can occasionally be identified in connection with the so-called group organization structure commonly found in larger and more complex organizations The group structure typically might emerge in one of two alternative ways One scenario takes place when a company grows in size and/or diversity and as a result the workload from day-to-day operation pressures might gradually become so great for the C.E.O. that he feels unable to adequately interact directly with all of the businesses. A response to this is to create sets of groups of businesses, so that each of the businesses may report to one out of several group vice presidents. The group management will in turn report to the chief executive. This type of group structure formation is thus created primarily to ameliorate pressures on the C E.O. The roles of the group vice presidents should therefore be seen as extensions of the corporate office of the chief executive, i.e., as ones of sharing in the responsibility to develop a portfolio strategy As an alternative scenario, groups might also be created when a company expands within the same business through several channels, such as acquiring and/or developing several organizational entities that will tend to operate essentially within the same business. One example of this was a highly diversified corporation which acquired several companies that were in the pleasure boat business Instead of integrating these into one division, none the least of corporate management's concerns being to avoid disruptions in the operations of each of the organizations by breaking up the well established patterns of functional interaction, a pleasure boat group was formed. In this case a group structure might be seen as a vehicle to coordinate the related organizations' efforts within essentially the same business area The group structure here becomes the vehicle for still being able to develop a coordinated business strategy. In the instances of both types of group structures, however, these might create problems for maintaining a proper strategic direction

of the planning process. In the next paragraphs we shall discuss these
issues in turn

When a number of business divisions report to a group executive who
in turn reports to the corporate chief executive, it seems at the outset
as if we might have created a four-level strategic hierarchy, adding the
task of developing strategic direction for the groups. In many companies
this is in fact exactly what is happening, the group vice president
attempts to develop a "mini-" portfolio strategy for his sub-group of
businesses with a strategic balance between the businesses that this
implies. The group plan which is in turn presented to the corporate
management will, together with the inputs based on the other groups serve
as the basis for the development of a corporate portfolio strategy. The
corporate strategy, then, will have as a primary focus the balance among
the groups By decomposing the portfolio strategizing task into two
stages, which is implied by the scenario just described, there will be a
possibility that serious dysfunctions may occur First, each of the group
executives will see only a subset of strategic business opportunities and
threats, namely those that occur within his own business sphere There
may consequently be better strategic opportunities in other parts of the
firm that conceivably may not receive sufficient resources. For instance,
suppose that one of the groups is fairly heavily dominated by relatively
funds-rich, slow growth "cash-cow" type businesses. Instead of planning
to make these funds available for a high-growth business with proven
potential within another group, there will be a natural tendency within
the group plan to attempt to develop its own growth opportunities, which
of course will be largely unproven On the other hand, a group which faces

the prospects of ample growth opportunities may have to scale down its plans in its pursuit of this due to lack of funds. Thus, the tendency towards at least some balancing of the groups' portfolios will imply that the corporate level no longer can see the entire pattern of business opportunities and/or threats when attempting to determine where to allocate its resources. The company does of course still consist of the same portfolio of businesses However, senior managers may no longer see it, only a set of filtered group aggregates This obstruction of the corporate level's opportunity to deal with the relevant portfolio pattern is a serious obstacle to meaningful corporate portfolio strategy development and to the top-down strategic resource allocation task

A related potential dysfunction from this source will be that the risk-taking of the firm might become unintentionally biased, typically leading to overly conservative strategic choices. This might come about as follows· In developing his group "sub-portfolio" plan, a group vice president might evaluate his risk-taking "capacity" for going after a particular business opportunity as being contingent upon the "safety" levels that he feels he can count on from the other businesses in his portfolio. If he already has involved his group in a few risky but potentially high-payoff ventures he may therefore be reluctant to take on another project. Another group within the corporation may however have been looking "with magnifying glass" for opportunities of this kind given a relatively low overall risk exposure of that group The development of group plans might easily lead to a tendency for each of the group managements to consider a risk in the context of its own smaller base, and not in the larger context of the risk-taking capability of the company as a whole. Thus, overly strong conservatism might creep into the strategizing picture This is indeed a serious problem in case, in that it might prevent a large firm from going after and capitalizing on one of its major advantages over smaller firms, namely that it typically will be in a position where it might better be able to take on a few selected projects with high risks and correspondingly high return potentials. A clear corporate portfolio strategy focus is essential for achieving this The group structure thus might add to the difficult problem of how to address the issue of risk-handling in planning

A common notion in the planning efforts of many companies is that risky alternatives are "bad" and that a major purpose of planning should be to contribute towards the reduction of risks. A more relevant approach would probably be that selected high risks/high return opportunities should be sought out so that the overall risk-taking potential of the firm can be taken advantage of. To pursue this, however, it is important to establish an explicit view of the actual as well as desired overall risk-exposure of the firm. If not, it might easily be led into a too conservative path, such as just described. Alternatively, the firm might be unaware of major environmental changes which may actually lead to increased risk exposure Socio-political developments, for instance, may have such effects We shall, however, not pursue the issue of how to conduct such a risk assessment for a corporation further here, but will return to this later in this chapter when we discuss managers' personal risk preference patterns as strategic filters. Instead, let us discuss approaches for modifying the planning system to cope with the other planning dysfunction issues raised in connection with the group structure

As a starting point let us ask ourselves two questions Which aspects of the planning capabilities might potentially be weakened the most by decomposing the portfolio strategizing task into two levels? Further, we need to question for each given situation which of the two major rationales for the introduction of the group level will be the closest to actuality The answers to these two questions might provide us with a useful way of delineating the role of the groups in the planning process in such ways that several of the "filter" problems can be minimized In terms of the first question it seems to be a particularly serious consequence that corporate management might be obstructed in its view of the overall, relevant portfolio picture, particularly when it comes to the <u>adaptation</u> planning task. Successful portfolio adaptation depends, as we know, on a realistic overall corporate portfolio outlook above all. As such it will be essential to take the complete picture of opportunities, threats, risks and environmental exposures stemming jointly from all the businesses into account

Turning now to the second question of what was the nature of the groups' roles, we recall that in one instance the groups were instituted in order to relieve corporate management from some of the day-to-day burden of coping with an exceedingly wide spectrum of businesses. Thus, the planning task transferred to the groups in connection with this decentralization move would fall primarily within the <u>integration</u> area. What therefore emerges is the following The chief executive and his close corporate level aides should elect to be dealing directly with the businesses when it comes to the objectives-setting stage, where the major impact of adaptation planning on the portfolio should be centered Each respective group executive should of course also take part in this interaction, but primarily as advisors to

the C.E O   Thus, when it comes to objectives-setting they should act as
"team-mates" of the C.E O , being "extensions" of the corporate office.
Corporate management should make every effort to stress that there exists
no group structure when it comes to establishing a corporate portfolio
objective consisting of a set of business objectives as the "building
blocks"   There is no short cut around the need for the C E.O. to be
directly involved in the development of the adaptive adjustments of the
overall corporate portfolio, despite the fact that this might require a
significant fraction of the C.E O 's time.

In certain instances one might of course expect that some group vice
presidents might resist this redefinition of their roles and view it as if
their importance is being down-played. However, when it comes to the
planning for the implementation of this strategic picture, the group
managements should play a much more active role. The development of
strategic programs as well as the subsequent development of budgets should
be coordinated by the group executives   This predominantly integrative
planning task can usefully be carried out within the group structure
The corporate level C.E O. will of course be involved in these planning
stages too, in reviewing the groups' strategic program suggestions as well
as their budgets   Considerable time will be freed up for the C E O by
relying on the group management structure in the strategic planning process
in this way   At the same time the potential dysfunction of weakening the
portfolio adaptation capability associated with a two-level portfolio
planning approach can be controlled.

Let us now turn to a discussion of the planning implications associated
with the facing of the second type of group structure creation, namely when

several divisions which de facto are in more or less the same business form
one group   In this case the group level is analogous to what we have been
calling a division throughout this book from a strategic decision-making
viewpoint. Consequently, the group management should take a major
responsibility for the development of one coordinated business strategy
involving all the related "divisions". If, on the other hand, each of the
"divisions" would be left with the task of developing its independent
business strategies on their own, we might expect to come up with plans
that in all likelihood will be suboptimal, particularly when it comes to
the execution of consolidation attractiveness-related integration planning
needs. In cases like this, the planning system might be an excellent
vehicle for initiating coordination and consolidation moves among the
various organizational entities so that one consistent strategic business
direction can be followed, but without at the same time giving the units
too heavy an impression that they are losing their semi-autonomous entity.
Too often in instances like this, however, a "group" business strategy is
not pushed heavily enough, the result being that consolidation synergy
benefits from one overall business strategy are being lost

     Let us now turn to another potential strategic filter source frequently
associated with the evolution of planning. Effective planning might be
hampered when the SBU pattern of the firm is "illogical". A logical SBU
pattern from a corporate planning viewpoint should facilitate the identification of logical strategies   Thus, a SBU should ideally be independent of
other SBU's to the extent that this might facilitate the development and
implementation of a business strategy in a reasonably straightforward
manner. Often, however, a SBU's strategy is being exposed to major effects

from actions taken within the strategic domain of other SBU's. We shall
discuss how to modify the planning system to ameliorate some of the
problems stemming from this in the next section.

6-6   Illogical SBU Patterns

The major problem with respect to the structure of the SBU pattern,
seen from a planning systems design and evolution point of view, is that
the organizational structure might not bear a high enough degree of
resemblance to what might be the most logical pattern to reinforce the
strategies that the businesses are being intended to plan for As an
example, we might have a situation with a rapid evolution of a firm's
product mix, implying that some businesses that might have been added
within a particular SBU might become increasingly important, while some
of the traditional businesses might have become relatively insignificant.
A particular SBU might even gradually start to resemble a smaller scale
portfolio of businesses on its own, merely through an evolutionary process
of "mushrooming" However, while the natural tendency for most companies
to evolve in terms of emphasis on different businesses over time might be
quite profound, a corresponding modification of the formal organizational
structure might often be lagging and hence not adequately reflect where
the actual business strategizing pressures are

The structural fit might be further diffused when extensive acquisitio
activities are going on. It usually will be impossible then from a practic
point of view to dismantle acquired firms structurally and to "parcel out"
its businesses in terms of fit with already existing SBU's, new SBU's only
being established in cases where the parent is not already actively involve

Needless to say, reasons such as concern for employee morale, hesitancy to "downgrade" certain strong managers, desire to reach for "know-how" reserves, and reluctance to cause too significant immediate changes in the funds flow patterns associated with an acquired company all might call for advancing carefully with the task of integrating newly acquired SBU's into its existing formal organizational structure. The consequence again, however, would tend to imply an increased discrepancy between where the de facto business strategizing pressures and challenges are and the formal organization pattern

Why is it that from a planning systems point of view that we propose that the formal organizational structure should reflect the actual business strategizing activities in a relatively accurate manner? Several studies have shown that strategy and structure seem to be highly interrelated. Not only is the organizational structure itself an essential management tool for facilitating the development and implementation of strategic direction. Even more, it seems as if companies with an explicit match between its intended strategies and organizational structure tend to perform better than companies with less of a match. This problem probably comes about in particular because of lack of being able to take advantage of the information-handling capabilities associated with a formal organizational structure. The pattern of communication is normally largely influenced through the formal organizational structure, thus, if this pattern reflects the strategic communication needs it might be a definite advantage when it comes to the implementation of strategic planning If not, the planning system itself will have to "open up" the relevant channels of communication.

Another planning implementation problem might arise when the
organization structure is illogical in terms of managerial practicality.
This might happen when the sizes of the various SBU's in a corporate
portfolio are dramatically different   For instance, when a company is
faced with a portfolio strategizing setting where there is one or a few
large SBU's which contribute the bulk of the firm's sales and revenues,
and, in addition, a relatively large number of smaller SBU's, we still
are faced with the requirement that large and small SBU's should both be
reporting to the C E.O. in a "proper" portfolio mode   In practice, however,
this might lead to the potential problem that the firm's critical businesses
might receive relatively too little and inadequate top-down input in its
strategizing process, given that the C.E.O easily might be "distracted"
by the strategic problems of the smaller businesses. This might be a
dilemma, given that in narrow business strategizing sense a smaller
business too might justifiably need much top-down interface   Managerial
time and efforts spent on a business' strategy formulation and implementation
will not be a proportionate function of business size   A small business in
a strategic turn-around situation might require as much or even more of top
management's time than a larger business   However, the cognitive capability
of the C.E.O. and his closest associates might be a bottleneck when it comes
to dealing with these small SBU's while still giving the larger SBU's the
required attention, given the overall importance of the latter for the
overall corporate success.

We shall discuss two approaches for modifying the design of the formal
planning system so as to ameliorate the often serious problems stemming
from strategic overlaps or excessive size differentials among businesses,

as reflected in the formal organizational structure   First, it should be underscored that any acquisition program should be carried out with this issue being kept in mind   For instance, it might thereby make sense to establish a minimum size for what acquisition candidates to look for   In line with this, some of the smaller businesses presently in a firm's portfolio might be divested, largely for reasons of lack of corporate management capacity. This is in fact not an uncommon reason for larger companies' divestiture of small and peripheral SBU's that do not fit closely with the other business activities of the firm. Another approach would be to put several of the smaller SBU's together into one "miscellaneous" ventures group   This relieves the C.E.O. from the pressure of dealing directly with all the small SBU's in the planning process. However, as discussed in the previous section, this introduces another potential strategic filter, namely that the overall corporate-wide business portfolio pattern might get blurred. There may, however, be instances in which senior management judges the benefits from ameliorating the first type of strategic bottleneck to outweigh the disadvantages of creating the second type of strategic filter. Some companies do not fully recognize, however, that they are creating a new strategic filter through a "miscellaneous ventures" group approach. One major oil company, for instance, recognized that the sheer size of its major business lines -- the integrated oil operations, as well as coal and chemicals businesses -- would make it difficult to create the momentum for developing new businesses beyond mere extensions of what the company's traditional businesses   Lack of enough senior management attention would be one inevitable problem in case of diversification   The strong business style or culture within the traditional business areas of operation

as well as the existence of ample attractive investment opportunities
within the traditional businesses might further complicate a viable
diversification drive   To ameliorate this, the oil company established
a separate new venture organization as a very autonomous group. This
"miscellaneous ventures" group soon resembled a small conglomerate in many
respects   This new venture group approach proved to be quite successful
in that it gave the company a vehicle for acquiring new venture companies
as well as pursuing further new internal developments. Given the small
size of the group's activities relative to the major business activities
of the firm, it would have represented a close to unacceptable toll on
senior management's attention to treat the new units in the planning process
on a basis more similar to the larger elements of the company's portfolio
The potential problem of overall portfolio pattern distortion has not been
serious thus far, due to the small size of the new activities   However,
as the new venture group grows the issue of portfolio strategy distortion
should be of increasing concern and the autonomous mode of planning within
the "miniconglomerate" may have to be modified

The approach for ameliorating the potential strategic filter problem
associated with strategically illogical formal organization structure
patterns, stemming from evolution of the business mix shift, mergers and/or
SBU size distribution imbalances, should partly be to create an alertness
towards the need for undertaking a reasonable degree of reorganization
changes focused specifically on containing this problem. The other part
of the amelioration approach, then, will be to specifically focus the design
and/or evolutionary improvement on meeting these problem areas, so that
communication channels might be opened to develop relevant strategies

despite of mismatch with the formal organization structure, so that
recently merged units can be gradually brought into the "mainstream"
strategic planning system of the firm, and so that a reasonable
differentiation can be reached when it comes to expending management
resources on the planning of larger, highly critical business elements
versus on smaller, less important businesses. Thus, to restate our
position, a certain amount of reorganization of the formal organizational
structure might be necessary even before the introduction of a tailormade
corporate planning attempt. However, it will be a delicate judgement to
decide how extensive a reorganization would be appropriate   On the one
hand, as previously explained that the scope of the organizational changes
must be kept under control. On the other hand, if the formalized
organizational structure is not modified to make it somewhat easier to
have it reflect the actual strategic tasks, there might not be enough of
a formal framework to build on in order to implement a meaningful planning
system.

    We thus need to reconcile the lines of argument given with respect to
reorganizing to ameliorate an illogical SBU structure as a potential
strategic filter with our basic premise that a strategic planning system
which is managed in an evolutionary sense should facilitate a reduction
in the frequency and degree of reorganizations. In this respect we shall
find it useful to introduce a distinction between two types of reorganization
steps. On the one hand, initial reorganization steps may have to be taken
in order to bring the organizational structure into such a shape that it
allows for a minimum degree of communality with the de facto strategic
tasks. This should be done before strategic planning is pursued, and
should be seen as a one-shot reorganization undertaking. On the other hand,
a firm's management is faced with the strategic responses that the company
has to make towards its environmental opportunities and/or threats on a more

or less ongoing basis. The corporate planning system should plan an important role in facilitating the responses to these pressures. Planning should be a major vehicle for allowing adjustments or shifts in the organization's capability to meet changing needs. For instance, when the environment seems to open up for a more aggressive pursuit of new opportunities, the need for adaptation will increase relatively The planning system should be modified accordingly in order to respond to these needs Similarly, in cases where the economic climate seems to become harder, a relative shift towards more integration needs is taking place Again, the planning system's capabilities should be modified in this direction as a consequence.

Traditionally, a major element of organizational response to major environmental pressures, as the ones just indicated in the previous paragraph, has been through reorganization. For instance, in order to strengthen adaptation a company might "break off" from traditional divisions several lines of business that it considers particularly promising in terms of growth opportunities and create new divisions out of these Alternatively, to strengthen integration it might attempt to combine divisions to improve efficiency by eliminating duplication of, say, sales forces and/or distribution channels. Typically, however, given the relatively static nature of an organizational structure, to adjust this way would mean a pattern of "stop and go" in terms of impacts on the organization Thus, this mode of response offers relatively little opportunity to carry our incremental responses on a more continuous basis With the emergence of an evolving planning system, this will represent a complementary tool to the more far-sweeping organization response route Therefore, we should have much less need for, and be much more careful about initiating large and usually disruptive reorganizations. However, although the frequency of using reorganization as a response to environmental changes thereby should go down, this should of course not eliminate entirely the need for

To reiterate, our approach to reorganization emphasizes its role of assisting managers to carry out their changing strategic tasks We do not advocate reorganization as a tool for enhancing a more "logical" organizational structure per se   On the contrary, we have emphasized that longer time commitment to a particular strategy is difficult to enhance in an atmosphere of frequent organizational changes and rapid job rotations Also, an attempt to strive at an overly "pure" and narrow business strategy focus, arrived at for instance by reorganizing so that all the business activities of each SBU fall into one segment of the business life cycle, does not necessarily produce the intended improved strategic performance By not being forced to manage the SBU as a somewhat broader composite of growing and maturing elements, managers might develop unrealistic attitudes Managers in complex strategic settings need the assistance of the strategic planning system in order to see clearly this strategic position and how to facilitate implementation of strategic progress in this setting. Thus, the organizational units should be able to maintain a reasonable strategic focus through planning, reducing the need for major reorganizations by not over-emphasizing "logical" business units. Unfortunately there seems to have been a tendency in many organizations to ecuate reorganization and job rotation with improved strategic performance capability, exactly the opposite is probably true. An improvement of each manager's understanding of how to operationalize strategic management is essential, and the pressure should be on management to facilitate this through the strategic planning process, not through reorganizations.

6-7. Modifying the Planning System to the Matrix Organizational Structure

Let us briefly touch upon a third area of potential organization structure-related strategic filters in connection with the evolution of effective strategic planning systems.[4] This might occur in connection with the emergence of a so-called matrix-structure found in some organizations. This type of structure has come about primarily as a response to the need to recognize interdependence among many SBU's. For instance, when it comes to businesses which share a common (typically process-oriented) intermediary production facility, but which might be sold through distinctive marketing channels, a matrix structure might be very useful, so that duplication of production efforts can be avoided. Certain specialty chemcial corporations might fall into this category Similarly, when it comes to high-technology companies that are active in several businesses but based on predominantly the same technological ase, a matrix structure might be applicable. The implication of such a structure is that an explicit set of interdependencies will be created between, say, a functional activity and several business-related activities. Thus, a pattern of "two bosses" gets created. A manufacturing manager, for instance, will not only be responsible to the vice president of manufacturing but also to the manager of the particular business for whom he attempts to provide his manufacturing output. We can identify three classes of dimensions that might be interrelated in a matrix mode, the business dimension, the geographical area dimension and the functional dimension. We shall not discuss now to design and implement such a matrix structure here, nor assess its appropriateness This is amply analyzed elsewhere and is outside the scope of this book. Our concerns relate to the potential strategic filter problems stemming from a matrix structure as part of the planning process.

While a matrix structure certainly will have important benefits in selected applications there are also several problems that might arise when it comes to planning in such a structure. For instance, it may become increasingly time-consuming and burdensome to carry out the interactions among management which typically are so essential to the development of good plans. Given the dual lines of responsibility patterns that predominate both the frequency and size of planning meetings might increase. A more fundamental problem might easily arise when it comes to carrying out major adaptation-related strategic moves within a structure of this kind. It should be kept in mind that an underlying rationale for developing a matrix structure is the sharing of selected functions and facilities, thereby diminishing duplications of efforts. Thus, a integration-oriented concern is being adhered to. Partly because of the "tilting of the balance" towards integraiton, but partly also due to the fact that extensive compromising between relatively larger number of executives when it comes to setting strategic direction, as we will have in a matrix structure, might make it difficult to come up with major deviations from the present direction, it is often difficult for matrix structures to adapt effectively.

One way of at least partially amelioratirg this problem is to develop a somewhat clearer "division of labor" among the matrix dimensions in the planning process. If we for instance consider a manufacturer of specialty chemicals the matrix organization might consist of a set of two dimensions, the functional activities such as manufacturing, marketing, distribution and R & D, as well as the business activities which will consist of several distinctive product-markets. When it comes to carrying out the planning tasks withing this particular matrix structure we might ask which of the two dimensions that primarily would be chartered with

the integrative planning tasks, and which dimension that would primarily
have to be focussed on adaptation We see that in this example the
functions can be characterized as the integrative dimension while the
business can be seen as the adaptive dimension While the efficiency
of this matrix organization's strategy primarily depends on how well the
functions are performing their tasks, the strategic effectiveness will
above all depend on how successful the organization will be in developing
and maintaining a good business product mix. We thus see that there is
a natural division of labor between the two matrix dimensions, one being
focussed primarily on the adaptation planning tasks, the other on integration planning tasks.

It often tends to be the case that we can identify such a duality in
the planning tasks among the dimensions in a matrix organization. It is
however necessary to determine which will be the adaptive and which will
be the integrative dimension in each case - we do not necessarily have a
similar division of labor to the example in the previous paragraph in
other settings A facilitating factor in the task of isolating the adaptive and integrative dimensions stems from the fact that matrix structures
with more than two dimensions tend to be rare. In most cases a combination
of only two of the functional, business or area dimensions tends to be at
work Thus, we can normally work with one adaptive and one integrative
dimension

We recall that the objectives-setting stage would play a major role
in facilitating the development of an adaptive strategy Conversely, the
budgeting stage tends to be central in the development of the integrative
aspects of a strategy This, however, implies that the adaptive dimension and the managers associated with this should be centrally involved

during the objectives-setting stage. The integrative dimensions's involvement at this stage should be more limited, merely focussing on providing awareness of potential internal constraints that might make a
particular adaptive move difficult The managers associated with the
integrative dimension would however be centrally involved in the budgeting
stage, while the adaptive dimension managers would not. In Exhibit 6-3
we have indicated the shift in involvement in the planning process between
the two matrix dimensions.

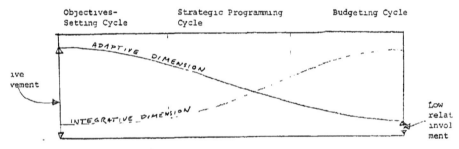

Exhibit 6-3   Shifts in Matrix Dimensions Involvement in the Planning Process

We see that the "division of labor" among an adaptive and an integrative dimension might provide a useful vehicle for the simplification of
the task of carrying out planning within a matrix structure. The pattern
of interaction among managers can be simplified and the frequencey and size
of planning meetings might be reduced. Only when it comes to the development of strategic programs during cycle two will there be a full-fledged
simultaneous involvement from both matrix dimensions. While in all likelihood this will continue to be a difficult and "messy" step in the planning process, the degree of ambiguity and complexity will at least have
been reduced when it comes to the objectives-setting and budgeting stages.
Not only will this be important in order to trim the managerial burden of

planning down to reasonable proportions. Even more importantly, the adaptive as well as integrative points of focus will have been strengthened. Thereby a potentially serious barrier to strategic planning within matrix organizations will have been reduced.

6-8. Planning Considerations in Multinational Corporations.

Needless to say the field of multinational management is exceptionally broad and complicated. It would not only require an inordinately extensive discussion to cover all substantive aspects of this field that might potentially be relevant for strategic decision-making in the multinational firm, but this would clearly also be outside the scope of this book given that our concern centers around the design of the planning process, not the development of a multinational strategy. What does fall within the scope of this book, however, is to identify a few critical aspects of the multinational planning setting that typically need to be considered in order to avoid barriers to the implementation of a planning process in such companies. The basic conceptual scheme for planning applies to the multinational firm as well. A few planning process capability issues need to be considered in addition.[5]

Specifically, we shall deal with four critical planning issues unique to the multinational firm. Two of these apply most directly to the portfolio level planning task. These are the increasing lack of flexibility in making significant changes in a company's portfolio due to socio-political pressures outside the control of the firm, as well as the added complexities in developing the funds transfer aspect of a portfolio plan due to currency valuation changes. At the business planning level a third factor to take into account are potential patterns of differences when it comes to the attractiveness and competitive strength for a business

from one country to another. A final factor relates to the "culture" of
strategic management in different countries, where several of the five
stages of the planning process play a more limited role than presumed in
the discussion thus far in this book, particularly when it comes to the
roles of incentives, monitoring and budgeting. We shall discuss each
four classes of factors in turn.

There seems to be a growing sense of increasing lack of flexibility
among many multinational corporations when it comes to significantly being
able to modify their portfolios. The problem is not only that to invest
to increase the activity level in a particular country may become increasingly difficult in that there will typically be a growing number of "strings
attached" to such investments. Potentially much more serious is the lack
of flexibility to scale down or change the nature of a particular operation.
In most of the European countries as well as in such developing countries
as Venezuela, for instance, tough labor laws make it next to impossible
to fire part of the work force, thereby making it very difficult to scale
down unprofitable operations. Political and union pressures also tend to
stifle such relatively near-term portfolio adjustments Leaving the substantive strategic choice question aside as to whether it in fact will be
attractive to have a presence in a particular country at all, the problem
calls for several modifications of the planning process. First, even
more elaborate prior analyses would probably have to be carried out before
sources are committed to a particular project. This is a self-evident
consequence of the lack of flexibility of subsequent corrective response
possibilities, and does not need to be elaborated on further. Secondly,
senior management must pay particularly careful attention to signs of potential deterioration of any of its businesses located in such restrictive
national settings. If a weakening of the position of a particular business

is detected a long-term strategic program of internal development for re-positioning this business should be initiated. By vigorously pursuing structural change challenges before they become a crisis the changes will be so much higher that a problem situation can be avoided. Given that internally generated development projects for restructuring typically take long time before reaching fruition it is important to start as early as possible. One European company has extended on this philosophy in its planning efforts by having developed alternative usage pattern plans for each of its physical facilities and also pursuing an extensive central de-velopment program intended for coming up with new activity options that might be transferred to existing plants in need for restructuring. A third area of modification in the corporate planning approach will be the increased emphasis of direct corporate-government contact typically taking place to resolve major structural portfolio issues. The government typ-ically plays a more active role in many countries in influencing corpo-rations' portfolio choices. It is important to attempt to provide as accurate government inputs as possible into the portfolio plans of com-panies in such settings.

A second major area of modification of the planning system of a multinational corporation will be with respect to the planning of the portfolio level funds flow patterns, so that potential disturbances due to currency fluctuations can be dealt with. Again, it will be beyond the scope of this book to discuss issues of international finance. What however seems important is that a company explicitly addresses the riskiness of its planned international funds flow transfers Given that an added element of uncertainty thereby has been added to the portfolio strategizing task one would expect that planning routines should get developed for pro-viding the appropriate information with respect to this aspect of the

strategy as well as for the monitoring of this factor. Too often there
tends to be too much of a split between strategic planning and multinational financial planning. The latter is clearly an important element
of the former. The planning system should be designed to recognize this.
Failure of achieving such a coordinated view might lead to several dysfunctionalities. The potentially most serious one is probably a tendency
to become too risk prone in both portfolio strategy decision-making as well
as in international finance strategizing. The reason for this is that
by seeing each of the strategic tasks in isolation there might be a tendency to overlook the constraints imposed from the other strategy, thereby
being led to believe that one might have more flexibility to maneuver to
ameliorate a problem than actually will be the case.

Turning now to the business level planning task within the multinational corporation there are several important issues that should be
addressed. One issue relates to how to measure business attractiveness
in situations where several countries are involved. We recall from our
discussion in Chapter Three that a product's position on its life-cycle
might be expected to be a major determinant of the growth rate that it
will enjoy at a given point in time and thereby determining the attractiveness of the business. It has however been demonstrated that a product's life-cycle position might differ from country to country, depending
on the level of economic development that each country enjoy, on the
country of origin of a product's original introduction, as well as on
other factors. For instance, a product which has reached a highly mature
stage in the US may still enjoy limited growth in Europe and Japan, while
enjoying strong growth in various developing countries Thus, the attractiveness of the product will differ from country to country, and so will
the adaptive planning needs - from relatively low adaptive planning

needs - from relatively low adaptive needs in the mature US market to highly adaptive needs in the developing economies.

There might also be important differences from country to country when it comes to a company's competitive strength. We recall again from our discussion in Chapter Three that market share typically will be a major determinant of competitive strength, and that experience curve advantages are likely to benefit the company the most which enjoys the highest market share. We also recall, however, that experience curve advantages do not tend to come automatically, but only when actively being pursued through an interaction planning effort. An important issue which follows is to determine the extent to which and, in case, for what reasons the experience curve benefits might differ from country to country. One determinant will be the absolute size of the market. With large production runs the experience curve effect is expected to be greater. Another determinant which will be less obvious but potentially more important is the "slope" of the experience curve, as found with respect to the same product in different countries. A country which has a highly learning-oriented work force will have the steepest experience curve and enjoy the biggest benefit. Factors to determine this are probably not only the general educational level of the work force, but also such factors as the relevance of the work forces training and experience, degree of absenteeism, attitude towards innovations, flexibility of labor laws and union attitudes, and so on. Further, cross-country experience curve comparisons would probably have to be done on an industry-specific basis, in that for some industries other countries might lead. Finally, a country's comparative experience curve advantage might change over time relative to other countries.

We see that a complex and challenging worldwide business strategizing picture emerges from the global business attractiveness-competitive strength analysis   This will probably have significant consequences for where to invest in new production capacity, where to attempt to develop new "star" positions, where one's "cash-cows" ideally should be located, as well as from which areas to withdraw   Only through a careful planning need-capability analysis, in line with what we have outlined in this book, might we expect that planning can be carried out in a relevant manner to facilitate a worldwide business strategy across a large number of countries.

Let us finally turn to our fourth major consideration with regard to modifying a company's planning system to fit multinational setting. This has to do with planning's "acceptance" as a management tool in different business cultures. As several multinational corporations might testify there might be even quite strong resistance to planning within their sub-sidiaries in certain countries. While the reasons for this may be numer-ous and in fact not necessarily much different than for when it comes to resistance to planning in general, we shall point out three factors that may be more or less unique to the multinationals. The first reason for resisting planning might be due to the fact that many of the organizations in concern might have been familiar with a relatively limited number of formal management systems beforehand. Thus, exposure to planning easily becomes a "culture shock," not a meaningful evolutionary step. When, say, an organization has just started its struggle to implement budgeting, it becomes without doubt a serious problem, to be able to implement a plan-ning system on top of this. There is no definite solution to this prob-lem. The major issue will be to stress the overall logic of the planning approach, which in its simplicity should be both appealing as well as more or less reconcilable with their intuitive ways of managing   Paradoxically enough it may actually turn out to be an advantage not to have been too much ingrained with an overly integration-biased budgeting culture

The second reason for resistance to planning is more fundamental. The notion of holding single executives accountable for strategic performance, and thereby not only explicitly associating him with measures of strategic progress but also incentivating him based on his individual performance might be resisted in many business cultures. This is largely due to the emphasis on group cultures and group success rather than on the individual in these business settings. To some extent too the personal income taxation system may be such that financial incentives at least mean little to an executive. There is little one can do to get around value norms like these. To be explicitly aware of them will at least save a company from problems arising from attempting to simply "transplant" their original planning system.

The final reason for resistance that we shall discuss is due to an increasing resistance to centralized decision-making in many countries The notion of lower levels' participation in a firm's strategic decision-making has been winning ground widely. We see no necessary conflict between this and following a planning approach as outlined in this book. In fact, the strong emphasis on developing interactive communication channels that is a key element of the planning approach outlined here should provide a strong impetus to more participative management. It may therefore largely be due to traditional preconceptions that planning means centralization that this kind of resistance exists.

We have now concluded our discussion of barriers to implementing planning in multinational corporations. Given that we restricted ourselves to issues related to the planning process and did not deal with key substantive strategic choices that might face the multinational, our discussion has been intentionally brief. While a broader treatment of these issues should be given elsewhere, there is one difficult problem that remains to be discussed, namely how to develop an operational measure of risk in complex corporate settings. This will be the topic of our final section of this chapter.

6-9. An Operational Measure of Risk.

We have discussed the significance of risk in several instances throughout this book. Our emphasis has been on the importance of formulating a relatively explicit assessment of one's risk exposure. This might facilitate the pursuance of strategic resource allocation in such a way that a risk-return tradeoff might be achieved. Our task in this section is to suggest ways for developing a more explicit assessment of risk exposure. It is our experience that risk-taking often might be seen as something "bad" when it comes to planning, and that minimizing risk often becomes an implicit objective of the planning effort A more appropriate apporach would be to <u>seek</u> selected relatively risky investments such that the overall risk-return posture of the firm may become in line with a firm's overall capabilities for risk-taking. By not doing this a company might be forgoing to utilize a potential competitive advantage that it elsewise would have over less resourceful companies.[6]

We shall discuss these aspects of risk-taking in this section. First, we shall suggest a method for operationalizing the assessment of risk in plans. Secondly, we shall discuss how a formal strategic planning approach actually might encourage excessive risk-averseness in large, diversified, hierarchical organizations unless risk assessment is being approached more explicitly. Thirdly, we shall briefly address the need for having management's own risk-taking preferences reflected in planning choices, what might be the "right" resource allocation choice for one decision-maker may be too risky for another

We recall that we have developed an approach for assessing a strategy's environmental exposure by attempting to identify a set of critical environmental factors that might influence a strategy's implementation, by attempting to establish to what extent and in what way each of these critical factors might be predicted, and by exploring what potential response opportunities that the firm realistically might pursue. We also saw how one's approach to monitoring and control would need to be tailored so as to reflect different predictability/response combination settings. But it also follows that different predictability/response combinations imply different exposures to risk. In seeing this let us consider Exhibit 6-4 By being able to both predict a critical environmental phenomenon rather well, as well as being in a position to have the discretionary freedom to respond so as to ameliorate an adverse effect or capitalize on an opportunity, we may conclude that the risk to a strategy by being exposed to this particular environmental factor will be relatively limited. On the other extreme, when the degree of predictability of an environmental factor is quite low and one's response potential is lacking as well, then the riskiness of the strategy will be relatively high due to the exposure to this environmental factor We have indicated different degrees of risk exposure in Exhibit 6-4 stemming from variations in the predictability/response postures.

<u>Degree of Predictability</u>

High   Low

	High	Low
High	<u>Low Risk</u>	<u>Medium Risk</u>
Low	<u>Medium Risk</u>	<u>High Risk</u>

e of
nse
tial

<u>Exhibit 6-4.</u> <u>Risk as a Function of a Strategy's Environmental Factor</u>
<u>Predictability-Response Posture.</u>

  In attempting to evaluate the riskiness of a strategy the nature of
the exposure from each critical environmental factor will have to be assessed. The manager will then subjectively have to weight the various
aspects of the risk exposure which thereby emerges. The approach should
of course be seen as a relatively crude instrument for facilitating risk-
return considerations in resource allocation. What is important, however,
is that the approach intuitively makes sense to most decision-makers. This
is often closer to their operational needs than sophisticated statistical
techniques. Also, the approach lends itself very well to inclusion in
planning documents, providing a basis for discussion of risk exposure
considerations in the planning reviews. This is of course important,
given that discussions of risk exposure elsewise easily might become unrealistic.

  Having now established a pragmatic measurement of risk assessment
let us discuss how this might be used to counteract the tendency towards
too much risk-aversion often found in large, hierarchical organizations.
Let us first, however, illustrate why risk aversion might become a problem. When an organization is considering taking a risk it will evaluate
whether it is strong enough or not to pursue this exposure. This will

largely depend on how much discretionary reserves the organization will
have at its disposal Thus, what might seem to be an overly high risk
for a manager at the SBU level, given his limited resources as well as
typically an incomplete perception of the resources of the company as a
whole, may seem a reasonable and appropriate risk to take when seen from
an overall corporate perspective. Thus, there may be a natural tendency
towards more and more risk aversion the further down one descends among
the general management levels in the organization.

There are particularly two aspects of the design of a strategic planning that might facilitate the counteraction of such "bottom-up" risk-
aversion As discussed in earlier paragraphs of this section an explicit
statement of risk exposure might facilitate the review of plans at higher
organizational levels from a risk-taking perspective. It might thereby
be upper level management to both get a more complete view of the range
of risk-return strategic alternatives that exist, not only the more conservative ones, as well as to endorse risk-taking on a selective basis.
Secondly, a portfolio strategy point of view is essential when it comes
to the corporate level's risk-return assessments Each major resource
allocation decision will have to be evaluated in the context of the nature
of the risk exposure that the firm already has been committed to Only
by taking such a corporatewide view can the firm's resource capacity to
be exposed to risks be matched with its actual risk/return commitments.

Let us now turn to the role of the individual decision-makers' preference towards risk-taking in planning We recall that an individual's
attitude towards risk is in fact part of this person's personality While
there are ways to determine executives risk preference functions we do
not feel that it will be necessary in most cases to go through such procedures. Instead, it typically suffices to develop some broad classification

of each key manager's risk-taking attitudes, both in terms of general risk-
taking philosophy as well as in terms of degree of consistency in risk-
taking over time. Over time, then, as management is becoming more experienced in making use of strategic planning as a management tool, a gradual
establishment of a risk preference image will take place for each executive. Thus, when a particular executive submits his plan corporate management will be in a position to review and evaluate this within the context of the manager's general risk-taking attitude   Corporate management
may then also become in a position to pay particular attention to the
plans of those managers who have shown to be oscillating in their risk-
taking attitudes.

This concludes our brief discussion of the handling of risk as a
potential barrier to the evolution of effective planning   Needless to
say the roles of the various executives as participants in the planning
process will have a major impact on the risk-taking patterns that actually
emerge in an organization   We shall have an opportunity to pursue this
further in Chapter Seven when we discuss in more detail the roles of
various executives in the planning process.

6-10. Summary

In this chapter we have discussed a number of important issues with
respect to managing the evolution of a strategic planning system so that
the system can remain current and effective over time. At the outset we
established the need for the task of managing the evolution of a corporate
planning system on a more or less continuous basis. The necessity of this
was due to the fact that a firm's situational setting, and thereby its
needs for planning, typically would be changing frequently, due to environmental changes as well as due to the fact that strategic decisions

taken internally might also impact the firm's own setting. Thus, the design of a planning system would be in need of frequent updating in order to facilitate the development of new planning capabilities to meet the emerging needs.

We also stressed the need to manage not only the evolution of a planning system in a narrow sense but to recognize that an important aspect of this management task will be to ensure consistency among the elements of the broader strategic management system. Given that the changing situational setting and the firm's evolving needs thus will be the basis for the tailormaking of all the subsystems it is pertinent to run a "consistency check" of how the design of the various subsystems fit together. Given that the responsibility to maintain the various subsystems typically rest with different people in the organization, say, the planning system with the corporate planner, the budgeting system with the corporate controller, and so on, it easily becomes a difficult issue to maintain an adequate cross-sectional systems consistency.

In the remaining six sections of the chapter we then discussed a number of issues that might become barriers to the implementation of effective planning systems. A common problem can be found when the planning system becomes so detailed, elaborate and inflexible that it simply represents too high a burden on line management's time and energy. We discussed several ways of cutting down such "overloading" of the planning system and also pointed out that the development of a more focussed strategic direction actually might allow senior management to free up some of the time that elsewise probably would have to be spent on near-term direction setting.

We also discussed various "strategic filters," notably a group structure's tendency to lead to sub-optimal portfolio strategies as well

as the problems that might arise in developing sound business plans when
the definition of SBU patterns was illogical. In both these cases we could
see that the organization's structure might be such that the development
and implementation of sound strategies would be hampered.

The so-called matrix organizational structure which is often found
in complex organizations creates special problems for planning, above all
because of the excessive time-involvement normally required by management
for carrying out planning in such a setting. We discussed how a "division
of labor" between an adaptive and an integrative dimension might facilitate
keeping this planning task within a more reasonable context.

Finally, we discussed how the concept of risk needed to be explicitly
dealt with in the planning process, not only in order to facilitate a
corporate-wide risk-return strategic resource allocation strategy, but
also to attain a proper degree of risk-averseness within an organization.
Finally, the risk preferences of key individual executives would have to
be taken into account when reviewing planning proposals.

Chapter Six - Footnotes

1. The following articles and books address important aspects of the task
    of managing the evolution of the strategic planning system Newman,
    William H., "Strategy and Management Structure", Journal of Business
    Policy, Winter, 1971-72, Greiner, Larry E., "Evolution and Revolution
    as Organizations Grow", Harvard Business Review, July-August, 1972,
    Ansoff, H. Igor, Rogert P Declerck and Robert L Hayes, "From Strategic
    Planning to Strategic Management," in Ansoff, H Igor, et al., (editors),
    From Strategic Planning to Strategic Management, Wiley Interscience,
    New York, 1976, Jantsch, Erich and Conrad H Waddington, (editors),
    Evolution and Consciousness Human Systems in Transition, Addison-
    Wesley, 1976, Hedberg, Bo L T , Paul C. Nystrom and William H. Starbuck,
    "Designing Organizations to Match Tomorrow", in Nystrom, Paul C and
    William H. Starbuck, (editors), Prescriptive Models of Organizations,
    North-Holland Publishing Co., Amsterdam, 1977, Malm, Allan T ,
    "Approaches to Social Systems Design," in Benningson, Lawrence H , (editor)
    Management Studies, Student litteratur, Lund (Sweden), 1977, Schein,
    Edgar H , "Increasing Organizational Effectiveness through Better
    Human Resource Planning and Development", Sloan Management Review,
    Fall, 1977, and Zaltman, Gerald and Robert T Duncan, Strategies for
    Planned Change, Wiley Interscience, New York, 1977

2. Several authors have addressed the issue of consistency among a firm's
    internal structure and external environment and/or among subsystems
    within the internal structure, see, for instance, Chandler, Alfred D., Jr

Strategy and Structure, M.I.T. Press, Cambridge, 1962, Likert, Rensis,
The Human Organization, McGraw-Hill, New York, 1967, Dalton, Gene W.,
Motivation and Control in Organizations, Richard D. Irwin, Homewood,
1971, Newman, William H., "Strategy and Management Structure", Academy
of Management Proceedings, August, 1971, Rumelt, R. P., Strategy,
Structure and Economic Performance, Division of Research, Harvard
Business School, Boston, 1974, and Kotter, John P., "An Integrative
Theory of the Behavior of Formal Organizations", Harvard Business
School Working Paper, Boston, 1976.

3. See Athanassiades, J. C., "The Distortion of Upward Communication in
    Hierarchical Organizations", Academy of Management Journal, June, 1973.

4. For the roles of a matrix organization structure as part of the
    strategic system, see Galbraith, Jay R., "Matrix Organization Design:
    How to Combine Functional and Project Forms", Business Horizons,
    Summer, 1964, Galbraith, J., Designing Complex Organizations, Addison-
    Wesley, Reading, 1973, Clelland, David I. and William R. King,
    "Organizing for Long-Range Planning", Business Horizons, August, 1974,
    Davis, Stanley M., "Two Models of Organization: Unity of Command
    Versus Balance of Power", Sloan Management Review, Fall, 1974, Goggin,
    William, "How the Multidimensional Structure Works at Dow-Corning",
    Harvard Business Review, Jan.-Feb., 1974, Davis, Stanley M. and Paul R.
    Lawrence, Matrix, Addison-Wesley, Reading, 1977, and Davis, Stanley M.
    and Paul R. Lawrence, "Problems of Matrix Organizations", Harvard
    Business Review, May-June, 1978.

5   See Schwendiman, Jonn S., "International Strategic Planning: Still
    in its Infancy", Worldwide P & I Planning, Sept.-Oct., 1971, Ringbakk,
    K A., "The Corporate Planning Life Cycle - An International Point of
    View", Long Range Planning, September, 1972, Wells, Louis T., editor,
    The Product Life Cycle and International Trade, Division of Research,
    Harvard Business School, Boston, 1972, Lorange, Peter, "La Procedure
    de Planification dans les Entreprises Multinationales," Revue Econo-
    mique et Sociale, March, 1973, Lorange, Peter, "Formal Planning in
    Multinational Corporations", Columbia Journal of World Business,
    Summer, 1973, Mazzolini, R , "European Corporate Strategies", Columbia
    Journal of World Business, Spring, 1975, Steiner, George A and
    Schollhammer, Hans, "Pitfalls in Multinational Long Range Planning",
    Long Range Planning, April, 1975, and Lorange, Peter, "A Framework
    for Strategic Planning in Multinational Corporations", Long Range
    Planning, June, 1976.

6. Drucker, Peter F., "Long-Range Planning Means Risk-Taking," in Ewing,
    David W., editor, Long Range Planning for Management, McGraw-Hill,
    New York, 1972, and Ball, Ben C and Peter Lorange, "Managing Your
    Strategic Responsiveness to the Environment", Sloan School of Manage-
    ment Working Paper, Cambridge, 1978.

CHAPTER SEVEN

Executives' Roles in Planning

7-1. Introduction

As stressed throughout this book, the planning process is a strategic decision-making process Thus, it will be only through proper involvement from real-life executives that the strategic process will work. It is therefore necessary to discuss what might be appropriate roles of various groups of executives in the planning process. There will of course never be one "best" role model that would be equally applicable to all situations Here again we shall face a contingency-approach issue For some corporate settings, with particular needs for planning, what might be appropriate role-models for executives' involvement in the planning process might be substantially different from what would constitute workable modes of involvement in other situations. Thus, although it obviously would be inappropriate to consider executives' styles as factors that can be controlled as part of the planning systems design process, we are still facing a set of issues analogous to the ones discussed in the previous three chapters, namely that the appropriateness of different managerial styles for involvement in planning will depend on the given situational setting. The purpose of this chapter, then, is to point out what might be major role choices for various executive positions and in different situational settings, so that the various executive team members can strive at self-development of appropriate styles of involvement.

As a preclude to our analysis, we shall start with a further delineation of some of the behavioral aspects of planning. First then, we shall discuss the specific role alternatives facing the C.E.O. as well as the senior line executives, such as group or division heads. Then, we shall

focus on the different potential roles that the corporate planner might

have. He might be involved with the design or improvement of the planning

process itself, on the one hand. On the other hand, he might be offering

substantive advice to the line on what strategic decisions to take as well

To conclude the chapter we shall discuss briefly the roles of the board

of directors as well as outside consultants in the planning process.

7-2   A Behavioral Process

As we have seen throughout this book, the diverse set of business

activities being pursued within a large corporation will be calling for

specialized input from those who are closest to the business At the same

time there will be a need for coordination of this potentially diverse set

of actions so that the company can move in the most favorable direction

A major purpose of a corporate planning system is to serve as a facilitator

of the setting of such a sense of common direction-setting within a diverse

organization Without some mechanism for developing a sense of direction

for a company with its many power constituencies and factions, it will be

difficult for an organization to move substantially in a desired strategic

direction Without a common focus which is at least understood and shared[1]

among the management team to some degree, a sense of factionalism is likely

to develop. Well-intended organizational talent and energy might be spent

pulling in opposite directions Even the most brilliant, insightful and

persuasive C E.O cannot unilaterally succeed in setting the strategic

direction that his company should be going in He will have to depend on

some sense of shared agreement and understanding of this course among his managers. The planning approach discussed in this book is intended exactly for facilitating this organizational direction-setting task

It should therefore be stressed again that one important condition for being able to reach an overall strategic sense of direction internalized among its managers, is that the planning process must be interactive and iterative It is necessary that the specialized skills and viewpoints of various managers throughout the line should be allowed to interact with the more general management viewpoints of the organizational levels above For instance, the C.E.O will depend on the specialized business inputs of his various division managers, who will be closer than he to their particular business settings, he, however, will consider these inputs in an overall corporate context. Similarly, the head of a particular division will have to rely on the specialized inputs of his various functional department managers He, however, will have to be the one who takes the overall point of view of the business, above all in attempting to channel the functional strengths into cross-functional strategic programs that enhance the strategic progress of the business as a whole. The planning process should therefore serve as a vehicle for unlatching the firm's specialized as well as general management resources. It therefore seems essential that there is a relatively free-flowing two-way interaction in order to achieve good planning Blockage of such communication channels might have deteriorating effects on the quality of planning

Before discussing guidelines for making the planning process an effective communication vehicle, let us raise another related behavioral concept, namely that the process should be iterative. Given the typically

complex nature of strategy formulation and implementation task, it is,
of course, unlikely that the various participants in the planning process
should be able to come up with their finalized inputs as the result of
their first attempt Few, if any, is able to see the ultimate strategic
solution "in a crystal ball" A more likely set of events will be that
plans are developed through a series of iterations, back and forth among
the managers of the planning process This can only be achieved through
a relatively open two-way communication channel

A significant requirement to all effective systems for communication
is that the various communication tasks are clearly identified and
delineated, which managers should be involved, what should be discussed,
when during the process should this be? The conceptual planning scheme
that has been developed provides exactly this type of focus It specifies
when objectives, strategic program or budget-related issues should be
discussed and what questions each group of managers should be concerned
with at each stage This should facilitate a clearer sense of role-
identification among the managers in the planning process

Similarly, by providing a set of rules for communication, the
planning system will provide a safeguard mechanism so that the various
managers will have a vehicle to be heard about concerns when appropriate
This is particularly important in a large corporation, where it often
might be difficult for managers down the line to raise a concern as part
of the "normal" way of operation. It is of course much easier for a
subordinate manager to present his points of view as part of the routine
yearly planning cycle than if he has to take the initiative to raise an
ad hoc strategic issue on his own on an exception basis Thus, the

planning system provides an important vehicle for formalized bottom-up communication mechanism A similar top-down communication mechanism is of course also critical, but this typically constitutes less of a bottle-neck in that senior management typically can feel more free to communicate with subordinate managers.

A relatively open two-way process of developing a course for the strategic direction of the firm will most likely add to the effect of instilling a sense of commitment to the attainment of this set of plans on behalf of management Not only will it be more difficult for a manager to depart from a widely communicated previously agreed upon direction in itself. In addition, there will be considerable group pressure on each executive to "deliver". A SBU manager, for instance, will know that fulfillment of his part of the overall corporate plan will be essential to the overall corporate success, and that a slip might have broad repercussions throughout the organization. A disciplined team spirit for strategy fulfillment accountability might emerge.

In our experience the disciplinary pressure of having to stick to a committed direction might frequently provide a particularly sombering experience for the C.E.O. and his senior management. This will mean that he will not be as free to impose unilateral ad hoc shifts in the strategic direction in jeopardy of the plans. In many cases this might represent a definite potential for strengthening the quality of decision-making, in that spur-of-the-moment decisions that will break with a systematically established prior strategy might less easily be taken. Even though some loss of flexibility might be the result, it often pays off to take time to assess why the old strategy would be invalid Ad hoc superimposed strategic

changes by the senior management will frequently be seen as "breach of
the planning contract" by the rest of the company's management   Such
decisions will typically be resisted by the organization and might be
difficult to implement irrespective of their merit. Needless to say,
such unilateral top-down spur-of-the-moment strategic decision-making
taken outside the context of the planning system tends to be the safest
way to undermine the effectiveness of the planning system as a de facto
strategic decision-making vehicle   Ironically, the C E.O. will probably
be the one to lose the most on this

Being fundamentally a behavioral process, planning is likely to
affect management's style in several ways. First, the typical effective
manager within the operating context of a strategic planning framework,
will probably be the one who possesses such personal qualities as flexibility, open-mindedness, ability to listen and tolerance   Less flexible
management types are less likely to succeed within a planning context.
Secondly, patience and discipline are necessary style ingredients for
managing within a planning context   Often it turns out to be particularly
difficult for action-oriented line executives to reconcile themselves to
the fact that orderly strategic decision-making typically takes time.
Finally, it should be stressed that good planning means hard work   It is
normally an intensive effort, time-consuming process to go through the
planning process. Participating in review meetings and undertaking
revisions might seem as a never-ending effort, before finally reaching
an agreement on a strategic direction to follow. Only when the managers
are realistic about the amount of time that planning will take, being
willing to commit sufficient time and intellectual involvement, will there
be a realistic possibility that effective planning might materialize.

What has been briefly touched upon in this section is tne need to recognize several general implications for management's style stemming from the fundamental fact that we are dealing witn a behavioral process. Let us now move to a discussion of the specific roles of tne various manager groups in planning, starting with the C.E.O

7-3   The Chief Executive Officer's Role in Planning

The C.E.O. is the one person ultimately responsible for strategic decision-making within the firm. Although he might have delegated larger or smaller parts of this task, he is still responsible. Given that a strategic planning system is intended to facilitate better strategic decision-making, it is clear that a strategic planning system must be designed in such a way that it suits the needs of and the decision-making style of the C.E.O.[2] Unless the C.E.O. is able to understand and feel comfortable with the rationale for the particular planning system's design, he will probably not make much use of the strategic planning system as an integrated part of his decision-making In line with this, he must be reasonably comfortable that the system reflects his own basic business aspirations and beliefs Let us structure our discussion around the following three issues, then: What management style characteristics should be taken into account when designing the planning system, how can the planning system be integrated as a tool into his decision-making process, and, what will be the C.E.O.'s role in the actual design of the planning process?

It does not require extensive observations to conclude that there is a wide diversity of management styles among the C E O.'s of large corporations. This will of course depend on many underlying factors, among which

might be the career pattern of the C.E O., his ambition on behalf of his
company, pressures from outside interest and power groups, and so on
Let us for instance consider the following two hypothetical C E.O.'s and
see how their management styles are likely to be different. On the one
hand we might have a C E O who has risen to the top spot of a large,
capital-intensive corporation through a series of internal promotions
He may be around 60 when he takes over as C.E.O , and the mandatory
retirement age may be 65. The financial situation of the company is
comfortable. The board of directors is relatively passive and there is
no one single large stockholder A C.E.O. in this position might well
adopt an outlook of "not rocking the boat". His major concern is probably
to preside over a firm which is continuing in its steady success and basic
mode of operation of the past and to be in a position to "hand over the
helm of a sound ship" to the next C.E.O when mandatory retirement occurs.
There will be little pressure for changes from the predominantly inbred
organization (of which the C.E.O. is a typical representative) Similarly,
the C E O. sees little reason to take major long-term risks that might
pay off a long time after his retirement. On the contrary, about the only
real pressure the C E.O. occasionally might feel is from financial analysts
and the stock market. no short-term surprises, steady quarterly performance
The basic outlook of this C.E O is therefore relatively short-run. He
will feel more comfortable with a planning system which emphasizes integration rather than adaptation. He typically does not see much of a need for
a planning system that would put explicit emphasis on surfacing and
ameliorating structural and/or financial portfolio pressures.

The contrast might be a C.E O. who takes over the top spot at a
relatively young age, so that he has, say, about 20 years of tenure ahead
in the job. Further, he might have been brought in from the outside some
years ago and has had extensive experience running several different
businesses as a SBU and a division manager The company may be fairly
diverse, and because of a high degree of growth through acquisition there
may not be one distinct internal corporate style of management. The
company has shown a strong financial performance in the past, however,
during the recent few years its performance has slackened somewhat when
compared with a selected number of other relatively similar companies.
This C.E.O. is having strong ambitions for his company, putting pressure
on the corporation for higher performance and being willing to make long-
term commitments that might take the firm into quite different strategic
directions. The planning system that this C.E.O. would find useful and
be comfortable with would probably emphasize relatively more adaptation.
It might facilitate the putting of pressure for longer-term strategic
performance excellence on its divisions, accentuated by explicit "competition" among the divisions for the available corporate resources for
their expansion The system might further emphasize structural portfolio
readjustment pressures by supporting the C.E.O.'s efforts in occasional
channeling of funds to acquisitions.

The above examples are merely intended to suggest that the C.E.O.'s
style and aspirations for the company and himself will be critical when
it comes to what will be a useful design of a planning system. Among the
factors that might affect the design of the strategic planning system
through impacting the C E O.'s style might be, as suggested in the examples,

the length of remaining tenure in the C E O 's position and whether the
C.E O is "inbred" or not   What is necessary in each particular corporate
situation is to carefully attempt to delineate what might be critical
elements of that C E O.'s particular style ard preconceptions.

Let us now move to the second issue relating to the C.E.O.'s role in
planning, concerning how for him to integrate planning into his decision-
making style. We shall claim that as a prerequisite for that to significantly take place, the C.E O. must accept that he will only get as much
out of the system as he puts into it   Thus, if not willing to interject
himself actively into the process, but rather taking a more or less neutral
or aloof role, critical top-down inputs will then be missing from the
planning process   In addition to thereby biasing the decision-making
process itself, there might also be adverse psychological effects on his
organization through this form of planning behavior. Consider for instance,
a C.E O. who has announced to his organization his intention to strengthen
strategic decision-making through promoting a strategic planning system
When the actual work on the planning cycle takes place, however, it turns
out that the C.E.O. takes a relatively low-key position when it comes to
providing inputs to and review of the substantive matters of the objectives-
setting and strategic programming cycles. In contrast, when the culminating
step in the narrowing down process -- the budget -- is being presented, the
C.E.O. comes on heavily with sweeping suggestions for change. This causes
modifications rot only of the buaget itself, but also of several strategic
programs and it raises doubt about the fundamental relevance of some of
the objectives   The strong, indirect signal to the organization in this
case is probably clear. Despite his lip-service commitment to strategic

planning, the C.E 0. will in fact be more oriented towards relatively shorter-term, internally oriented, and integration-related issues. The line is likely to remember this in subsequent years, being likely to prepare objectives and programs in such a way that these will fit into an anticipated budget, dominated by the C.E.0 's integrative emphasis. Thus, we see that the entire core purpose of the planning process as a vehicle for identifying the relevant strategic options and of narrowing down these options is likely to be biased. Lack of participation by the C.E.O. in this case becomes a major barrier to effective strategic planning.

It follows tnat the C.E 0. must be willing to devote a sufficient amount of time and degree of intellectual involvement to the planning process in order for it to function. Some C.E 0 's might state that although they ideally would want to devote the time required, tney simply do not have enough time available and cannot free up this either, due to other pressing activities The real irony of this quite common line of argument is not only that it signals that planning is likely to fail, but that it frequently is based on a false assumption. The key question when it comes to time spent is whether planning might facilitate the freeing up of time now spent on ad hoc firefighting activities as well as on disentangling a strategically unfocused budget In one large, success-ful, highly diversified company we studied, we found that exactly this had happened to the C E.0 's time-spending pattern The added strategic focus being brought to the company through the increased empnasis on the objectives setting and on the strategic programming gradually allowed the C.E.O. to free up time he previously had to spend on what was previously

an exceedingly elaborous and cumbersome budgeting process In another
company the C.E.O was able to free up considerable time previously devoted
to capital budgeting approval aspect of budgeting as he was able to snift
his emphasis from a detailed review and approval/rejection of each particular investment project proposal to a review of the strategic programs.
Given that an investment would be part of an already approved program and
that the strategic relevance of the investment thereby would have been
established, the C E O. became in a position to treat the individual
proposals in less detail. Thus, a considerable part of the C.E.O.'s time
was freed up, given the shift in proposal review purpose to become fine-
tuning and a "safety mechanism"

An effective strategic planning system is above all then a tool for
the C E O., intended to assist him in doing a better job in his overall
strategic decision-making task   It follows that tne C.E.O. therefore will
have particularly strong incentives for contributing to making planning
work   If not willing to let his strategic decisions unfold within the
framework established by the planning system, the C E O is handicapping
himself above all   Similarly, if not willing to commit the necessary
amounts of his time and his intellectual involvement, the C E.O handicaps
himself again.

Let us now turn to the third issue raised in relationship with the
roles of tne C.E O in the planning process, namely what should be his
involvement, if any, in the design of the strategic planning system
Further, to what extent should he have a knowledge of the detailed
functioning of this system? Most C E O 's will probably state that the
design of the strategic planning system as well as the monitoring of this

system is a task that belongs to the corporate planner and his department
Given the lack of time that typically plagues a C E O , this is a very
understandable position. However, the design of the strategic planning
system and the way it is managed will have a vital impact on how strategic
planning might function, as we have seen throughout this book Consequently,
it is necessary that the C E.O be reasonably certain that the planning
system is designed and managed in a way that facilitates a planning
emphasis consistent with his intentions. There are two concerns that need
to be raised in order to facilitate this.

First, it seems necessary that the C.E.O must know enough about the
general aspects of planning so that he can feel reasonably comfortable
about how the process in fact broadly seems to work within his company
Without this "pit of the stomach" feeling about what has been going on in
order for the planning outputs to have been developed, it will be difficult
for him to feel entirely comfortable about taking a position with respect
to the substantive strategic issues he will have to decide on through the
process. In particular, he will have to have a reasonably good perception
about the amounts of efforts, degree of professionalism and sincerity of
commitment to the plans that has gone into the planning documents he
receives. By understanding the functioning of the process the C.E.O. can
better calibrate what emphasis to put on the various planning outputs as
basis for his strategic decisions.

Secondly, it follows that the power to control the actual design
and execution of the strategic planning system is an important one, since
influencing the planning system might be an effective if indirect way of
promoting strategic direction. Hence, the C E O. should maintain the

broad responsibility for this task in his own domain   This would mean that he should stress that the corporate planning department, which often has the task of designing and managing the planning system, is operating strictly as an extension of his own office   Changes in the planning process should have the clout of being sponsored by the C.E.O., although prepared through the staff support of the corporate planning department Thus, the C.E O. should retain "ownership" of the strategic planning system

Neither of the above two issues should significantly tax the C.E.O.'s time. The critical issue is more a matter of sensitivity to these issues on the part of the C E O and of delegating tasks to the strategic planning department consistently with this. Some C.E.O.'s, however, might not feel content with taking such a passive role of minimum acceptable involvement in the development and management of the planning system. These C E.O 's have found that the design of the planning system has the potential to offer such an effective indirect tool for changing the strategic direction of a company that they want to keep themselves directly involved in this function   If for instance a company is facing an increasingly complex environment, say, because of acquisitions or because of increasingly turbulent business surroundings, the C E O might approach the issue of how to take advantage of this indirectly by modifying the planning system so that it more adequately might cope with the new setting. One move in this direction would for instance be to institute more sharply targeted formalized environmental scanning procedures. Increasingly, we have examples of C E O 's who actively and deliberately are modifying the structure of the strategic planning system in order to achieve a change in the strategy that they want their firm to follow

As stated throughout this book, an important strategic planning
system situational design issue is to tailormake the structure of the
strategic planning system to the particular strategy that is being
followed. There is seemingly a contradiction between this and what was
stated in the previous paragraph, where it was implied that a strategy
emerges as an output from the planning system Does structure follow
strategy, or does strategy follow structure? We shall elaborate on
several key issues behind this apparent contradiction, and we shall see
not only that the two viewpoints can be reconciled, but that this will
have consequences for the C.E.O.'s role in planning.

Former Secretary of Defense Schlesinger has said about planning that
the task is to develop strategies that are sufficiently robust so as to
in turn allow for opportunism within the general confines of the robust
strategic direction. The issues arising from this are twofold. how does
a corporation develop a good and sufficiently robust strategy, and, how
does the company go after opportunities (and avoid threats) within the
general confines of such a robust strategy? We have previously stressed
that the formulation of an initial strategy seldom tends to be developed
from scratch through a formal strategic planning cycle Instead, the
implicit strategic decision-making pattern of the firm's past typically
will play a significant role as inputs to an explicit strategy statement.
In addition, ad hoc special purpose studies on specific strategic issues
will typically play a major role as inputs in sharpening of a formalized
statement of the firm's strategic position As examples of such ad hoc
strategic positioning attempts we have discussed the ad hoc strategic
audits A more robust formal statement of the firm's general strategic
posture will come out of this.

The role of the strategic planning system, then, would be to further facilitate operationalization and "fine-tuning" of the basic robust strategic thrust by providing the mechanism for reassessing the rationale for one's strategies through the annually recurring adaptation and integration-related stages of the planning cycle Given this, there should ne no doubt that the design of the structure of the strategic planning system must be tailormade to the basic robust strategy at hand, i.e., that structure should follow strategy

However, at some point down the evolutionary path of implementation of the robust strategy, there might be a perception of a need to modify the basic strategic thrust, beyond the incremental fine-tuning that will be the result of the completion of each year's planning cycle It will be in such instances that the C.E O. may want to modify the structure of the planning system in order to indirectly have an impact on changing the robust strategy. Thus, when seen in such an evolutionary context we might say that structural changes might precede strategic changes in order to facilitate major but relatively rare strategic reorientations.

To summarize our position with respect to the C.E O.'s role, then, we generally find it useful that the C.E.O. actively influences the design and evolution of the strategic planning system in such a way that it reflects the situational reality, and that he also makes use of his leverage to make modifications in the strategic system at discrete intervals in time in order to induce major strategic changes.

7-4   The Line Management's Roles in the Planning Process

Let us now turn to a discussion of the roles of the other line management groups in planning, excluding of course the C E O that we

discussed in the previous section   We shall find it useful to distinguish
between the role of line general managers, such as those who head a
division or a SBU, and line managers who represent a particular function

A line general manager, such as a division or SBU head, should
normally be in a position with little or no ambiguity in terms of the
role that he is expected to play in planning process. Given that the
overall pattern of the planning process has been established from the
corporate level, it will soon become apparent to the corporate level as
part of the top-down/bottom up interaction if a division manager is out
of phase with his planning attempts. The line general manager will face
a strict schedule for when to prepare what aspects of his business plan.
The effects of being out of phase time- and quality-wise might be twofold,
and might have quite serious consequences. First, the corporate level
will have to make portfolio strategizing and resource allocation decisions
based on a pattern of business opportunity data which in fact will not be
comparable across all the businesses, given that the quality and
reliability of the inputs will vary from division to division   This
might cause serious dysfunctionalities in the portfolio strategizing
Secondly, a division with insufficient quality of its planning thrust
might end up shortchanged in the interdivisional competition for funds.
It is therefore important that a division manager be able to develop
relatively accurate and relevant plans, and that he approaches the task
of planning in a professional manner. His challenge is to perceive the
key adaptive and integrative strategic issues facing his business as well
as possible and from a general management point of view

Given that the effectiveness of the company's planning process as a
whole might suffer when one division manager does not carry out his
planning task, it is indeed pertinent to try to prevent this from taking
place. We shall look at two types of causes for potential lackluster
divisional planning and also indicate what might be appropriate senior
management action for ameliorating this problem. One reason might be a
resistance by the division manager to adequately cooperate in the planning
effort Such a situation is not entirely uncommon, particularly during
the initial start-up periods of planning This might be caused by such
emotions as "I've been successful in this business for a long time -- why
should I do it differently", "I do not have time for this, because someone
has to run the business", or "this is just another of corporate management's
fads; next year there will be something else'" Alternatively, the
resistance might be a more calculated one, based on the perception that
planning might diminish the power of the division manager. A strong
division manager, for instance, might feel that a less explicit resource
allocation process based on a one-to-one, not a portfolio-type, divisional-
corporate interaction might provide him with more leeway. The corporate
level can of course not tolerate such forms of resistance The C E O
might partly communicate this to the division manager directly, say,
during the corporate review period. This will imply that resistant
divisions will be requested to go "back to the drawing board" and come
back adequately prepared Partly too the point might be communicated
indirectly by penalizing those divisions in the funds allocation divisions
that have not satisfactorily documented how the funds are intended to be
spent strategically. Such an approach might be expensive, however, and

the C.E.O. will typically not want to carry too far a policy of "education" by distorting the resource allocation process   Given the seriousness of divisional non-cooperation, the C E O. will sooner or later have to face up to the issue of when to relieve those division managers from their positions that do not want to cooperate. Lack of action by the C.E.O. on this point might seriously strain the usefulness of planning as a meaningful strategic decision-making tool

We are of course here dealing with an aspect of the more fundamental issue of strategic planning's effect on potential redistribution of power within the organizational hierarchy of a corporation. Given that a more explicitly focused corporate portfolio strategy opens up the potential for a more systematic redistribution of resources among the elements of a portfolio, one might deduce that comprehensive formal planning in many instances might imply a redistribution of power away from previously more autonomous divisional business-centered nuclei and towards the corporate office. As such, it is not surprising that division managers might resist planning. For the same reason it should be equally clear, however, that such resistance must be kept within limits by the C.E.O

Another major reason why division managers might not perform satis-factorily in planning has to do with lack of familiarity with the task of thinking in a strategic mode on the part of division managers. For many there will have to be a period of learning before becoming comfortable as business strategists For others, however, the likelihood might be slight, at best, that their development will catch up through learning. Such a lack of aptitude to function as a good business strategist would indeed be a serious deficiency on the part of the division manager. Eventually, this is likely to lead to his removal.

In summary, then, a division manager does not have to be concerned about the issues of how to design and manage the planning system, per se, this task has been taken care of at the corporate level. However, the division manager must be able to understand the rationale for the design of the planning system well enough to be able to provide those substantive planning inputs that the system requires When it comes to participation within the system he will have no choice other than full cooperation, in order to excel substantively.

Let us now turn to the functional line executives and discuss their roles in planning As pointed out earlier, the functional departments will typically be playing a rather informal role during the objectives-setting stage. During the strategic programming stage, however, they will play a key role in bringing to the process specialized functional skills, hopefully of an outstanding quality. The yearly programming cycle will primarily serve as a vehicle for summing up the status of a more or less continuous and primarily interfunctional set of unstructured or semi-structured activities. This is intended to conceive of new programs, as well as improve and implement existing ones. The focus or general direction for the company to take is more or less given; the issue for the functional executives is how to come up with program suggestions to make this happen This process typically calls on highly creative inputs This is generally not easy, none the least because it will generally be difficult to prescribe a common structure in terms of steps to follow in this part of the process Thus, the functional executives' roles in planning tend to be generally less formal and quite ambiguous as well

The "interface" between the functions and the annual formal plan can at times be a traumatic and frustrating experience for the functional

managers. This "planning stress" might be brought on them partly because
of the typically high requirement for communication and coordination along
intuitive and diffuse patterns across clearly defined functional boundaries,
partly because the temporary nature of strategic programs prevents the
development of more long-term and permanent interpersonal ties, and partly
because of the difficulty in seeing the overall strategic rationale from
a narrow, functional perspectual basis.

7-5. The Role of the Planner

In our discussion of the role of the planner, we shall find it useful
to distinguish between the corporate level planning executive and planners
at the division and functional levels.[3] This is in line with what was
proposed during our discussion of the roles of the C.E.O and the line in
the planning process We distinguished there between the task of developing
a strategic planning system that would fall primarily under the C.E O.'s
jurisdiction versus the tasks of operating within the system by providing
the substantive inputs to the planning process, to be performed by the line.
We shall discuss the roles of the corporate level planner first.

We shall point out two major groups of tasks that might be conceived
of for the corporate level planner There will of course be a need to
contribute to the various substantive strategic decisions that will have
to be taken at this level too. Examples might be to assist in acquisition
studies, or to give advice to the C.E.O on the relative merits of the
planning documents submitted by each division We shall however delay
our discussion of the corporate planner's role in substantive strategic
decision-making, and instead initially focus on the other major group of

tasks, namely to play the instrumental role in the design and implementation
of the strategic planning system as well as to administer or manage the
planning process This task is in essence at the center of what this book
is all about. Issues in this context would be to facilitate the design of
a strategic planning system through choice of an appropriate conceptual
scheme for strategic planning and through tailormaking this scheme to the
particular situational setting at hand Other central issues would be to
facilitate the implementation of the planning system by discussing it with
the line executives and assisting the line in making use of the system
This leads to a third set of issues, namely to be responsible for the
improvement of the system, such as modifications, extensions of scope, or
changes in emphasis. Finally, we have the task of physically coordinating
the often vast number of diverse activities associated with a company going
through a planning cycle, such as the preparation of an updated planning
manual, dissemination of a planning calendar, distrubution of common background assumptions to the line such as common economic assumptions,
collecting divisional output drafts at each planning stage, arranging for
time, place and agenda for planning review meetings, and so on The job
of running the planning function is exhaustive and challenging.

Maybe the biggest challenge with respect to the planner's job of
managing the system stems from our emerging recognition that rather than
dealing with a planning function in the narrow sense, planning should
rather be seen as one of several critical elements of an overall strategic
decision-making system. This, as we have seen, attempts to encompass in
a coordinated and consistent fashion the tasks of identification of
strategic options, of narrowing down these options, of monitoring progress

towards the fulfillment of the targets set, and of reconciling the
motivating of individual managerial behavior with the strategic direction
desired It will probably become exceedingly critical that the emerging
managerial function of managing the evolution of this broader strategic
system is being well performed It is particularly important to take a
unified point of view when it comes to this management function, given
that lack of consistency among the elements of the broader strategic system
in all likelihood might jeopardize its overall effectiveness as well as the
effectiveness of its parts, despite the fact that a given subsystem when
seen in isolation might appear to be performing entirely satisfactorily.

Traditionally, different corporate level staff functions have been
responsible for managing aspects of this overall strategic system For
instance, the corporate planner might be responsible for the parts of the
system relating to objectives setting and strategic programming the
corporate controller might have been responsible for the budgeting and
monitoring stages, and the executive development function might be
responsible for the management incentives aspects. There is a need to
unify and coordinate these responsibilities. Whether the corporate
planner or one of the other staff members should be the one to be
designated to head up this task is not relevant, the key is that one
executive actually is given the overall responsibility.

The task of managing the planning system, i.e., of being an effective
custodian of planning as a strategic decision-making process, is thus not
only an increasingly important one, but an increasingly complex one as
well It is increasingly important because of the exceedingly central
role the planning system is expected to play in facilitating strategic

change within the company It is increasingly complex because of the fact
that we are dealing with one overall strategic system that needs to stay
consistent and current, not a set of separable, more or less independent
subsystems. It might be reasonable to speculate, then, that the position
of being responsible for the overall strategic corporate planning process
should be held by a senior staff executive This person should be working
in close cooperation with the C.E O , in order to be able to manage the
thrust of the system in a direction that corresponds with the C E.O 's
strategic outlook Given that the increasing importance of such an overall
strategic decision-making system is likely to become recognized by a wider
strata of managers, it is also to be expected that some of the apprehension
that line typically might have for the corporate planner might be weakened

Let us now turn to the other major task of the corporate planner,
namely to be involved in analyzing and even in deciding on parts of the
substantive issues that are brought up through the planning process. There
might be several aspects of this that might raise concern, out of which we
shall point out three. One is the corporate planner's role in providing
common background assumptions on certain factors such as the overall
economic outlook as well as what common figures might be relevant to use
for wage rates, interest rates, currency rates, and so on A second is
the planner's role in consolidating substantive planning inputs from the
divisions, checking for "mechanical" type errors such as in the arithmetics,
as well as performing a general analysis of the effects of the proposed
planning inputs, with particular emphasis on funds flow feasibility from
a corporate point of view. A third role would be the planner's responsibility to pass judgment on the appropriateness of various substantive

strategic decision alternatives. The nature of the first of these roles
is such that it should be seen in isolation from the other two, in that by
calling for making available background information to the planning process
in a unified manner this function does not represent a direct involvement
in the strategic decision-making process as such. This is in contrast to
the latter two roles which intervene more directly in the functioning of
the strategic decision-making processes themselves. While the second role
refers to the functioning of the management process, and the third role
refers to the substantive strategic choices that will have to be made,
there is room for confusion with respect to these two interrelated roles,
as we shall see below

The dynamic and industrious corporate planner will of course attempt
to play a dual role, emphasizing an involvement in the management of the
planning process as well as attempting to have an impact on the substantive
strategic issues that will have to be decided on as part of the planning
task. Unfortunately, however, this dual task involvement pattern might
cause friction within the organization, and ultimately might diminish the
corporate planner's ability to carry out both his process-related and his
substance-related tasks We shall see that there are several reasons why
it might be difficult for the corporate planner to fulfill the two types
of tasks. First, the process of identifying relevant strategic options
and deciding which of these options to pursue and in what ways, is a task
which might potentially significantly change the strategic direction of
the firm. The line will have to be the vehicle to carry out these changes
It would therefore also be appropriate to place a significant part of the
responsibility for fulfillment of strategic performance squarely on the

line. The line executives, who are the ones who subsequently will have
to live with the plans, should also feel that they are dealing with their
"own" plans. Consequently, accountability for one's stated strategic
positions is probably an integral element of the interactive "narrowing
down" planning process. Line executives will be likely to resist the
notion that staff executives have a major influence on critical strategic
choices. The typical feeling prevailing would be that these executives
will not be as close as the line to the businesses and also that the staff
more easily might "walk away from" their decisions   The likelihood of
such line resistance to inputs from the corporate planner is probably
particularly high when the corporate planner is new to the company, as
well as when he does not have a line background from within one or more
of the company's businesses.

A second and related reason why the corporate planner might run into
resistance if attempting to have an impact on the substantive strategic
direction-setting stems from the interrelationship with his other task,
managing the planning process. We have already discussed how modification
of the structure of the planning system might affect the firm's strategic
direction   Thus, the corporate planner might have an indirect impact on
the substantive strategic course that the firm takes   To carry out
rational and pragmatic modifications of the planning system is of course
within the domain of the corporate planner's task, and should not be
challenged by the line. If, however, the corporate planner also tends to
get heavily involved in substantive issues, then a feeling might easily
develop among the line that the corporate planner is attempting to both
"set the rules of the game" and "is a player in the game" as well   The

line will naturally resist letting one of the "players" have such a
substantial advantage of "controlling the rules"

What emerges is that there seems to be a trade-off situation when
it comes to this potentially dual role of the corporate planner. On the
one hand he should undertake the task of managing the planning process
well However, his task effectiveness with respect to this is likely to
diminish if he allows himself to get involved in substantive strategic
decision-making matters in addition. On the other hand, he might be a
staff confidant of the C.E O., relied on and respected by the C E.O. for
his sound judgment on substantive matters. If a staff executive in such
a position in addition is chartered with undertaking the corporate
planner's task of managing the planning process, he too will probably
fall into the trap of wearing two hats. The result is that he most likely
will have to compromise either on his effectiveness in his substantive
strategic decision-making involvement or on his effectiveness as a custodian of the strategic planning process.

Given the difficulty of combining the two potentially conflicting
roles of the corporate planner, a sensible solution might be to explicitly
assign the two tasks to two different executives or offices. The executive
in charge of corporate planning would then concentrate on the task of
managing the strategic planning process As already pointed out, this is
a critical management task in itself, and will probably take on even
higher importance given the emergence of the notion of having to reckon
with an overall strategic system, as we have advocated in this book. It
definitely does not seem prudent to risk the possibility of this planning
function being carried out less effectively by creating a potential role

conflict by adding a substantive strategizing task element to the corporate planner's responsibilities. His key priority should be to improve the planning system's effectiveness

The task of counseling the C.E O on substantive strategizing matters should rest with one or several corporate staff assistants to the president These should be executives whom the C.E.O. feels comfortable with, both in terms of respecting their judgment as well as in having no doubt about their loyalty Ideally, such executives should have strong backgrounds in the operations of the company, and they will normally hold quite senior titles. Together with the C E.O. they form the senior management team.

Let us illustrate by means of an example how the dilemma of the duality of the corporate planner's role was tackled within a large oil and energy related company. In this firm the two types of tasks were delineated in considerable detail, providing for a clear split between the two purposes This was done by letting the corporate planning group consist of not two but five distinctive subunits A unit called "planning process administration" oversaw the functioning of the planning process, and was the only process-oriented unit The other four emphasized aspects of substantive planning Notably, there was one group for strategic analysis of the submitted business plans Another group called "corporate strategy analysis and development" focused on strategic aspects of the corporate portfolio's properties. Thirdly, an acquisition/divestiture analysis and coordination group focused on assisting in the implementation of such tasks Finally, a group was charged with macro-economic analysis and compilation of special-purpose background statistics, primarily for

serving as common inputs to the line's planning process   This company
seems to have been quite successful in delineating between the process-
related and the substance-related tasks so that these do not weaken each
other. Also, there seem to have been benefits from instilling a mode of
specialization in terms of who should be carrying out different aspects
of the substance-related tasks. Given the formidable work-load typically
at hand when it comes to substantive planning issues' analysis and
resolution in companies of this size, this degree of delineation might
be a sheer necessity too.

In practice, there unfortunately tend to be at least two common types
of forces that tend to jeopardize the clear division of labor that we have
recommended for achieving effective role definitions of the planner's
tasks. First, a corporate planner, entrusted with the management of the
planning process might find it exceedingly difficult to discipline himself
to stick to his low profile "hands-off" role by not becoming excessively
involved in substantive strategic issues. There might be a natural
tendency for him to attempt to build up his influence on substantive
matters as he perceives that he is progressing in managing the planning
process to the extent that he is in a position of reasonably firm control
of this   It might indeed be mentally hard for the successful corporate
planner to stay away from a gradually increasing involvement in substantive
issues as he matures in the process job. He might even see this as the
only direction he can go in order to continue a satisfactory professional
development. Unfortunately, such a misconception might easily be the
first step towards the "downfall" of the planner   Instead, he should
pursue his professional development within the planning process area, by

taking on greater responsibility for developing a better overall
integrated strategic system.

Another potential type of problem stems from the common tendency
among corporate planners to allow themselves to get temporarily involved
in a "firefighting capacity" during the period of start-up of strategic
planning to do a large part of the planning themselves   It may seem
evident to the corporate planning group and be particularly frustrating
that the line executives are felt to be still so far away from thinking
and acting strategically   In their frustration about what they perceive
as slow progress towards the development of more involved strategies, the
corporate planners may not be able to resist the temptation to step in
and "help" the line in the development of their plans. This may happen
even though the corporate planner might be perfectly clear about the fact
that planning should be a function of the line. However, the planner will
justify his temporary substantive involvement as only intended to "get
things started" so that progress can be made faster   Unfortunately, the
effects from this type of well-meant but less well conceived intervention
by the corporate planning groups are almost universally negative. The
line will typically fail to accept the plans that are being developed for
them   They will typically feel a lessened pressure for developing
strategic thinking on their own   The corporate planning staff will be
perceived as mingling in substantive matters, and may be seen by the line
as a threat   There is also the danger that the planner's own perception
of the importance of a strict process involvement posture might be com-
promised as time goes on   In short, the entire basis for making a
satisfactory progress with planning through evolution might easily be

undermined at the outset through such actions. At best, the misconceived eagerness by the corporate planning staff might have led to a delay of planning progress; at worst they might have significantly diminished altogether the chances of making planning work.

Let us now shift the focus of our discussion to the roles of the planners at lower organizational levels within the corporation Let us first consider tasks of the planner within a business division. Let us recall that the role of a division in planning, above all, will be to be chartered with contributing bottom-up inputs for the resolution of where the company and its parts should go and for choosing alternative strategic programs for the business for how to get there. The systems framework for developing and delivering these substantive planning contributions has been provided by the corporate planning department. Thus, the role of the division planner, or the business planner, will be one of **assisting** the general manager of the division in the development of his substantive business plans. The division planner's role in many ways will be analogous to that of the C E.O.'s corporate level senior staff assistants The focus is on substantive strategic choices. The rationale for the need for a planner's position is, above all, to relieve the division manager from some of the substantive strategic analytical work that he otherwise would have to carry out. Further, the division planner might be of use to the division manager with advice on evaluating and choosing among the substantive alternatives.

It follows that the actual role definition of a division planner will critically depend on his particular division manager. Therefore, it is difficult to give general suggestions with regard to the division planner's role. The success of his task will depend on whether he is able to develop a highly personalized relationship with his division general business manager. This will largely be dictated by whether the division manager finds him useful in the analysis and advice on substantive strategic alternatives.

Let us turn finally to a brief discussion of the roles of planners at the functional level. As stressed before, the strategic role of the various functional departments occurs primarily through their participation in the strategic programming activities, where the emphasis is heavily on interfunctional cooperation. Thus, at the functional level it might be useful to assign a planning executive the responsibility for the planning of a particularly important strategic program. A major focus for such planning would be to facilitate better cross-functional integration. A unique feature of these strategic program planners' tasks would be the temporary nature of their planning missions. As soon as a particular strategic program has come to completion, the planning task will be finished. It seems essential that the planners in question recognize the temporary nature of their roles. Too often a planning organization might add some sense of permanence to the management of a strategic program, thereby distracting from more realistic management actions to keep the programs moving.

In many organizations we find even large staff executive groups carrying out marketing planning, production planning, R&D planning, and so on. Given the point of view taken in this book regarding the strategic roles of the various functions, we do not see a need for functional planners as such. Rather, the planners should be assigned to strategic programs, as discussed above. Often, however, labels such as production planning or marketing planning are quite misleading; these tasks often refer to quite well-defined, near-term tasks that will have to be carried out within strategic program contexts. A major part of these activities may be related to the development of inputs for the operating budget, and to the execution of these "action-programs" as well. Let us, however, stress that long-term functional planning in isolation from the other functions, per se, seems to have little merit.

As a way of summarizing the span of role alternatives for planning executives it is useful to consider Exhibit 7-1. As can be seen, we have

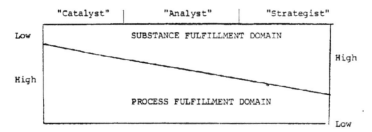

Exhibit 7-1. Tradeoff Between Process Effectiveness and Content Effectiveness for Different Role Alternatives of Planning Executives.

indicated three role alternatives for the planner, "catalyst," "analyst" or "strategist." Also we have indicated two major types of tasks for the planner. He may contribute more or less effectively towards the fulfillment of a better functioning of the planning process. Also, he may be more or less effective in enhancing sound, substantive strategic decisions. As we have argued, the corporate planner might find himself in a tradeoff position if he tries to do an effective job along both dimensions. It is not easy to "wear two hats" in a satisfactory manner. Thus, we also argued that the primary task domain to be prioritized by the corporate planner should be process effectiveness. Hence, the most

appropriate as well as normally the most "safe" role profile for him
would be to act as a "catalyst." Only rarely will he succeed in maintaining his process involvement effectiveness while attempting to increase
his role in substantive strategic decision-making The C.E.O.'s corporate level planning assistants, on the other hand, should be expected to
emphasize the role of "strategist," providing advice and recommendations
on strategic decisions that are to be taken. Thus, we see that when it
comes to the roles of the corporate planners at the corporate level there
seems to be a dichotomy between process and substance, and it may in
fact be unrealistic to attempt to combine the two roles. Exhibit 7-1's
continuous trade-off picture may, therefore, not be realistic. To make
our summary complete, let us finally stress again that planners at lower
levels in the organizations will be primarily concerned with substantive
issues, and will consequently not face a similar role tradeoff dilemma
as is the case at the corporate level

7-6. The Role of the Board of Directors in Planning

Let us now turn to a brief discussion of the role of the board of
directors in the planning process, assuming in the ensuing that the
board is composed primarily of outside directors   (The inside directors
will presumably play the roles laid out for the C E.O and the senior
line officers already discussed in sections three and four of this
chapter) We see two distinct roles for the board. One might be on
influencing certain types of strategic decisions, by facilitating the
recognition of corporate-level needs for changing the portfolio-direction
due to financial pressures as well as, above all, due to structural
pressures. In fulfilling this role the board members typically would be
benefiting from some understanding of how the rudiments of the strategic

planning process works   A second role would be as a "watchdog" to check
whether the strategic decision-making process seems to satisfy a minimum
aspiration level of excellence and professionalism   We shall discuss
each issue in turn.

The board of directors traditional mode of operation is that it typically will be involved in the "signing off" on next year's budget, as
well as in the formal approval of large capital expenditure decisions.
We have previously discussed how capital expenditure decisions should be
evaluated in terms of their fit as elements of broader strategic programs.
As such, the judgment of the merit of various strategic program alternatives is what represents the crucial strategic decision, not the
capital expenditure appropriation per se.   Thus, the traditional role of
the board is often de facto not focused on the strategic issues, but
will instead be closer to what we might call rubber-stamping.   A poten-
tailly more useful role for the board would be to be involved in the
evaluation of the decisions of the major strategic thrusts of the firm.
As such, the board should play a role in the approval of the emerging
corporate-level outcomes from each of the objectives-setting, strategic
programming and budgeting cycles.   The board's role should of course be
primarily one of being informed, in order to be able to achieve a better
understanding of the strategic direction of the firm, not one of playing
an active role in strategy formulation as such

The benefits from a more focused strategic involvement by the board
might be useful in two areas in particular.   As has been discussed widely,
the board is expected to take a strong lead when it comes to overseeing
the company's stance on social responsibility issues.   Such issues can
probably only be meaningfully analyzed, however, when it is applied to
the social acceptability of strategies.   To focus on evaluating the

acceptability of events that are taken out of their strategic context
might more easily lead to biased judgments. Thus, the board needs to
understand the rudiments of the overall strategic direction in order
to better be able to carry out its role when it comes to social accountability

A second useful area of contribution for the board members might be
in providing the company access to information about a wider set of opportunities This might be particularly valuable when filling the corporate level planning gap Here, opportunities for acquisitions and/or
divestitures in particular might be brought up by members of the board.

There is another important function to be played for the board when
it comes to planning, namely the one of overlooking that the professionalism of strategic decision-making is being maintained in the corporation. As such, board members might for instance ask themselves
whether its management in fact manages strategically and possesses a
sufficient sense of strive for excellence. Such probing by the board
should help keep alive the issue of whether the aspirations of the senior
management for the company are satisfactory It is above all within the
context of the probing into the firm's planning activities and the review of the plans that the board typically will have its primary chance
of adding a more long-term view to senior management's aspirations.

It follows from the above that it will be desirable that board members normally should have a minimum degree of understanding of how the
planning system functions in order to be able to perform the tasks discussed. One approach that was taken to this by one company, with sales
of three billion dollars and active within the high technology business,
was to hold a workshop with the board and senior management in attendance
to discuss the structure and the functioning of the planning system.

The board members felt that without such a background understanding of how the strategic processes work it was becoming next to impossible for them to provide a positive contribution to the strategic direction-setting.

7-7. The Role of Outside Consultants

Not unexpectedly, the area of strategic planning and analysis has become a thriving field of management consulting. In our opinion there is quite a span of potential roles for consultants to play in this area. Confusion about these roles might be dysfunctional. Let us therefore delineate at least three distinctive areas of consulting tasks that should call for different modes of involvement by the outside consultant.[4] First, we might have the task of carrying out an assessment of one's strategic strategic setting in order to update one's needs for planning either at the business level, the corporate level, or at both. We recall that such assessments typically will not be carried out every year, and that they often require the familiarity with specialized analytical techniques (as seen in Chapter Three). Analogous to a "medical check-up" such an analysis, if coming up with problems, might frequently touch upon issues that would be highly sensitive to the management involved. All these considerations should suggest that it might be beneficial to make use of outside consultants to ensure an objective approach when carrying out the strategic assessment analysis. It will of course be necessary for the consultants to establish close cooperation with the firm's own management in such instances, in order to ensure a realistic input of company-specific background information.

A second area where outside consultants might play a useful role would be when it comes to carrying out specific, one-shot, analyses of

substantive strategic choices   Here the consultants would work in a
capacity similar to the C E O 's staff assistants for analysis and re-
commendation of substantive strategic issues   He will in fact be in a
working capacity quite similar to the strategic substance oriented corporate or division level planner.

When it comes to bringing in outside consulting assistance   to
facilitate improvements in the functioning of the strategic planning system, however, our position is that consultants' role typically might be
more limited. In order to be useful in such instances a careful role
and task delineation should be undertaken. The only way to operationalize
the implementation of a planning process within a company implies that
this strategic way of thinking must be adopted by the line management.
Thus, we are dealing with the task primarily of changing a style, or a
process, not a task of searching for some specific solution to a problem,
as we had in the two previous situations. For such a change to develop
there seems to be no way around impressing on the line that it must help
itself through learning by trial and error. Thus, there will be no short-
cut or substitute to having the line, including senior management, to be
intimately involved in the establishing of the planning "culture" themselves. A consultant might however play a useful role as a facilitator
of this "help to self-help" approach   Specifically, he can be of assistance in suggesting the design of aspects of the process, keeping in mind
however the caveat that the "design" of the system should be done under
the auspices of the C E.O. and the line   Issues that might fall into this
category might be relating to the preparation of planning instructions
(often labelled the planning manual), the establishment of a planning
calendar, as well as delineation of how to modify the budgeting, monitoring, and incentive systems in order to become consistent with the

planning system. Further, an outside consultant might play a useful role as an educator during the start-up period, by not only explaining aspects of the system to various line units, but also in communicating the overall rationale of the approach He might also play a role as a "catalyst" during the planning reviews, particularly when it comes to facilitating a more open-ended and free-flowing mode of communication among the executives involved. Thus, we see that an outside consultant can be a useful although peripheral resource in advising and guiding the line during their attempt to self-implement the planning process.

Unfortunately, there still seems to be a quite widespread misconception among some companies that a planning system can be installed through a "short-cut," by means of what will amount to an intensive outside consulting effort, and that even outside consulting resources can beneficially be drawn on in preparing the actual plans. In our opinion this will typically not provide the line with a sufficient opportunity to internalize the strategic management process mode Nor will plans primarily developed by outsiders be likely to create a necessary sense of internalization, commitment and "ownership" among the line. In summary, then, while outside consultants might play useful roles in carrying out strategic audit tasks and in analysing and reaching recommendations on specific substantive strategic issues, the outside consultants' roles in when it comes to influencing changes on the strategic planning process itself should generally be more as advisory catalysts.

7-8. Summary

We have discussed the roles of various executive groups in the planning process. A few general conclusions emerge from this which seem to be particularly important. The first is that the C.E.O.'s role in planning is a central one; in fact he is the "owner" of the planning system.

It is hard to justify the costs of developing a planning system unless the C.E.O. intends to make use of the system for substantive decision-making directly as well as for influencing strategic direction through evolving the system. Secondly, the line plays a key role in the development of plans. The planning documents should represent the line's views of their strategic positions and tasks, and as such should be developed by the line itself. While a corporate planner should be responsible for the management of the strategic planning process, he should leave it to the line to get involved in the substantive strategic decision-making. If not, his effectiveness as custodian of the strategic planning system is likely to diminish rapidly. However, while the substantive planning issues at the corporate level thus should be dealt with by the C.E.O. and his team of top management advisors, planners at the divisional level should be seen as an assistant to the division manager on substantive matters

The board of director's role in planning was seen as one of attempting to understand the planning process enought so that they might be in a better position to "sign off" on the firm's strategic direction, in contrast to a more or less common "rubberstamping" of capital expenditure projects and the annual budget. Also, the board might play a role in facilitating the necessary degree of professionalism in strategic management. Outside consultants' roles were seen as potentially useful in carrying out strategic position audits as well as in doing specific strategic issue substance analyses. However, the outside consultants' role was seen as more limited in directly carrying out the planning process itself.

Returning to the role of the corporate planner, it was stressed that his role might be expected to increase in importance with the growing

recognition is important for two reasons: partly because the planning
system needs to be seen as part of a broader set of systems, presenting
a more challenging managing task, and partly because of the importance
of managing and manipulating the strategic system as an indirect way
for achieving strategic change.

Chapter Seven - Footnotes

1. See Morrow, A., D. Bowers, and S. Seashore, editors, Management and
    Participation, Harper & Row, New York, 1967, Beckard, R. D., Organiza-
    tion Development: Strategies and Models, Addison-Wesley, Reading,
    1969, and Bennis, W. G., Organizational Development: Its Nature,
    Origins, and Prospects, Addison-Wesley, 1969.

2. See Tannenbaum, R. and F. Massarik, Leadership and Organization,
    McGraw-Hill, New York, 1961, Fiedler, Fred E., A Theory of Leadership
    Effectiveness, McGraw-Hill, New York, 1966, and Neuschel, Robert F.,
    "Corporate Strategy: The C.E.O. as Kingpin", McKinsey Quarterly,
    Summer, 1977.

3. See Schein, E. H., Process Consultation: Its Role in Organization
    Development, Addison-Wesley, 1969, Steiner, George A., "Rise of the
    Corporate Planner", Harvard Business Review, Sept.-Oct., 1970, and
    Ackerman, Robert W., "Role of the Corporate Planning Executive", in
    Lorange, Peter and Richard F. Vancil, Strategic Planning Systems,
    Prentice-Hall, Englewood Cliffs, 1977.

4. See Schein, E. H., Process Consultation: Its Role in Organization
    Design, Addison-Wesley, 1969, and Kolb, David A. and Alan L. Frohman,
    "An Organization Development Approach to Consulting", Sloan Management
    Review, Fall, 1968.

CHAPTER EIGHT

Corporate Planning - A Synthesis

8-1. Introduction

In this concluding chapter we shall summarize the book's major thrust
and discuss where planning stands today   First, we shall briefly restate
the major purpose of this book namely to set forth a concept of corporate
planning which is based on matching the capabilities of a company's planning system to the particular needs for planning stemming from this company's strategic setting. The major theme of the book has been to create
an operational concept of effective corporate planning, not only by pre-
scribing how such a planning needs-capability match might be reached, but
also in terms of what it might take to maintain such a level of planning
effectiveness.

Having restated the book's purpose we shall briefly review the major
components of our planning approach. Then, we shall discuss how this approach can be useful in providing a planning capability for meeting some
of the major planning problems that companies face today, notably a need
to adapt to environmental opportunities and/or threats, as well as to integrate more efficiently around its internal strength and weakness pattern.
Finally, we shall attempt to see planning in a prospective view, without pretending that we know what the future may bring we shall point out
certain trends that we think may occur   We hope that this will bring about
a notion of the benefits and costs of corporate planning as a strategic
decision-making tool for management   Only through a planning approach
will companies be able to succeed in the years to come, we believe, not
only because the planning approach offers an operational set of tools to
cope with emerging challenges, but also because of the competitive advantage to those firms which make effective use of planning.

8-2. A Rationale for Corporate Planning

There should be a number of important benefits to a corporation from instituting a strategic planning approach. The real test as to whether planning is worth its efforts, of course, will be whether planning will contribute to the improvement and stabilization of the firm's "bottom line" results over an extended period of time. It is for all practical purposes impossible to measure the benefits of planning in such a direct way, and we have not even attempted to come up with a direct benefits/cost measure in this book.

One might instead attempt to develop an indirect measure of the benefits from planning, partly by specifying what might be a set of useful outputs from the process on substantive strategic decision-making, and partly by indicating what would be the nature of (hopefully) positive changes in the firm's managerial decision-making process from adopting planning as a tool. Although we have not attempted to develop such an indirect benefits analysis either, we shall briefly list what we feel might be a key list of benefit factors for improved substantive strategic decisions as well as for an improved strategic decision-making process.

In terms of positive impact on strategic decision-taking the planning approach should provide a better sense of strategic direction of an organization, not only in terms of more strategically focussed decisions at the business level stemming from a better understanding of the businesses, but also in terms of providing a corporate portfolio context allowing for a more directed allocation of strategic resources in order to actively influence the long-term overall direction and structure of the firm. In addition to developing a better sense of direction within the company planning will also typically provide an early sensitivity of problem areas. The strategic decisions that thus are being

taken should not only be more strategically focussed in general, but also
lend themselves to translation into resources needed, tasks implied and
by whom, measures of progress, as well as time-specific schedules of progress.

   In terms of positive impacts on a firm's decision-making process, in
general, we shall indicate four, although there certainly will be several
others. First, the process might significantly assist at arriving at a
proper strategy. This is of course exceedingly important in that those
"old salts" tend to be very few who are able to develop superb strategies as
a natural, informal and highly personalized process. Secondly, a benefit
should be that more explicitly understood strategic direction for the
company is likely to emerge. Thirdly, a planning approach might provide
the discipline for periodic strategic review - actions to ameliorate potential strategic problems typically do not easily get initiated, in
contrast to "firefighting" actions to tackle day-to-day problems Finally,
a planning process should provide a basis for a more explicit "division
of labor" among management at various organizational levels, thereby also
providing a basis for a greater decentralization of operating decisions.

   The benefits from planning listed in the two preceeding paragraphs
should be relatively plausible to accept at this stage. We have seen,
throughout the book, how these and other benefits are likely to emerge
from planning We have however not attempted to come up with some explicit benefit measures in this instance either. Given the vast diversity
of corporate settings and styles we feel that it would be difficult at
best, and probably quite useless to attempt to measure the effectiveness
of planning this way Instead, attempting to develop a "proof" for why
planning is good, we have instead assumed that this is so in this book
Based on the premise that planning makes sense in general, we have instead

advocated an approach to planning which states that the maximum benefit
a given firm might get from planning depends on how well the planning
system's capabilities will match this company's particular needs for
planning Thus, our position is that to measure the effectiveness of
planning in an absolute sense has relatively little meaning, given that
some companies will be in better positions than others when it comes to
achieving such benefits Rather, we have argued, a more meaningful measure of planning effectiveness would be to assess how well a given firm
is doing in meeting its particular potentials, i.e. how well it is able
to match its planning capabilities with its planning needs

Both of the concepts of needs for planning as well as planning capabilities were operationalized by means of measuring adaptation and integration Adaptation, as we recall, refers to the identification and
pursuance of opportunities and/or threats in the firm's environment Integration, on the other hand, refers to the pursuance of the long-term
internal, ongoing activity patterns of the firm in such a way that internal strengths are being taken advantage of and developed while internal weaknesses are being ameliorated The needs for planning, both
adaptive as well as integrative, stem from the particular strategic setting
of the firm, as we have seen. The adaptive and integrative capabilities
to meet these needs depend on the particular design and structure built
into the planning system. A major purpose of this book, then, has been
to come up with an operational approach to how to determine an organization's needs for planning, as well as for how to design a planning system
in such a way that its capabilities become as relevant as possible. A
second major purpose of this book has been to develop the argument for
the necessity to maintain a planning system i e to manage its evolution

over time. Given that most firms' needs for planning will tend to change, often quite rapidly, as a function of environmental changes as well as due to reallocations within the firm itself, it will be necessary to keep on modifying a planning system so that it may maintain its effectiveness.

Having now restated the rationale for our approach to planning let us briefly revisit the major elements of our approach.

8-3   The Elements of the Approach

The first element for our approach is the emphasis on an overall strategic decision-making system consisting of five interrelated elements objectives-setting, strategic programming, budgeting, performance monitoring and motivating. The task of this system, then, seen as a decision-making tool for allocation of strategic resources, is to facilitate the identification of relevant strategic options; narrow down these options by making gradual commitment of resources to particular strategic directions culminating in a set of action programs coordinated for the company as a whole, monitor progress towards the fulfillment of objectives, long-term and near-term programs, and provide management with rewards for contributing the fulfillment of strategic direction The system, then, attempts to facilitate adaptation ot environmental opportunities and/or threats as well as integration of the company's pattern of activities so as to capitalize on internal strengths and ameliorate internal weaknesses

The second element of our planning approach provides a basis for a "division of labor" within the management hierarchy with respect to strategy formulation and implementation, specifically, three levels of strategy are being operationalized. At the corporate level we have a portfolio strategizing task which balances the various business activities that the company is in Thus, the key strategic issue here is to allocate the firm's resources to the businesses in such a way that the desired overall portfolio strategy can be reached.

At the division level the strategic emphasis will be on succeeding competitively within a particular business. The key strategic issue here too is resource allocation, but the focus of strategic choices will be fundamentally different, in what aspects of the business shall we invest in the creation of competitive strength, say building market share? A successful company cannot be involved in everything, strategic management implies making strategic choices and a sharpened strategic focus.

The third level of strategy involves the functional departments. The task here is to develop strategic programs for implementing a particular business strategy. These strategic programs will typically be interfunctional. This level of strategizing, thus, differs from the other two levels in at least three important respects. First, strategizing at the corporate and division levels implies a general management point of view, but specialized, functional viewpoints are the bases for strategic programming, brought together under the auspices of a business strategy "umbrella." Secondly, although the tasks of portfolio and business strategizing are permanent, a functional strategic program will be much more temporary in nature Thirdly, this strategic programming will have a key role in determining "how" to implement a strategic direction set at higher levels, but will not be fundamentally concerned with "where" to go.

The third element of the conceptual scheme is the notion of a behavioral process, with emphasis on learning and information-handling. Thus, the scheme acknowledges the necessity to bring a relatively large number of managers into the planning process, to share responsibility for and commitment to a particular direction for the firm. In order to achieve this the system must provide an opportunity for each relevant manager to set forth his arguments and for an orderly pattern of interaction. Given

planning system provide an effective communication pattern among managers. It is also critical that the system allows for the accumulation of useful managerial experience among its participants. It is not a trivial task to develop and maintain a good strategic posture; only through learning and improvements over time can this be done.

The "five by three" communication framework for strategic planning should provide the basis to pursue planning. Giving an overall logical consistent focus it permits the various aspects of planning to be addressed separately at different points in time, while still enabling all of it to fit into an overall strategic trust. Having thus developed a "sceleton" for a strategic planning system the next task is to discuss how this scheme might be implementable in such a way that the system might respond to the needs of the firm today.

8-4. Responding to Today's Needs

Although there might be an unfortunate tendency among management to claim that the problems one is facing today are more complex than ever and that the future is more uncertain than ever, there is still a truth in the fact that a few basic environmental shifts seem to have taken place. The "growth forever" syndrome of the decades up until the early 1970's certainly seems to be gone. The culmination of this point might have been labelled "growth without profits." Similarly, energy shortages may inflict more structural changes on the business environment than we have yet seen. Certainly, the need to keep up with and respond to the environment seems to have increased. Similarly, competitive pressures seem to be as strong as ever in calling for efficient modes of operation - today more than ever there seems to be a "survival of the fittest." As a consequence, today's planning challenge should be seen in a dual perspective

It should enable the company to <u>adapt</u> better to environmental opportunities and/or threats. Also, however, it should facilitate the handling of the integrative challenges facing the firm. In a given situation to strike a proper balance between the adaptation and the integration emphasis of planning thus becomes critical.

There are several issues which emerge which are important in influencing the adaptive/integrative planning capability balance viewpoint, we shall point out five examples of such issues that we see as particularly pertinent to today's setting.

First, there is a need to emphasize an appropriate top-down participation by senior management in "starting off" the planning process so that a realistic picture can emerge of the C.E O.'s expectations for the firm and his preconceptions as to how far and in what direction the firm might go. Secondly, there is a need for responses by the divisions to the C.E.O 's initiative by assessing the nature of opportunities and/or threats within one particular business. This would involve an analysis of how to predict and respond to a particular environmental factor to which a business strategy might be exposed. Thirdly, a corporate review of the business opportunity assessments should be carried out within the context of a portfolio strategizing task, i.e., a review of all divisions' inputs to an overall portfolio pattern as well as response to and interaction with each division contingent on the other inputs. Thus, a sequential corporate review of the divisions would not be satisfactory. Fourth, the attempt to formulate a set of objectives should be kept in a decision-oriented focus, in that it will be necessary to choose which businesses to emphasize relative to others. The expected effects from such shifts in emphasis within the portfolio will be to close the planning gap between the C E O.'s initial expectations and the expected performance

output of the tentative portfolio. A fifth aspect of the design tools
which seems to become increasingly critical is the development of "strategic control" to monitor progress not only towards the fulfillment of
budgets but also towards the fulfillment of budgets but also towards the
fulfillment of specific strategic programs as well as more general objectives.

In addition to the above "tools" which seem to have become increasingly important for directly influencing the adaptive/integrative balance
thrust of a company's planning, we have operational ways of improving adaptation or integration through indirect means, as well as by influencing
the relative emphasis on adaptation in relation to integration. Let us
briefly discuss each. The indirect way of influencing adaptation is through
linking the various planning elements together. Specifically, the monitoring of progress towards objectives-fulfillment might be strengthened.
A relatively larger share of the management incentives too might be tied
to objectives-fulfillment.

The strength of adaptation relative to integration can be influenced
by strengthening the steps in the planning process that might weaken integration aspects of planning, primarily within the strategic programming
and budgeting stages of the planning process. Also the linkage of performance monitoring of these cycles might be de-emphasized The role
of these cycles in determining managerial incentives might be deemphasized
as well.

A proper perspective of corporate planning as a management tool today,
then, recognizes that the state of the art is sufficiently developed to
provide critical support for strategic decision-making. This results from
our increasing understanding of how to focus the planning system in a

particular direction, towards a more appropriate adaptation/integration balance, as well as our ability to specify in operational terms the nature of the particular needs for planning.

8-5. Emerging Trends and Challenges

About the pressures facing the firm during the years to come we can of course only speculate. However, it seems reasonable to expect that the need to be able to strategize will become even stronger during the years to come Thus, a corporate planning system will increasingly become a tool for senior management to influence the strategic direction of the firm. In this respect three considerations should be made. The first reinforces the need to manage the evolution of a strategic planning system in order for it to remain sufficiently up-to-date to stay effective, as would be required given the planning system's role as a critical strategic tool. The second deals with the need to manage the planning system to anticipate strategic shifts that management wants to carry out, i.e., as a vehicle to facilitate and reinforce strategic change. The third deals with the new and important role of the corporate planner as a custodian managing the planning system in this context

The need to manage the evolution of the planning system will probably become increasingly important due to a combination of two forces. First, a strategic planning system which is reasonably effective in the first place will have an impact on the actual strategic choices and decisions that are being taken. These strategic decisions will in turn change the situational setting of the firm. This, however, will probably imply changes in the needs for planning, i e , a need to revise the planning system too Thus, the system needs to be updated in order not to "destruct itself " Equally important in this respect will be the realization that the planning system no longer can be seen as a relatively broad-gauged, crude tool but as an increasingly precise, multifaceted vehicle. Hence, the need for a more continuous updating effort emerges, where less frequent revisions of the planning system previously might have sufficed.

The issue of making use of the planning system as a vehicle for re-inforcing strategic changes is an important one. Increasingly there seems to be a realization that strategic change seldom occurs as a consequence of "dictate" by senior management when it comes to the substantive aspects of a decision, but rather as a function of senior management's manipula-tion of the administrative systems of the firm. Particularly, organiza-tional changes have been used by senior management as a vehicle for in-ducing new strategic direction. Instead of using such a sweeping tool exclusively, the planning system might emerge as another useful vehicle for the C.E.O to set strategic direction. Particularly important is the opportunity that this offers to change the planning system in advance to ensure more immediate and focused strategic shifts.

This brings us to the role of the corporate planner The corporate planner should continue to focus on maintaining the system and not become more involved in the substance of strategic decision-making. However, his task of managing the planning system is likely to become increasingly important In order to do an adequate job on this he will need to have a good sense of the strategic direction which senior management is pur-suing. Thus, the corporate planner might be seen as a member of the senior management team, close to the C.E.O.

In summary, it seems reasonable to predict that a strategic planning system might become a distinctive competitive advantage to those companies able to develop effective systems. This, however, will require an in-creasing emphasis on keeping the system's evolution under close scrutiny

and control, as well as ensuring that the system's focus is consistent
with the strategic direction acually comtemplated by senior management.

8-6   Summary

We have put forward in this book a discussion of strategic planning
as a decision-making tool which can be summarized from three angles   From
a retrospective point of view the "bits and pieces" of elements of planning that have been introduced might be summarized into a unified conceptual scheme which integrates three distinctive strategic levels, five
distinctive stages of tasks, and one interactive as well as iterative
communication process.   From a perspective point of view the system can
be seen as a vehicle for responding to particular planning needs that
have been identified, notably the increased need to pay attention to a
proper adaptation/integration that commonly face today's firms.   From a
prospective point of view we can expect a planning system to become more
and more the central tool for facilitating strategic change.

Milton Keynes UK
Ingram Content Group UK Ltd.
UKHW022320170124
436226UK00005BA/160

9 781017 730449